The Strong State and the Free Economy

The Strong State and the Free Economy

Werner Bonefeld

ROWMAN & LITTLEFIELD
INTERNATIONAL

London • New York

Published by Rowman & Littlefield International Ltd
Unit A, Whitacre Mews, 26–34 Stannary Street, London SE11 4AB
www.rowmaninternational.com

Rowman & Littlefield International Ltd. is an affiliate of Rowman & Littlefield

4501 Forbes Boulevard, Suite 200, Lanham, Maryland 20706, USA
With additional offices in Boulder, New York, Toronto (Canada), and Plymouth (UK)
www.rowman.com

British Library Cataloguing-in-Publication Data
A catalogue record for this book is available from the British Library

ISBN: HB 978-1-7834-8627-4
         PB 978-1-7834-8628-1

Library of Congress Cataloging-in-Publication Data Is Available

Names: Bonefeld, Werner, 1960– author.
Title: The strong state and the free economy / Werner Bonefeld.
Description: London ; New York : Rowman & Littlefield International, [2017] |
    Includes bibliographical references and index.
Identifiers: LCCN 2017007962 (print) | LCCN 2017016249 (ebook) |
    ISBN 9781783486298 (Electronic) | ISBN 9781783486274 (cloth : alk. paper) |
    ISBN 9781783486281 (pbk. : alk. paper)
Subjects: LCSH: European Union countries—Economic policy. | Liberalism—European
    Union countries. | Free enterprise—European Union countries.
Classification: LCC HC240 (ebook) | LCC HC240 .B64145 2017 (print) |
    DDC 337.1/42—dc23
LC record available at https://lccn.loc.gov/2017007962

∞™ The paper used in this publication meets the minimum requirements of American
National Standard for Information Sciences – Permanence of Paper for Printed Library
Materials, ANSI/NISO Z39.48–1992.

Printed in the United States of America

This book is dedicated to my son Declan.

Contents

Acknowledgements

I had the good fortune to present some chapter drafts at conferences, including the workshop on the New Right at Queen Mary University, London, September 2015; the conference Is There No Alternative: The European Union, Global Crisis, and Authoritarian Liberalism? at Kings College, London, March 2016; the conference Ordoliberalism as an Irritating German Idea, the Hertie School of Governance, Berlin, May 2016; the Manchester Graduate Conference, Is There No Alternative to Europe?, Manchester Jean Monnet Centre of Excellence, Manchester University, June 2016; and the Festkolloquium in celebration of the seventy-fifth birthday of honorary Senator Prof. Dr. h.c. Horst Weitzmann, Der Ordoliberalismus: Chance oder Gefahr für Europe, University of Freiburg, September 2016. I thank all participants for their insightful comments, discussions and helpful criticisms. Special thanks are due to Allison Howson, Ray Kiely, Richard Saull, Neil Davidson, Nicola Short, Daniel Woodley, Alexander Avienas, Alex Callinicos, Magnus Ryner, Lucia Pradella, Tim Stanton, Christian Jörges, Josef Hien, Thomas Biebricher, Frieder Vogelmann, Angela Wigger, William Harvey, Gabriel Siles-Brügge, Angeliki Stogia, Dimitris Papadimitriou, Lars Feld, Victor Vanberg, Tim Krieger, Phil Cerny, Volker Berghahn and Brigitte Young. I am most grateful to Peter Burnham and Hugo Radice for their advice, and especially to Greig Charnock and Huw Macartney for reading and commenting on the whole manuscript, seeing things that I had failed to see. The responsibility for this piece of work is of course entirely my own.

The book was made possible by a Leverhulme Trust Research Fellowship. I am grateful to the Leverhulme Trust for its award.

The Leverhulme Trust

Chapter 1

The Strong State and the Free Economy: German Ordoliberalism, Political Theology and European Democracy

The program of liberalism . . . summed up in a single word, should read: *property*, that is, private ownership of the means of production. . . . All the other demands of liberalism derive from this fundamental demand.

von Mises 1985, 19

The term *laissez-faire* is a highly ambiguous and misleading description of the principles on which a liberal policy is based.

Hayek 1944, 60

Of Rules and Order.

German ordoliberalism (*The Economist* 9 May 2015)

ORDOLIBERALISM AND EUROPEAN DEMOCRACY

Ordoliberalism has been identified as the villainous presence at the heart of Europe (Dardot and Laval 2013). It is said to be behind the austerity politics that the EU has actively promoted recently (Blyth 2013; see also Mirowski 2013). According to Nedergaard and Snaith (2015) and Biebricher (2014) the influence of ordoliberalism extends beyond the politics of austerity. It also shaped the institutions of economic governance in the Eurozone. Indeed, it is said to be the theoretical foundation of European monetary union and ideological force behind the entirely misguided response to the euro crisis, which ruined the economies of the weaker member states and led to conditions of abject misery, particularly in the Southern member states (see Stiglitz 2016). For these critics ordoliberalism stands for an imperious 'German ideology'

1

(Ojala and Harjuniemi 2016) that transformed the Eurozone into an 'ordolib-eral iron cage' (Ryner 2015).

Other critics characterise the European Union as a contemporary mani-festation of a tradition of authoritarian liberalism that goes back to Carl Schmitt's political theology and expresses the political project of the found-ing ordoliberal thinkers. In this argument the Europe that has come to pass is an exception to law-based policy making by democratic government. Jonathan White (2015, 314) thus speaks about an 'emergency Europe' that replaces law-based policy making with 'emergency politics' or with 'mana-gerial decisionism' (Everson and Jörges 2013; Jörges and Weimer 2014) by the European Council, which is the meeting of the heads of government.[1] Jürgen Habermas is the most prominent critic of what he calls the emergence of a European 'executive federalism'. He charges that ordoliberalism has 'more confidence in economic constitution than democracy' and that execu-tive federalism amounts to a 'faceless exercise of rule behind closed doors by the European Council' (Habermas 2012, 102, 129). He rejects Eurozone governance as a 'post-democratic exercise of political authority' (Habermas 2012, viii). Wolfgang Streek (2015, 361) summarises this argument about European policy making well. In his judgement the European Council now 'closely follows the liberal – authoritarian template devised by Schmitt and others in the final years of the Weimar Republic'. What Streek refers to as 'the others' are the founding ordoliberal thinkers (see also Oberndorfer 2012, 2015; Wilkinson 2014, 2015).

The book expounds the principles of ordoliberal political economy and analyses the character of an ordoliberal Europe. The identification of ordo-liberalism with austerity is not helpful and does not hold up. The ordoliberal argument is not about this economic policy and that economic technique. Rather, it is about the construction of what Müller-Armack (1976, 231–242) called a definite 'economic style' of moral sociability.[2] It is an argument about the liberal state as a market constituting and preserving power. It is to civilise and moralise the economic conduct and restrain competition to rules. Ordoliberalism recognises the political state as the concentrated power of economic liberty. The book argues that the European Union is founded on and integrates the role of the federated member states as 'market police' (Rüstow 1942). This term is central to the ordoliberal conception of political economy and places the argument about 'emergency Europe' into the context of a his-tory of authoritarian liberal thought, from Benjamin Constant to Carl Schmitt.

ON ORDOLIBERALISM

The founding ordoliberal thinkers are Walter Eucken (1891–1950), Franz Böhm (1895–1977), Alexander Rüstow (1885–1963), Wilhelm Röpke

(1899–1966) and Alfred Müller-Armack (1901–1978). Against the background of the turmoil of the Weimar Republic, they asked what needed to be done to (re-)assert and sustain a free labour economy.[3] Like traditional liberalism they accepted that laissez-faire is the economic concept of freedom. Yet, in distinction to the popular understanding of traditional liberalism, they argued that the economy does not comprise an independent reality. Rather, in the ordoliberal argument, market regulation by the invisible hand amounts fundamentally to a political practice of government. In ordoliberalism the state is the primary and predominant institution of the free economy.

The founding ordoliberal thinkers reprimanded laissez-faire liberalism for its neglect of the state, which led to its abandonment to social democracy and the lobby of powerful economic interests, including the trade unions. 'What', asks Rüstow (1954, 221), 'really distinguishes our neoliberalism from the long vanquished paleo-liberalism of . . . laissez faire? The distinction is this: we do not expel the state from the economy only for a much weakened state to come back through the backdoors of interventionism, economic subsidies, and protectionism. Right from the start, we assign to the strong and independent state the foundational task of market-police to secure economic freedom and complete competition'. The ordoliberals recognise that free economy is a social construct, an 'artificial order' (Müller-Armack 1947a, 86), that has to be actively constructed and maintained by means of state. Ordoliberalism asks about the conditions of liberty and what needs to be done to achieve and maintain them, and what can one hope for?

In the ordoliberal argument the freedom to compete defines the essence of Man (Eucken 1989, 34). They argue for a system of complete competition and identify unrestrained greed, protection from (labour) market pressures and the democratic welfare state as a threat to human freedom. The ordoliberals reject any talk about the state as a weak night-watchman state. The weak state does not govern for complete competition. Rather, it is overwhelmed by the powerful rent-seeking private interests (see Rüstow 1963, 258). The ordoliberal state is a strong state. It does not allow itself to become the prey of the competing social interests, nor does it allow a mass democratic citizenry to influence the liberal utility of government. Only the strong state is able to maintain its distinction from society. The strong state is the limited state. The primary meaning of the ordoliberal state lies precisely in this dimension. The ordoliberals conceive of the state as a 'planner for competition'.[4]

What then, according to the ordoliberals, can one hope for? The hope is for a harmonious social order of free economy, which they conceive of as ORDO. ORDO is *cosmos*. It constitutes an essential correspondence, some consonance and adequacy between the presumed essence of Man, the freedom to compete, on the one hand, and the world, the structure of being, on the other. ORDO 'accords with reason' in that it combines the nature of man with the social structure (Eucken 1959, 239). An ORDO does neither come about by 'spontaneous actions' nor by the laws of history, God or nature. An ORDO is a political creation and amounts to an eminently political practice of *Ordnungspolitik* – of ordering. Its purpose is the 'moralization of economic life' (*Versittlichung des Wirtschaftslebens*) (Müller-Armack 1947b, 147).

In distinction to traditional political economy analyses, ordoliberalism does not define the state by its relationship to the economy, and conversely, the economy by its relationship to the state. This view implies a conception of market and state as two distinct modes of social organisation. The perennial question about such a conception is whether the market has autonomy vis-à-vis the state or conversely whether the state has autonomy vis-à-vis the market, characterising its retreat or resurgence as a power vis-à-vis the economic. For the ordoliberals, the relationship between economy and state is an innate one, and within their 'inner connection' or 'interdependence' (Eucken 2004) the state is fundamental. Indeed, free economy has no independent existence. Rather its independence amounts to a 'political event' (*staatliche Veranstaltung*) (Miksch 1947, 9; Böhm 1937, 101). Ordoliberalism recognises the state as the political form of the capitalist social relations and conceives of it as the concentrated power of bourgeois society.[5]

In this context, contemporary analysis of the European Union as resembling an ordoliberal iron cage is most intriguing. The European Union is not a political union. It is a supranational union founded on common market rules and common market institutions. The euro is a stateless currency. In the context of the European Union the ordoliberal argument that economic liberty amounts to a political practice and that the state is the predominant power in the relationship to free economy appears dated. This is, however, not the case at all. The book argues that the European Union incorporates the role of the state in sustaining 'Europe' as a seemingly stateless market liberal framework. The euro is a politically constituted and sustained currency. It rests on the capacity of the federated member states to operate in concert as executive states of monetary union. The notion of an executive state belongs to Carl Schmitt's political theology and characterises the ordoliberal idea of freedom as a political event, as a practice of government.

The remainder of this introduction places ordoliberalism in contemporary and historical contexts to establish points of reference, set the analytical framework, introduce however briefly its founding thinkers and review its character and relationship to neoliberalism.

ORDOLIBERALISM IN CONTEMPORARY DEBATE

The 2008 global economic crisis reinvigorated debate about the character of neoliberal political economy and its future. In this context, ordoliberalism came to the fore as a contested account of post-neoliberal political economy. While some commentators came to reject ordoliberalism as undemocratic and dogmatic in its relentless pursuit of austerity in Europe, others endorsed it as a progressive alternative to neoliberalism (Sheppard and Leitner 2010; Wagenknecht 2011). These contrasting views follow in the footsteps of earlier assessments, in which ordoliberalism was discussed either as a project of a socially just market order (Nicholls 1994; Glasman 1996) or as an authoritarian liberalism (Haselbach 1991; Ptak 2009).

Conventionally, neoliberalism has been associated with buccaneering deregulation, especially of financial markets, and a weak state, which was accepted even when the argument held that the retreat of the state amounted in reality to a transformation of the national state towards a market enforcing, enabling and embedding state.[6] In this perspective, the neoliberal character of the relationship between economy and state comprised the global economy as an independent force.[7] Analysis of the capitalist social relations was set aside for an argument about the relationship between two apparently distinct structures of social organisation, that is, state and economy (see Gill 2003). At its core was the question of whether the economy had achieved unassailable power over the state or whether the state retained some degree of influence over the national economy.[8] The financial crisis of 2008 was thus identified as the demise of neoliberalism. It heralded the return of the state as a principal actor vis-á-vis the economy (Jessop 2010).

It was in this context that ordoliberalism resurfaced as a term of reference for a state-centric post-neoliberal political economy. According to Peck (2010, 275), it stands for 'a more orderly, restrained form of market rule' that might now be 'back in favour'.[9] Sheppard and Leitner (2010, 188) argued that ordoliberalism subjects the economy 'to controls' and on the basis of this insight they draw a line between neoliberalism as pro-capitalist and anti-state and ordoliberalism as critical of capitalism and pro-state. In their view ordoliberalism is an anti-capitalist alternative to neoliberalism. Their identification of capitalism with neoliberalism is widely shared, including third-generation ambassadors of ordoliberalism, for example Oswalt (2012) and Wörsdörfer (2012), who view the ordoliberal critique of monopoly power and cartels as evidence of its anti-capitalism.[10] Some left-wing critics argued likewise. Sahra Wagenknecht (2011), for example, urged the successor party of the former ruling party of the GDR, *Die Linke*, to adopt the ordoliberal idea of a social market economy to achieve social justice, full employment and wage-led economic growth.[11] According to Maurice Glasman (1996, 54–56), who was appointed a Labour-peer to the British House of Lords in 2011 and who coined the phrase 'blue labour' as the small-'c' conservative successor of social democracy, the ordoliberal idea of a social market economy is not a market economy at all (see also Giddens 1998). Rather, it stands for a socially responsible economy that protects individuals from the strife that markets bring about.

Glasman's account highlights the elements of cultural conservatism in ordoliberal thought. Ordoliberalism includes a critique of what Jesse Norman (2010) calls the *rigor mortis* economics of numerical equations and government by central targets. Röpke (2009, 57, 66) in particular rejects what he calls economism. He likens it to a 'religion of scientific positivism' that, intoxicated by 'mere numbers', reduces the supposedly human quality of the free economy to a mathematical numbers game at worst, and to an argument about economic technique at best. The latter is the means of the former, that is, economic argument about technique is about the most effective means of achieving, say, productivity gains, be it by means of socialist economic technique or capitalist technique. For Röpke political economy is fundamentally a moral philosophy about the freedom of Man through the institution of private property.[12]

In ordoliberal thought, economy policy is fundamentally social policy (see Eucken 2004, 303). It rejects what the intellectual conservative Guglielmo Ferrero (1963) called a 'quantitative civilisation'. The ordoliberals identified this 'civilisation' as a proletarianised mass society. They portray this society as one in which the individual is absorbed into a literally gigantic socio-economic machinery defined by mass production, mass parties and a mass state that governs in the interest of mass Man for material security. Ordoliberalism seeks, as it were, a 'qualitative civilisation' – one that is founded on the entrepreneurial vitality of the market participants. Indeed, ordoliberal social policy amounts to a *Vitalpolitik* (Rüstow 1942), a politics of vitality or a biopolitics (Foucault 2008). *Vitalpolitik* has to do with the establishment of an enterprise society in which the freedom to compete is second nature. *Vitalpolitik* is about the incorporation of competitiveness into a 'total life-style' (Müller-Armack 1978, 328).[13]

Foucault's (2008) lectures on biopolitics in the late 1970s recognised ordoliberal social policy as an original contribution to the practices of liberal governance and liberal governmentality (Foucault 1991). Foucault considers ordoliberal social policy as a countervailing effort to the destructive effect of the free economy on human community. However, in distinction to Foucault's view, ordoliberal social policy is not a policy against the destructive character of economic competition. Rather, ordoliberal social policy intervenes in the 'human disposition' to enable a competitive economy. Ordoliberal social policy is therefore not directed against the market. Rather it is a means of market freedom. Foucault argues on the basis of two distinct though interdependent logics, the logic of the market and the logic against the market.[14] It is because of this duality that Foucault's account of ordoliberalism does not draw it out fully. He identifies the logic of the market as a competitive market economy that is ruled by the laws of perfect liberty – free competition, pursuit of economic value and regulation of entrepreneurial preferences and innovation by the free price mechanism. He conceives of the logic against the market as comprising the principle of ordoliberal social policy, which for Foucault somewhat compensates for the heartless logic of economic competition (2008, 242). However, for the ordoliberals, *Vitalpolitik* is a market facilitating, enabling and embedding policy, which, in the face of the destructive sociological and moral effects of the free economy, has to be pursued relentlessly to sustain and maintain the free economy. The ordoliberals recognise that, if unchecked by the power of the state, the free economy destroys the moral and social fabric of society, leading to proletarianised social structures, politicised economic relations and erosion of (entrepreneurial) morality. Ordoliberalism therefore demands the provision of market sustaining and enabling ethical, moral and normative frameworks of individual behaviour, securing the mentality of enterprise in society at large. Ordoliberal social policy is a means of 'liberal interventionism' (Rüstow 2009, 51).[15]

The ordoliberal meaning of a 'restrained form of market rule' (cf. Peck 2010) was brought out clearly in an exchange between Hajo Riese and Franz Böhm in the early 1970s. Riese (1972), who was a leading Keynesian economist, had criticised the post-war programme of a social market economy as a project of a 'formed society' – a *formierte Gesellschaft* – which he rejected as totalitarian. Franz Böhm's rejoinder to Riese was most concise: free economy 'is an *eminently political decision*' (Böhm 1973, 39), which needs to be made time and time again to curtail the illiberal use of freedom. Economic freedom presupposes not only a law-governed and rule-based social order. It also requires the incorporation of an entrepreneurial culture in the mentality of the governed, formatting the will for freedom (Böhm 1937, 11; Müller-Armack 1978, 328).

In the British context, the ordoliberal rejection of the state as a weak night-watchman and its assertion of the liberal state as a comprehensive 'planner for competition' (Hayek 1944) were recognised early on. Thomas Balogh, who was a Keynesian economist and advisor to the Labour Party in the 1950s and 1960s, captured its idea of an ordered freedom succinctly when he defined ordoliberalism as an attempt at socio-economic planning 'by the "free" price mechanism' (Balogh 1950). Terence Hutchinson (1981) agreed with the ordoliberal critique of laissez-faire liberalism, saying that it concedes too much power to economic agents, whose greed, though required to oil the wheels of competition, is all consuming to the extent that it destroys its own foundation, the prevention of which, he says, is a political task (see also Joseph 1975). Andrew Gamble (1979) characterised the 'revival' of neoliberalism in the 1970s as a project of 'free economy and strong state'. With this characterisation Gamble traced the political stance of the incoming Thatcher government in 1979 back to this defining ordoliberal idea.

ORDOLIBERAL THOUGHT AND THINKERS
IN HISTORICAL CONTEXT

The issues raised by, among others, Riese, Balogh and Gamble point towards 'a rather different orientation from that usually attributed to the term' social market economy (Tribe 1995, 205). Indeed, Tribe (1995, 212) characterises ordoliberalism as an authoritarian liberalism that he associates with the political theology of Carl Schmitt.[16] Bentin (1972, 145 fn. 16) argues similarly: like Schmitt this 'liberal' school of thought looked at the strong state as the means of guaranteeing free economy. Given Schmitt's role in the Nazi dictatorship, this association does not sit well with ordoliberalism as the theoretical foundation of social market economy. Proponents of ordoliberalism, for example, Rieter and Schmolz (1993), have argued that ordoliberalism did not originate as an authoritarian liberal critique of Weimar democracy. Rather, for them the roots of ordoliberalism go back to the Nazi period. In this manner, ordoliberalism no longer figures as an authoritarian-liberal reaction to the Weimar Republic. Rather it appears as a liberal-democratic opposition to Nazism that planned for a liberated political economy, which, as Rieter and Schmolz (1993) argue, was to be lasting, free and humane. This attempt at cleansing ordoliberalism from association with the rightist rejection of Weimar is confronted by the paradox that its founding thinkers did neither write in defence of Weimar democracy nor in critique of Nazism. Rather they perceived Nazism as the consequence of the democratic character of the Weimar Republic.[17] Indeed, for the ordoliberals the lesson of history was that the 'evil of National Socialism should be laid at the door of anti-liberal policies of a state – Weimar – that had been grievously weakened by concessions granted to trade unions and other vested interests' (Lemke 1997, 242).[18] In the late 1920s/early 1930s, the ordoliberal argument that mass democracy leads to the tyranny of the majority was part of the rightist reaction against democratic government. In the 1950s, it became part of the 'anti-totalitarian' idea that mass democracy leads to tyranny, and that for the sake of an open society and individual freedom, mass democracy needed to be fettered to liberal principles.

Independently from each other Walter Eucken, Alexander Rüstow and Alfred Müller Armack published telling critiques of Weimar conditions in 1932. Most remarkably they do not engage in economic analysis of the then capitalist crisis. Instead, they saw the crisis as a consequence of Weimar democracy. Their accounts show a keen understanding of Schmitt's political theology, ranging from the critique of mass democracy to the endorsement of the state as the concentrated power of 'sound economy', from calls for a political decision for commissarial dictatorship to the use of language and phraseology. Müller-Armack (1932) writes about the laws of capitalist development and argues that its development is ultimately a matter of the 'actions' (*Tat*) and the 'decisions' (*Entscheidungen*) of those in power. In this argument, economic liberty expresses a political will and amounts to political decision. According to Eucken (1932) Weimar democracy had taken from the economy the 'whip of competition'. It had thus allowed the emergence of what he called 'an economic state', which he describes with reference to Carl Schmitt's quantitative total state, that is, the Weimar democratic welfare state (1932, 301 fn. 78). Eucken bemoans that 'the power of the state today no longer serves its own will but to a considerable degree the will of the interested parties'. Since 'the real independence of its will is missing' (307, 308), resolution to the malaise depended on the strength of the state to 'free itself from the influence of the masses and once again to distance itself in one way or another from the economic process' (318). Rüstow argued likewise. The Weimar Republic had succumbed to the pressures of politicised interest groups and mass democratic demands, and unionised workers, and was 'devoured by them' (Rüstow 1963, 258) with crisis-ridden consequences.[19] What is needed, Rüstow argued, is a state that 'governs, that is, a strong state' (258). The distinctive character of the founding texts of 1932 is that they define the economic crisis as a crisis of democratic disorder and call for the strong state to curtail democracy as a precondition of liberal economy.[20]

Berghahn and Young's (2013, 772) point that the founding ordoliberal ideas of the strong state are 'of interest primarily to tease out their "proto-fascist" components' is ill-conceived.[21] By linking the founding ordoliberal idea about the strong state to fascism, they obscure its character. The insight that the free economy amounts to a political practice is not peculiar to German ordoliberalism. It rather articulates a whole tradition of liberal political economy since Adam Smith.[22] The ordoliberals reasserted this insight in their political critique of the Weimar Republic. Ordoliberalism was the first sustained attempt at confronting collectivist challenges to the capitalist relations. It originated towards the end of the Weimar Republic, 1918–1933, in a context of hyperinflation, depression, mass unemployment, politicised labour relations and anti-systemic mass movements, political violence, social and political instability, Nazi storm-troopers and a politics of austerity that led to the characterisation of Heinrich Brüning (chancellor from 30 March 1930 to 30 May 1932) as the *Hungerkanzler*: the famine chancellor. With the exception of Müller-Armack, the funding ordoliberal thinkers did not call for the strong state in support of fascism. They called for the strong state as the concentrated power of a free labour economy.

Of the four principal founding ordoliberal thinkers, Müller-Armack was the only one who joined the Nazi Party in 1933. He had been an admirer of Italian fascism since the mid-1920s. In 1933 he published a book in praise of Nazism, entitled *Ideas of the State and Economy Order in the New Reich*. He worked as an advisor to the Nazi regime and the German army, and contributed to discussions about the post-war economic order. He was appointed professor first at Münster University in 1940 and then at Cologne University in 1950. After liberation from Nazism, he joined the Christian Democratic Union (CDU), published about the sociology of religion and was appointed chair of the Policy Department at the West-German Ministry of Economics in 1952. From 1958 to 1963 he was secretary of state for European Affairs, leading the German delegation at the negotiations of the Treaty of Rome and overseeing the early period of its implementation. Müller-Armack's writings concentrated on either political questions or the sociological and ethical preconditions of economic freedom. Akin to Sorel's conception of myth as a means of social integration, he advocated the ideas of nation, *Volk*, and movement as the 'metaphysical glue' (Fried 1950, 352) that is supposed to hold capitalist society together. After 1945, he turned to Catholicism as the 'ideological' means of social cohesion. Following Haselbach (1991), his advocacy of the different means of ideological cohesion was entirely functional. Myth was an essential means of social cohesion and as such a necessary component of rule in changing circumstances. Müller-Armack's lasting legacy is the phrase 'social market economy', which he coined in 1947. In the words of Rüstow, 'The only consequent, properly thought-out, unified and independent program of economic policy from our side known to me is the one of the so-called "social market economy", according to the fortunate coining of my colleague Müller-Armack. . . . It is a program my friends and I . . . have been working on for years' (1953, 101).

Alexander Rüstow argued forcefully for a strong state reaction to Weimar conditions and made his case with clear reference to Carl Schmitt's political theology. Unlike Schmitt who joined the Nazi Party once it was in government, Rüstow went into exile. He emigrated to Turkey where he took up a professorship at Istanbul University. He returned to West Germany in 1949 and became a professor for economics and social sciences at Heidelberg University in 1950 where he taught cultural sociology until retirement in 1956. It was Rüstow who coined the term neoliberalism in 1938 at a meeting of the Walter Lippman Colloquium in Paris. The term was meant to distinguish the new liberalism from the tradition of laissez-faire liberalism. He developed the term in sharp opposition principally to von Mises, whom he called a paleo-liberal because of his seemingly unerring belief in the natural capacity of the market to self-regulate itself (see Jackson 2010). Rüstow rejected laissez-faire as a theological idea. He advocated for a strong state as the precondition of liberty. In this first definition of neoliberalism, the system of liberty amounted to a sustained practice of government. From his exile in Istanbul onwards, he contributed to the development of the sociological framework of German neoliberalism, developing the notion of *Vitalpolitik* as a market enabling social policy. Rüstow was an early member of the Mont Pélerin society, which developed from the late 1940s onwards into the neoliberal think tank (Mirowski and Plehwe eds. 2009).

Wilhelm Röpke had a glittering academic career. At only twenty-four years of age, he was appointed a chair at Jena University in 1923. In 1929 he took up a professorship at Marburg University where he taught until 1933. During the 1920s, he feuded publicly with the contributors to the Nazi journal *Die Tat*, took out an advert in the *Niedersächsiche Landvolk* in 1932, in which he asked its readers not to vote for the Nazis, and after the Nazi takeover of government he reasserted his opposition publicly on 27 February 1933 when in his role as dean of the Faculty of Economics at Marburg, he spoke against them at the funeral of his colleague Walter Tröltsch. He emigrated in the autumn of 1933, first to Turkey where he took up a professorship at Istanbul University and then to Geneva in 1937, where he was a professor in what today is called international political economy. He was an early member of the Mont Pélerin Society. During the 1950s he was appointed personal advisor to Konrad Adenauer, the first West German chancellor. Röpke contributed to the development of the sociological framework of German ordoliberalism with three book publications during the early 1940s: *Social Crisis of Our Time* ([1942]2009), *The Moral Foundation of Civil Society* ([1944]2002) and *International Order and Economic Integration* ([1945]1959a). According to Röpke, the moral sentiments and social values of enterprise are indispensable preconditions for the civilised conduct in a free labour economy. Free economy tends to destroy its moral preconditions, and it falls to the state to sustain them for the benefit of enterprise.

Franz Böhm is with Eucken the main contributor to the development of the so-called Freiburg school that consolidated the economic account of German ordoliberalism during the Nazi dictatorship. Böhm trained as a lawyer and completed his postgraduate studies at Freiburg University in 1933. He objected to the discrimination and persecution of Jews and his stance might well have contributed to the fact that he was not offered a professorial position until after liberation from Nazism. Nevertheless, he acknowledged with obvious relief that the Nazi seizure of power had eliminated the chance of a Marxist government in Germany (Böhm 1936, 5). He worked for the regime in various advisory capacities to do with the financing of the war effort and achievement of an effective war economy. He was a co-founder of the Freiburg-based series *Ordnung der Wirtschaft* (*Economic Order*), the first volume of which was his *Die Ordnung der Wirtschaft* (*The Order of Economy*) (1937). With Eucken, he co-founded the yearbook ORDO in 1948. He also chaired the West German delegation for reconciliation with the state of Israel and the World Jewish Congress, and was a member of the Bundestag for the CDU from 1953 to 1965. His book *The Order of Economy* argues with great clarity that the state is the primary power of a free economy and that the constitution of a free economic order manifests a political decision and expresses a political will (1937, 11, 95). Böhm translated economic categories into legal concepts. In his account, the economy appears as an application of the rule of law. The ordoliberal argument about economic constitution enshrines the freedom to compete as a legal right, legal responsibility and legal obligation. It thus recognises the freedom to compete as a public duty. The economic constitution restricts the scope of democratic law making in so far as it posits foundational economic norms as a limiting framework for law making by parliamentary majorities.[23]

Walter Eucken was and remains the *spiritus rector* of ordoliberalism. He taught economics at Freiburg University where he opposed Heidegger's attempt at introducing the *Führerprinzip* to the university. He was one out of a group of eight prominent economists to advise the economics ministry about the financing of the war. His defining work, *Foundations of Economics*, was published in 1939 (Eucken 1959). It develops a critique of what he calls the 'economic state', by which he means the democratic welfare state of Weimar, and offers argument about the typology of economic orders. He identifies two basic typologies of economic order, the order of economic planning and the order of freedom. Each order contains a multitude of economic forms that express the character of interdependency between state, economy and society in concrete historical settings. Eucken argues for the order of freedom, of which the form of complete competition is the most desirable concrete manifestation. He was an early member of the Mont Pélerin Society and its first deputy chair. He died in London in 1950. Lionel Robbins had invited him to deliver lectures at the LSE about the virtues of the free economy.[24] Robbins was a sound opponent to all things Keynesian, including the commitment to a politics of full employment and welfare redistribution, which like other neoliberals, Hayek in particular, Eucken rejected as a first step towards totalitarianism.

SCOPE AND STRUCTURE

Contemporary analyses of European monetary union as ordoliberal in character call for a concise understanding of ordoliberal principles and argument.

The book lays out the character of ordoliberal political economy in chapters 2 to 5. Its exposition demystifies ordoliberal argument as an account of a socially responsible capitalism (Glasman 1996; Nicholls 1994; Sheppard and Leitner 2010). It also demystifies ordoliberalism as a 'German ideology'. Ordoliberalism is a theoretical expression of economic liberalism, which, in the words of von Mises (1985, 19), is the programme of the legitimate Rights (*Rechte*) of '*property*, that is, private ownership of the means of production'. Ordoliberalism is premised on the notion that for the sake of economic freedom, the state cannot have enough power. The book lays out the Smithean origins of this notion in his classical political economy, explores the ordoliberal conception of the economy as class-ridden and expounds its critique of democratic government as yielding to the demands of those who need to be governed, principally the labour movement. The containment of labour within the limits of what Smith called commercial society entails a definite conception of social policy. Concerning the contemporary ascription of the European Union as ordoliberal in character, the book argues that the ordoliberal elements of monetary union have to do with the establishment of the euro as a stateless currency. Its stateless character is a political decision and amounts to a continued political practice. The book argues that monetary union entails the member states as executive states of European law, money and market. This arrangement restrains conventional forms of parliamentary democracy in the member states and establishes the context for the contemporary nationalist backlash against the European Union.

The book develops the ideas and arguments mainly of the first generation of ordoliberal thinkers. The political experience of Weimar conditions is fundamental to the formation of ordoliberal thought. Contemporary ordoliberal writers argue in the shadow of the original accounts. The book incorporates contemporary ordoliberal contributions where relevant, in particular in the analysis of the ordoliberal character of European monetary union.

The character of ordoliberal thought cannot be determined by normative argument about the desirability or undesirability of its political economy. The book does not think *about* ordoliberalism as a feasible or purely imaginary, desirable or undesirable political project of capitalist organisation. Rather, it thinks *through* ordoliberalism to establish its rationality as an authoritative statement about the political preconditions of a free labour economy. Political concepts and ideologies are moments of a reality that requires their formation. The exposition of ordoliberal thought entails its critique as a theoretical expression of a definite form of society.

The approach taken here rejects the search for 'the' ordoliberalism as doctrinaire in its quest for authenticity. It is also fruitless. Indeed it is as fruitless as the search for 'the' neoliberalism, which does not exist either. It might well make sense to say that neoliberalism is more individualistic in its conception of free economy in contrast to the more state-centred ordoliberalism.

Yet, what really does this distinction mean?[25] Rüstow coined the term neoliberalism in 1938. He employed it in critique of von Mises, whom he characterised as a theologian of market freedom. German neoliberalism became known as ordoliberalism only in the 1950s. The name derived from the Freiburg-based journal *ORDO*, which was founded in 1948, with Hayek as co-editor.

The difference between ordoliberalism and Chicago neoliberalism is not one of doctrine. It is one of emphasis (Willgerodt 1986; Streit and Wohlgemuth 2010). Indeed the doyen of Chicago neoliberalism, Milton Friedman, argues with ordoliberal diction that the state will have to 'police the system [of private property], it will establish the conditions favourable to *competition* and prevent monopoly, it will provide a stable monetary framework, and relieve acute poverty and distress' (Friedman 1951, 11, 110; see also Hayek 1949, 107–118). The distinction in emphasis has to do with specific historical and social contexts in which they raised their questions, that is, what belongs to the concept of 'private property', and what needs to be done to sustain and maintain a free labour economy? With these questions in mind, the difference between ordoliberalism and neoliberalism is one of nuance, not distinction (Roth 2001). Müller-Armack made this point rather well when he argued that the 'economic theory developed by Walter Eucken, Franz Böhm, Friedrich von Hayek, Wilhelm Röpke, Alexander Rüstow, and others, led to the insight that in a mass society the functionability [*Funktionalität*] of the system of enterprise (*Wettbewerb*) requires the existence of a clear rule-based framework' (Müller-Armack 1956, 390). The framing of competition is a political task and defines the liberal state as a strong state. The purpose of the strong state is the 'policing [of] the *market* order' by means of a 'central authority strong enough to maintain formal exchange equality between all economic agents' (Gamble 1988, 37, emphasis added). It means also, and importantly so, the policing of the *social* order, including the ethical, moral and normative frameworks of individual behaviour.

Chapter 2 explores the class character of liberal economy and expounds the classical argument that the free economy and the strong state are interdependent categories of a free labour economy. It presents the ordoliberal case for the strong state, explains its critique of laissez-faire liberalism and contextualises its stance by exploring in particular the political economy of Adam Smith. The critical role of the state in capitalism is well brought out by Marx's argument in the *Communist Manifesto* that the modern state is nothing but a committee for managing the common affairs of the whole bourgeoisie. Ordoliberalism offers a most concise confirmation of this insight. Chapter 3 explores the ordoliberal critique of mass democracy and expounds its demand for state independence from mass society. It assesses its characterisation as an authoritarian liberalism and analyses the neoliberal critique of mass democracy in the 1970s as excessive in character and detrimental to individual freedom. Chapter 4 presents the ordoliberal argument that competition has to be restrained by rules and regulations to secure its liberal utility to the full. The ordoliberal argument for restraint articulates the classical argument that the passion for competition has to be constrained by laws and moral sentiments to civilise its conduct for the sake of the common wealth.[26] It examines the meaning of complete competition and economic constitution. Ordoliberalism argues for performance competition on competitive labour markets. Chapter 5 expounds ordoliberal social policy as a market enabling and embedding effort of social fabrication and character formation. It presents the ordoliberal argument that the free economy entails proletarianisation and analyses its proposals for deproletarianisation. The analysis of the ordoliberal character of the European Union starts with chapter 6. It establishes the ordoliberal arguments about federalism and subsidiarity as institutional means of maintaining the strong liberal state in conditions of mass democracy. In this context it presents Hayek's projection of an interstate federalism as a blueprint of monetary union. Chapter 7 assesses the institutional structure of the euro as a stateless currency and argues that despite appearances to the contrary, it is a politically founded and sustained currency. In monetary union the member states govern as federated 'planners for competition'. Monetary union incorporates the role of the state as the concentrated power of a free labour economy. Chapter 8 is the conclusion. It integrates the presentation of ordoliberal political economy with the analysis of European monetary union. In distinction to its original formulation in the early 1930s, which argued that mass democracy and liberalism are incompatible, the institutional structure of monetary union incorporates mass democracy within a European framework of economic liberty. In contemporary Europe, the tension between democracy and liberty manifests itself at its most regressive in the populist nationalist reactions to the European Union.

NOTES

1. In the words of president of the European Council, Herman Van Rompuy (2012, 17), '[t]he crisis has shown the need to strengthen [the Economic and Monetary Union's] ability to take rapid executive decisions to improve crisis management in bad times and economic policymaking in good times'. I owe this reference to Oberndorfer (2015).

2. Quotations from German language sources are the author's.

3. The freedom of labour is fundamental to the free economy and defines its system of liberty. These terms are used interchangeably. On liberalism as the theoretical expression of the capitalist social relations, see Clarke (1992a).

4. This phrase is Hayek's (1944, 31). It accords with the ordoliberal characterisation of the state as 'market police' (Rüstow 1942, 289; Röpke 2009, 52).

5. These formulations, concentrated power and political form, and also 'inner connection', belong to Marx's critique of political economy. See Bonefeld (2014, chapter 8). What Marx establishes in critique, ordoliberalism identifies as the political principle of capitalist society.

6. On the idea of the retreat of the state in neoliberal political economy see, among others, Strange (1998).

7. For a systematic account of the relationship between world market and national state, see Holloway (1995a), Burnham (1995) and Bonefeld (2000).

8. On the myth of national economy see Radice (2015, chapters 1 and 3).

9. Peck's (2010) account of the evolution of what he calls 'neoliberal reason' acknowledges the importance of ordoliberalism for the development of neoliberalism but does not go into depth.

10. The critique of monopoly, syndicates and cartels played an important part in the ordoliberal conception of the free economy. This critique was widely shared; see, for example, Simons (1948) who is a founding thinker of Chicago neoliberalism. It was also a common theme at the emergence of Mont Pélerin with Hayek as chair and Eucken as deputy. On this see the contributions to the volume edited by Mirowski and Plehwe (2009). On complete competition and critique of monopoly, see chapter 4.

11. Social market economy was to bring about 'prosperity through competition' (Erhard 1958). There is no doubt that West Germany's post-war political economy included elements of ordoliberalism. However, fundamentally, it amounted to a compromise between German liberalism, conservatism and social democracy, and Christian thought too. Key ordoliberal schemes, including an economic constitution of complete competition, failed to materialise in any meaningful manner (Abelshausen 1983; Wigger 2008; Manow 2008). Nevertheless, ordoliberalism germinated the new republic, not necessarily in terms of policy but, rather, in terms of ascription and mythology. The so-called economic miracle is the miracle of German ordoliberalism. What appears in the appearance of the economic miracle is the idea of a social market economy. It created the founding myth and legitimating basis of the new West German state (Haselbach 1994).

12. For Hayek, too, economics amounts to a moral philosophy. On this, see Samuel Brittan (2004).

13. Gary Becker's (1993) term 'human capital' rationalises the sentiments of the ordoliberal idea of social policy as an effort in character formation and expresses them in economic language. Becker's human capitalist is the self-responsible entrepreneur of ordoliberalism.

14. On this, see also Tribe (2009).

15. Foucault's (2008) account does not conceptualise the ordoliberal critique of Weimar democracy. He analyses ordoliberalism in the context of the social market economy of the 1950s. By removing ordoliberalism from its emergent Weimar context, he cuts it off from its constitutive political experience. Dardot and Laval (2013) argue with similar abandonment.

16. The characterisation of the 'new liberalism' that emerged towards the end of the Weimar Republic as an authoritarian liberalism is Herman Heller's (2015). See also Herbert Marcuse (1988).

17. This stance is commonplace in market liberalism. According to von Mises (1947, 75), 'The philosophy of the Nazis . . . is the purest and most consistent manifestation of the anti-capitalistic and socialistic spirit of the age'. Hayek argued that Hitler took advantage of the Weimar democratic welfare state, which manifested 'the decay of democracy' in favour of 'socialism' (Hayek 1944, 71, 31). He thus dedicated his book *The Road to Serfdom* to 'socialists of all parties' and argued that Nazism is the tyrannical consequence of a political commitment to social justice in the Weimar Republic. On market liberalism and democracy, see chapter 3.

18. As Foucault (2008, 116) remarks, they put 'concentration camps and social security records into the same critique'. See also the previous note 17.

19. The text was first published in 1932.

20. The founding ordoliberals favoured resolution to Weimar 'disorder' by commissarial dictatorship under the conservative politician von Papen (Haselbach 1991). For an account, see chapter 2. Franz von Papen was a German nobleman, officer and politician. After serving as chancellor in 1932, he persuaded the president Paul von Hindenburg to appoint Adolf Hitler as chancellor in 1933. Von Papen served as Hitler's vice chancellor from 1933 to 1934. The von Papen chancellorship was known as the 'cabinet of barons'.

21. See also Peck (2010, 59). He says that Rüstow's 'authoritarian strand of liberalism would later find a place within the National Socialist project'. Although authoritarianism and Nazism emerged from same society, they are distinct.

22. See chapter 2.

23. For contemporary constitutional economics, Böhm is an important reference. On economic constitution, see chapter 4.

24. The lectures are published in Eucken (1952).

25. See, for example, von Mises. He asserts that uninhibited market forces are the only remedy to resolving economic crisis, and then argues that 'fascism and similar movements [have] . . . saved European civilisation' (1985, 51). Hayek is equally drawn between the idea of individual freedom and the strong, authoritarian state (see Cristi 1998). Like Hayek, Friedman understood the Pinochet dictatorship in Chile as a dictatorship for freedom, and advised the regime on the necessities of freedom. Foucault (2008) rightly argues that Chicago neoliberalism developed core ordoliberal ideas in its own distinctive manner.

26. On the passions of the interests and the classical argument for constraint, see Hirschman (1977).

Chapter 2

The Free Economy as Political Practice

INTRODUCTION

The chapter explores the ordoliberal critique of laissez-faire liberalism and elucidates its conception of the relationship between the free economy and the strong state. Its critique of laissez-faire liberalism is ideological in that powerful intervention into economic life by public authority has never been absent from the liberal tradition. Nevertheless, against the background of what turned out to be the terminal crisis of Weimar the ordoliberals pointed the finger of blame at laissez-faire liberalism for the 'pathological' perversion and 'degenerate form' of Weimar capitalism (Rüstow 2005, 364). In this manner its own ideas about the free economy appear novel and distinct. In distinction to those commentators who consider ordoliberalism a progressive alternative to neoliberalism, its argument for a restrained form of market competition does entail neither 'less' competition nor abandonment of the idea of the invisible hand of market regulation. Rather, it recognises that both economic competition and the invisible hand entail the power of the state. Indeed, and as Adam Smith was well aware, without the power of the state the system of liberty descends into 'bloodshed and disorder' (Smith 1976b, 340). Ordoliberalism establishes a coherent account of capitalist economy as a practice of government. Indeed, it makes clear that the state is the concentrated and organised coercive force of the free economy.

The following section sets out the ordoliberal critique of laissez-faire liberalism. The next section examines the character of political economy in the classical tradition, which ordoliberalism reasserts in its political critique of the Weimar democratic welfare state. It establishes the indispensability of the liberal state as the political form of the capitalist social relations. The assertion of state power is a condition of economic liberty. The section introduces

Kant's argument for a civil constitution as perquisite of individual autonomy, explores Hegel's understanding of the class character of the bourgeois society and expounds the political character of Smith's political economy. The final section examines the ordoliberal characterisation of the strong state as 'market police'. The concluding section draws out the implications of the argument, according to which economic crises are in fact crises of – illiberal – interventionism. In the ordoliberal argument economic crises express a political failure. That is, the state failed in its role as 'planner for competition' or 'market police'.

ORDOLIBERALISM: CLASS, STATE, ENTERPRISE

The ordoliberals reject laissez-faire liberalism as an indefensible doctrine of faith in the magic of invisible principles. In their view, the liberal tradition since Adam Smith disregarded the role of the state as the concentrated power of economic freedom. According to Wilhelm Röpke 'Classical economic science had gone astray in conceiving competitive economy as autonomous', and he dismisses Smith's account as a 'disastrous belief in the sociological autonomy of competitive economy'. The belief in economic liberty as a self-contained system in which 'self-dependent processes [are] whirring away automatically' entails 'the cardinal error of the laissez-faire philosophers'. Röpke thus rejects laissez-faire as a 'deistic philosophy' (Röpke 2009, 51). Laissez-faire liberalism turned a blind eye to the sociological consequences of market competition on workers and vacated the struggle for the state, leaving it to social democracy. Rüstow concurs, 'Blind to the problems lying in the obscurity of sociology' laissez-faire amounts to a 'deist providentialism', which defines the 'theological-metaphysical character of liberal economics'. It asserted the 'unconditional validity of economic laws' (Rüstow 1942, 270–273) without enquiry into their social, moral and political preconditions. For the ordoliberals competition is not an end in itself. It is, rather, a means of individual freedom and individual autonomy. Indeed, competition 'does not breed social integration' (Röpke 1942, 6). Nor does it provide for 'the general framework of society. . . . It is unable to integrate society as a whole, to define those common attitudes and beliefs or those common value standards without which a society cannot exist'. In fact, if left to its own devises, it destroys 'the substance of binding forces inherited from history and places the individual in often painfully felt isolation' (Müller-Armack 1979, 152). They thus reject laissez-faire liberalism as a 'superstitious belief' in the providence of free economy, which 'prevented the necessary sociological conditions from being secured in economic life' (Rüstow 1942, 272). In the ordoliberal view, laissez-faire neglects to consider, let alone undertake, the political task of creating and sustaining the fundamental sociability of a competitive society.

Clearly competition is not a category of social unity. On the contrary, it is a category of disunity and strife, self-interest and greed, abuse and coercion. It includes both cutthroat self-interest and protection of self-interest by monopoly and cartels, and other forms of protection from competitive pressures.[1] Since competition 'appeals . . . solely to selfishness' the civility of a competitive society is 'dependent upon ethical and social forces of coherence'. One has therefore to look 'outside the market for that integration which was lacking within it' (Rüstow 1942, 272). That is, the free economy is a political matter. Although competition is the affirmed means of individual freedom, its conduct needs to be civilised by firm rules and regulations. The fundamental condition of a civilised system of competition is the equality of all market participants before the law and equal exposure to the dynamic of market competition, regardless of the inequality in property and economic power. In the ordoliberal account every single market participant has to be equally deprived of the power of shaping the rules that govern the conduct of society as a whole.[2] Competition is rule based or unruly, orderly or disorderly, performance based or skewed by the political assertions of private power, which compete for political influence to secure preferential treatment and special arrangements. It is either governed by firm rules or impeded by the participants who compete for special favours and privileges. Laissez-faire is no answer 'to the hungry hordes of vested interests' (Röpke 2009, 181). In the ordoliberal argument laissez-faire liberalism assumes as an eternal truth the divine reason of a supposed natural order of things, but does not inquire what needs to be done to sustain, secure and defend it not only in the hour of need but, also, and importantly, preemptively to prevent liberal emergencies from arising in the first place.[3]

The ordoliberals thus reprimanded laissez-faire for its neglect of the state as the only power capable not only of confronting the dangers to economic freedom that lay hidden in society and indeed within the economic itself, but also of sustaining free economy. In the free economy there is always 'a danger' that the liberal state is 'weakened or corrupted by economic power groups' (Eucken 1932, 307) who 'elevate cheating to a legislative or governmental programme' (Böhm 2010, 183). Laissez-faire liberalism is quite unable to prevent the state from becoming the powerless servant of interest groups and illiberal parliamentary majorities to the extent that it has 'absolutely no unifying thought and will' any more (Eucken 1932, 307). That is, capitalist society 'cannot function without authority [*Obrigkeit*]. . . . [I]t requires a support, which it cannot produce from within its own resources in order to function at all' (Böhm 2010, 167). Political power is required to police the conduct of the markets participants, retain depoliticised market relations and sustain the freedom to compete in the mentality of the governed. Free economy is not a natural occurrence. It is a social construct, which is the result of an '*eminently political decision*' (Böhm 1973, 39) about the character of economic life. The ordoliberals are clear that free economy amounts to a politics of order (*Ordnungspolitik*).

In the ordoliberal argument it is therefore important to recognise the limits of competition. Under no circumstances should it be applied as a universal principle to every aspect of social life. Since competitive social relations depend on the existence of a 'robust political-legal-ethical-institutional framework' (Röpke 1950b, 143) these frameworks are not negotiable; they cannot be subject either to market forces or to decision making by unpredictable parliamentary majorities.[4] Rather, they set the rules of the game, restrict the scope of legitimate regulative interventions into the economy and determine the fundamental values of the economic system. The issue is not whether the state should or should not intervene. Rather, the issue is the purpose and method, the objective and aim of state intervention. The ordoliberal state 'intervenes' not for specific social ends or on behalf of powerful socio-economic interests. Rather, it intervenes for undistorted exposure of the economic agents to competitive market pressures. It 'intervenes' into the 'economic sphere' and the 'non-economic spheres' to secure the social and ethical preconditions upon which '[complete] competition' rests (Müller-Armack 1979, 147). 'The problem', says Eucken (1952, 36), 'of economic power can never be solved by further concentration of power, in the form of cartels or monopolies.' The solution to the problem of economic power therefore *cannot* be found in 'a policy of laissez faire which permits misuse of the freedom of contract to destroy freedom' (37). Since free markets destroy the 'economic system based on freedom', the 'problem of economic power can only be solved by an intelligent co-ordination of all economic and legal policy. . . . Any single measure of economic policy should, if it is to be successful, be regarded as part of a policy designed to establish and maintain economic order as a whole' (54). The freedom of competition is essentially the freedom of ordered competition.

Following Eucken (2004, 254–289) the economic constitution of a free labour economy comprises seven constituent principles and four regulative principles. The constituent principles are a functioning price system, primacy of the monetary order, open markets, private property, freedom of contract, legal liability and continuity of economic policy. The four regulatory principles are antitrust policy, income policy, correction of externalities and correction of anomalous labour supply. The constituent principles organise the economy akin to an economic constitution. They reject central planning and exclude a policy of full employment, protectionism and (deficit-) demand management. Instead they require conditions of sound money and fiscal tightness, and enshrine the inviolability of private property and freedom of contract. They also make clear that freedom entails responsibility; that is, the economic agents are liable for the consequences of their decisions. The liberal state is not a public insurer for private risk-taking through, say, welfare provisions, state aid or bailouts.[5] Eucken's principles are manifestly anti-Keynesian; instead of demand management, they assert supply-side economics as the means of economic adjustment (Bofinger 2016).[6] The constituent principles frame the regulative principles, which are to facilitate the economic constitution 'in concrete historical situations' (Eucken 1959, 183).

Ordoliberalism conceives of free economy akin to a 'constitutional order', which places definite limits on the scope of parliamentary decision making (Vanberg 2011, 6). Clearly, economic freedom is not a function of social disorder. It is a function of social order. Order is not an economic resource. Order is a political category. In ordoliberal thought, the free economy amounts therefore to a political practice of economic order. Government is responsible for setting the conditions for economic regulation by the invisible hand (see Vanberg 2015, 29). The liberal utility of the state is not negotiable. It has to be protected from mass democratic intrusion, political lobby and public opinion. Competition has no lobby. In distinction to laissez-faire ideas about market self-regulation, ordoliberalism thus endorses the liberal state as the organised force of 'ordered competition' (Peukert 2010, 93).

Ordoliberal politics is first and foremost a politics of order (*Ordnungspolitik*), that is, an order of freedom (*Freiheitsordnung*). Freedom to compete is a means of individual autonomy. It does not permit recourse to special treatment by political power. Instead, it compels the economic agents to accept responsibility for the consequences of their non-coerced decisions. Order has a number of meanings. It refers first and foremost to the establishment of a definite economic order as the basic constitution of social life. It also refers to a legal order and a moral order which entail participation in free economy as a legal obligation and moral duty. Furthermore, it entails the notion of order akin to a political command that requires its agents to commit to the economic order and meet the challenges of a free labour economy by their own free will as self-responsible entrepreneurs – the entrepreneur of capital seeking to make a profit, the investor of great financial wealth seeking to make money out of money, the entrepreneur of labour power seeking to make a living by means of wage income. In this society of self-responsible entrepreneurs, everybody pursues his or her interests in freedom from each other. Everybody is therefore liable for the consequences of his or her non-coerced decisions. Finally, it entails the notion of a harmonious social order – an ORDO – in which the freedom to compete manifests itself both in the structure of society and in the mentality and conduct of the governed, as second nature.

The question at the heart of ordoliberal thought is, therefore, how to sustain the sociability of a society of 'greedy self-seekers' (Rüstow 1963, 255) and contain the 'natural tendency towards proletarianisation' (Röpke 2009, 218) within the limits of capitalist economy. Since competition is understood as the indispensable 'instrument of any free mass society', political authority is required so that the freedom to compete does not 'degenerate into a vulgar brawl' (Röpke 1982a, 188) that threatens to break it up. In this context, ordoliberalism develops the necessity of the state as the authoritative force of sociability; it is charged with sustaining unsocial interests on the basis of their fundamental sociability, restraining the 'greedy self-seekers' for their own good. A society based solely on egoism is impossible. They thus conceive of free economy as a political practice of sociability. For the sake of sociability, the state gives order to competition by establishing and safeguarding the rules of conduct. The rule of law does not apply to a lawless society. It is a function of order. The state thus appears as the force of order and law. It gives order to society and enforces the rules decided upon by law making political authority.[7] The disunited character of a society of 'greedy self-seekers' achieves unity, coherence and civility by means of state. In this conception of society, nobody is dependent on anybody in particular and yet everybody is obligated to everybody else. The state is the institutional embodiment of general dependency, public authority of sociability and institutional means of market freedom. It civilises the conduct of a society of self-seekers. Nevertheless, this conception of the liberal state does not go far enough. It is tied to the competitive relations between commodity producers whose interests are reconcilable on the basis of their fundamental dependency upon each other as agents of exchange.

The antagonistic character of society demands a different conception of state. For the ordoliberals, proletarianisation manifests the 'social irrationality of capitalism'. It is a veritable menace. If left unchecked, proletarianisation destroys the entrepreneurial vitality of the workers and turns them into 'the source of all evil' (Röpke 1942, 3). That is, in the ordoliberal argument, a proletarianised mass society confuses the freedom to work with the freedom from work. In this context, the ordoliberals speak about the 'revolt of the masses', which helped by the system of mass democracy tends to replace the sovereignty of the liberal rule of law with the sovereignty of the proletarianised demos, who subject the liberal rule of law to mass democratic demands for social equality and material security.

The polarisation of society into antagonistic class relations is fundamental to the ordoliberal conception of political economy. In fact, Rüstow defines the class of property-less workers in orthodox Marxist terms. He argues that the most severe sociological pathologies of capitalism belong to what 'Marx described most concisely as the transformation of labour power into a commodity, which results from the separation of the worker from the means of production' (2005, 365). The proletarianised worker is thus, as Marx had argued, doubly free – free of the means of subsistence and free to sell his or her commodity, that is, labour power, to acquire wage-based access to the means of subsistence (see Marx 1990, chapter 26).[8] As a class state, the state does not figure as the institutional manifestation of the fundamental sociability of society. Instead it represents the Rights (*Rechte*) of private property against the rapacity of the 'property-less masses' (Röpke 2002, 149). For the progress of the system of private property nothing is worse than a proletarianised mass society that rebels against the 'peaceful coordination' of millions and millions of individual preferences by means of the free price mechanism (Böhm 1937, 11). The formatting of this will defines the ordoliberal purpose of the state as the independent power of a class-divided society. The ordoliberal state governs not only over the social individuals but also through them to secure the 'psycho-moral forces' (Röpke 1942, 68), the 'moral sentiments' (Smith 1976b), at the disposal of a capitalist society, transforming rebellious proletarians into self-responsible participants on competitive labour markets.[9]

In sum, ordoliberalism asserts the authority of the state as the political master of the free economy. Only on the basis of order can a free labour economy flourish, and can a free people be trusted to be free, adjusting to the free price mechanism willingly and self-responsibly, each liable for their own actions and each seeking to meet their ends by means of voluntary exchanges on undivided and undistorted markets that are governed by the competitive price movements. The ordoliberal state is charged with removing all 'orderlessness' from markets (Böhm 1937, 150), that is, with 'depoliticising' the socio-economic relations and thus with achieving apolitical exchange relations between the buyers and sellers of labour power, and other commodities. It is therefore also charged with monopolising the political. There cannot be competing claims for political power in a free society. The state, says Müller-Armack (1981b, 102), 'has to be as strong as possible within its own sphere, but outside its own sphere, in the economic sphere, it has to have as little power as possible'.[10] However, as Müller-Armack (1933) was well aware, the depoliticisation of the socio-economic relations is an eminently political act. It presupposes the politicisation of the state as society's independent power and concentrated force.

STATE, ECONOMY AND SOCIETY

From Kant to Hegel

The understanding of bourgeois society as antagonistic in character was already accepted by Immanuel Kant. It was because of its antagonism that its reproduction required a specific political form to codify, regulate and moralise its conduct. For Kant the social antagonism was not one of class. His conception of antagonism was pre-modern. For him the social antagonism comprised the competitive relations between distinct branches of production and especially the competition between petty commodity producers. As he saw it, antagonism was entailed in the '*unsocial sociability* of men to come together in society . . . coupled with continual resistance which constantly threatens to break this society up' (Kant 1971, 44). The state appears here as a force that civilises the unsocial character of society, securing its fundamental sociability. The institutional independence of the state from society is vital to this task. It allows for the regulation of the competing private interests without prejudice on the basis of an impartial legal standard. The working class, or the Fourth Estate, did not inform his conception of the antagonistic character of society.

Kant's conception of the state rests on the positing of social antagonism not in the form of irreconcilable class interests but rather in the form of reconcil-able bourgeois interests. The private interests are 'unsocial' and therefore demand protection and cohesion on the basis of law. Law is the expression of a moral order. It moralises the conduct of a society based on the pursuit of self-interest. As he put it, 'The great problem for the human species, the solu-tion of which nature compels him to seek, is that of attaining a civil society which can administer justice universally'. At issue was the establishment of a 'perfectively *just civil constitution*' (Kant 1971, 46). Thus, the universal interests of the owners of private property are assured by the establishment of a 'law-governed civil constitution' (47). It resolves the '*innate capacities . . . of antagonism within society* [on the basis] *of a law-governed social order*' (44). In today's parlance, the necessity of the state as an institution of law and order arose for Kant out of the conflicts of interests, and he argued that the state has to retain its independence from these interests so as to moralise them in a civil society. The state sets the rules of the game and resolves the clashes of interests on the basis of these rules – it codifies property rights and regu-lates the conduct of the property owners within civilising intent. According to Kant, the state represents the general interest over the private interests in soci-ety. Its unsocial character will destroy what it presupposes: society's funda-mental sociability. For Kant, the mutual recognition of competing individuals takes the form of the rule of law, which is independent from their immediate interests and does not direct them in any particular manner. Individuals are free if they have to obey only the law, not particular persons or interests. The force of law is the state, which for Kant is a moral institution.

In distinction to Kant, Hegel understood the antagonistic character of bourgeois society as one of class. For Hegel, the fundamental condition of bourgeois society is thus no longer the competitive relationship between commodity producers. He conceives of bourgeois society as a class society.[11] His theory of the state thus differs from Kant's inasmuch as the recognition of labour's antagonistic presence in bourgeois society renders reconciliation impossible on the basis of a common interest. Class society is a society divided by irreconcilable interests. For Hegel, the state is with necessity a class state. The state is thus not only necessary as an institution of the general interests over and against the competing private interests. It is also necessary, and fundamentally so, to sanction and sustain the rule of private property against the 'rapacity of the poor'. Its purpose is the containment of the class tied to work within the limits of bourgeois society. For Hegel, containment is not only a matter of law. It is also a matter of coercive force, that is, the force of law making violence.

Hegel conceived of bourgeois society as selfish, competitive and antagonistic in character. Great wealth is accumulated by the few at the expense of the many. It condemns the masses to poverty. Hegel painted bourgeois society in the following term: '[the individual] is subject to the complete confusion and hazard of the whole. A mass of the population is condemned to the stupefying, unhealthy, and insecure labour of factories, manufactures, mines, and so on. Whole branches of industry, which support a large bulk of the population, suddenly fold up because the mode changes or because the values of their products fall on account of new inventions in other countries, or for other reasons. Whole masses are thus abandoned to helpless poverty. The conflict between vast wealth and vast poverty steps forth, a poverty unable to improve its conditions. Wealth . . . becomes a predominant power' (Hegel 1932, 232), fostering resentment and hatred. Bourgeois society appeared to him like the 'moving life of the dead. This system moves hither and yon in a blind and elementary way, and like a wild animal calls for strong permanent control and curbing' (240). The passions of this society required curbing to prevent it from imploding under the weight of its own contradictions. It requires, in short, the strong and capable state to render its conduct 'civil'. Fundamental to the establishment of a civil society is the containment of the 'poor' within the limits of bourgeois wealth.[12]

Hegel (1967) develops the class character of the state from the internal dynamics of bourgeois society. In his *Philosophy of Right*, he first introduces the notion of general dependency: the particular person is essentially related to other particular persons, each finds satisfaction by means of the others, and their reciprocal relationship means that the satisfaction of needs comprises a universal system of mutual dependency (122–129). There is thus a division of labour and satisfaction of needs by means of exchange. Concerning the state, his purpose here is the 'protection of property through the *administration* of *justice*' (126). However, and importantly, 'the infinitely complex, criss-cross, movement of reciprocal production and exchange, and the equally infinite multiplicity of means therein employed' goes beyond the division of society into individualised individuals, or in today's language, the so-called market participants. That is, the division of labour crystallises 'into a systems, to one or another of which individuals are assigned – in other words, into class divisions' (130–131). These divisions are of an antagonistic kind, and the development of bourgeois society leads to its polarisation into antagonistic classes (150). According to Hegel, the polarisation of society into two opposing classes is innate to bourgeois society. It belongs to its social nature, defines its concept and characterises its dynamic.[13] As he sees it, the market economy 'results in the dependence and distress of the class tied to [work]'. Dependence and distress are also entailed in the 'inability to feel and enjoy the broader freedoms and especially the intellectual benefits of civil society' (149–150).

It seems that civil society is civil only on the condition that the labouring class is excluded from it. However, exclusion is not possible for the simple fact that the expanded reproduction of bourgeois society results 'in the creation of a rabble of paupers' and the 'concentration of disproportionate wealth in a few hands' (Hegel 1967, 150). What is to be done 'when the masses begin to decline into poverty' and start to rebel (150)? He rejects redistribution of wealth as this 'would violate the principle of civil society' (150). He also argues that what today is called a policy of full employment is contrary to its logic. Rather than solving the problem, it would intensify it. Thus, 'despite an excess in wealth, civil society is not rich enough, i.e. its own resources are insufficient to check excessive poverty and the creation of a penurious rabble' (150). There is no economic answer to the polarisation of society. In fact, 'the inner dialectic of civil society . . . drives it . . . to push beyond its own limits' (151). How might the poor be kept at bay and the class antagonism be contained within the limits of its bourgeois form? For Hegel, there is only a political answer. He charged the state with the task of containing the class antagonism. Indeed, he argued that a civil society might well be assured by 'successful wars' that 'have checked domestic unrest and consolidated the power of the state at home' (210).

In sum, the dynamic of bourgeois society polarises society into antagonistic class relations. Maintaining it is a political task. It defines the state as the concentrated power and independent force of bourgeois society. 'Interventionism' in the forms of welfare provisions and employment guarantees is contrary to the logic of bourgeois society and is detrimental to its interests. Interventionism has to be in conformity with its logic and interests, or as Röpke (1936, 50) would put it, 'interventionism' has to sustain the character of bourgeois society and maintain its system of wealth, and it does so by enabling the 'natural tendency of the market', liberalising the economic relations, deproletarianising the social structures and securing the freedom of competition in the mentality of the governed.

Political Economy and the Market
Police: On Smith

The ordoliberal perception of Smith is blinkered. Rejection of Smith's political economy as a metaphysics has to be seen in the context of their battle with laissez-faire liberalism. The ordoliberals rejected laissez-faire liberalism not because of its endorsement of market freedom. They rejected it because of its alleged hostility towards the state and theological indifference to the social consequences of free economy, which contains a tendency towards the politicisation of socio-economic relations and proletarianisation, or both. For the sake of free economy, the state needs to be strong. For the ordoliberals, economic freedom is an empowered freedom. It amounts to a practice of 'market police' (Rüstow 1942, 289; Röpke 2009, 52) – a term Smith hints at in his *Lectures on Jurisprudence* where he asserts that securing the system of perfect liberty belongs to the police.

In Smith's theory of history the economic forces work their way through history towards what he calls 'commercial society'. He argues that in each historical stage, the political form of society, be it conceived in terms of authority or jurisdiction, necessarily flows from the forms of property. For Smith, private property is the consequence of the development in the division of labour, which, he argues, 'is not the effect of human wisdom but the slow and gradual consequence of the propensity to truck and barter' (1976a, 25). By force of its innate dynamic, the propensity to exchange leads to an ever greater division of labour, the extension of which increases the social surplus and gives rise to the growing social differentiation of society into distinct social classes, leading to the establishment of private property and the separation of society into the interdependent spheres of depoliticised society and political state in commercial society.

Adam Smith does not conceive of political economy as an economic theory. Rather, he defines political economy as 'a branch of the science of the statesman or legislator' (Smith 1976a, 428).[14] In Smith's conception of political economy, production and distribution are regulated through competitive exchanges, mediated by money. This regulation is achieved where there is 'perfect liberty'. The price mechanism that allows prices to rise and fall above and below the 'natural prices' is governed by an invisible hand, which informs individuals where to invest and what to sell. The invisible hand is a depoliticised devise of economic adjustment. Its ability to transform private vices into public virtues depends on the existence of undivided and undistorted markets. Given these conditions, individuals follow price signals in a manner of their own choosing and in pursuit of their own interests. Government or persons do not tell anybody what to do, when and where. Nevertheless, the magic of the invisible hand requires government. Impediments to market freedom have to be removed by means of state. There needs to be a functioning price system and an assured standard of money. Economic freedom requires the establishment of an order of freedom to sustain its sociability and prevent disorder. Smith understood that 'commercial society' is class-ridden and held the state to be indispensable for the organisation and maintenance of the entire system of liberty.

For Smith, 'Justice . . . is the main pillar that holds up the whole edifice' of commercial society (Smith 1976b, 86). Justice is a matter not only of law and the rule of law, which is the regulative force of the freedom of contract between ostensibly equal exchange subjects.[15] Fundamentally, it is a matter of order as the precondition of law. The rule of law does not agree with social disorder, and law does not enforce order. The police enforces order and in this manner renders the rule of law effective.[16] The system of justice is also dependent upon a moral order that commits individuals to the rules of justice. The rules of justice, then, presuppose a definite social order and unfold within a definite moral framework. The removal of impediments to the free movement of prices entails thus also the provision of morally committed participants in market freedom. In this sense, the invisible hand represents the promise of a system that is constantly striving for perfection by means of a political effort in removing obstacles from the system of liberty to establish its unimpeded operation. Liberty is a constant practice of government, rendering the unsocial character of society civil on the basis of law and order and containing the dependent sellers of labour power within the moral framework of bourgeois society. That is, the system of perfect liberty amounts to a constant effort at restraining the passions of competition according to the rules of justice, at configuring the moral sentiments of enterprise and competition, at governing for the 'cheapness of provision' and at containing the rebellious character of the poor to secure the further improvements of the productive power of labour upon which rest the prospects of the common wealth.

For Smith, the moral sentiments of commercial society are based on the sense of the 'propriety' of the beauty of a well-ordered whole. This whole gives purpose and benefit to the private individuals. It restrains their passions that are governed by 'self-love'. The private individuals are interested only in themselves, and yet each individual is obligated to all other individuals. The pursuit of their unsocial interests rests thus on the fundamental sociability of the whole. Its achievement restrains the conduct of the unsocial interests within the framework of a well-ordered whole. He argues that the basis of judging the propriety of the whole is 'sympathy'. Sympathy is the ability of individuals to adopt the position of the 'impartial and well informed specta-tor'. However, in Smith's account sympathy is not sufficient to contain the fundamental condition of commercial society, that is, 'self-love'. A society based on the pursuit of self-interest requires a moral foundation and an ethi-cal framework, to sustain it. The moral sentiments alone are thus insufficient for maintaining a society of self-seekers. On the part of the self-interested individuals, the moral sentiments express, firstly, the charitable site of com-mercial society or, as Marx (1975) put it in the *Holy Family*, its sentimental-ity.[17] Secondly, for Smith, the state renders the moral sentiments valid as the impartial and well-informed spectator of the system of liberty. That is, for Smith, the political state is not really an impartial and well-informed spec-tator. Rather, it is charged with making the system of perfect liberty valid. The state is thus endorsed as the impartial and informed enforcer of the rules of perfect liberty. Without such enforcement social disorder will result. For Smith, the state governs in the true interests of the *common* wealth, appeal-ing to and connecting with the honest core of individuals by restraining their immediate interests within a moral framework of law and liberty.

For the sake of liberty it is thus necessary to employ 'the power of the commonwealth', that is, the state, 'to enforce the practice of justice. Without this precaution, commercial society will descend into bloodshed and disor-der, every man revenging himself at his own hand whenever he fancied he is injured'. Punishment is the condition of justice. 'All men delight' to see injus-tice 'punished', and injustice needs to 'be punished . . . on account of the order of society'. Further, only those who do 'not violate the laws of justice [are] left perfectly free to pursue their own way, and to bring both their industry and their capital into competition with any other man, or order of man' (Smith 1976b, 89, 91, 340, 749). In the *Wealth of Nations* he argues further that the state is responsible for securing the proper use of freedom – by means of policing, it punishes the misuse of freedom, enforces the moral sentiments of freedom and intervenes into the moral make-up of individuals to restrain the passions of self-love for the benefits of the common wealth. In this context, he argues that the state is responsible for establishing the exact administra-tion of justice, adjudicating between clashes of interests and equal rights, erecting and maintaining public works and public institutions upon which the pursuit of commercial society depends (Smith 1976a, 723). Furthermore, the state is responsible for achieving the 'cheapness of provision', that is, for facilitating the progressive division of labour by means of greater labour productivity (Smith 1978, 6). Smith thus argues that the 'system of private property necessarily requires the establishment of civil government. . . . Civil government, so far as it is instituted for the security of property, is in reality instituted for the defence of the rich against the poor, or of those who have some property against those who have none at all', and he maintains therefore that the defence of private property against the poor is in fact undertaken in the interest of the poor (Smith 1976a, 770). In Smith's account, the state is the political power behind the system of liberty.

Smith introduces class struggle between capital and labour arguing that 'wages depend upon contract between two parties whose interests are not the same'. That is, the 'workmen desire to get a lot, the master to give as little as possible. The former are disposed to combine to raise, the latter to lower the wages of labour'. In this struggle, the masters have the upper hand because they 'are fewer in number, and combine much more easily; they can live for longer without getting their profits, the workers are starved' (Smith 1976a, 83). That workers rebel is understandable given their 'desperate conditions'. Yet, their action is foolish because 'the masters react with purpose and force the worker back and that is, the workmen very seldom derive any advantage from the violence of those tumultuous combinations'. The only way to raise wages and improve conditions is by sustained accumulation. 'Workers do well not to struggle', because with an increase in surplus, stock accumulates, increasing the number of workers, and an increase in revenue and stock results in an increase in national wealth. He argues thus that 'the demand for those who live by wages . . . increases with the increase in national wealth'. This, then, is the famous trickle-down effect – accumulation, he argues, increases national wealth and 'occasions a rise in the wage of labour' (Smith 1976a, 84, 85, 86–87, 87). Smith calls this the 'liberal reward for labour', and one consequence of his argument is, of course, that if there are poor, then this is an indication that 'things are at a stand', requiring state action to facilitate 'the cheapness of goods of all sorts', that is, to increase labour productivity and thus to improve price competitiveness on global markets. Smith thus attributes to government responsibility for the further progress of the system of liberty. Society at a standstill, or worse still in recession, expresses a failure of public policy, of liberal interventionism, of 'police'. In Smith's account resolution to the workers' desperate conditions and quarrelsome character does not lie in the admittedly unequal exchange relation between capital and labour. Resolution lies in the dynamic increase in wages that depend on the growth in the demand for labour, which results from the growth of the market and the increase in trade and commerce, and which is based on the further division of labour and fed by greater labour productivity.[18]

However, although according to Smith, 'national wealth' and 'workers' benefit from progressive accumulation, the owners of stock might not because 'the increase in stock, which raises wage, tends to lower profit' (Smith 1976a, 105). In this context, too, the state acts as the impartial enforcer of the system of perfect liberty. That is, higher wages benefit capital too by stimulating the growth of population, the expansion of trade and the division of labour and the industriousness of the worker. Nevertheless, capitalists pursue their own class interests and might therefore seek to maintain the rate of profit artificially, impeding the natural liberty of the market, for example, by means of price fixing or protectionism, dividing markets and disturbing its regulation by price movements. Furthermore, owners of stock in some countries might achieve higher rates of return on their investment than owners in other countries, 'which no doubt demonstrate[s] the redundancy of their stock' (Smith 1976a, 91, 109, 333). In order for their stock to be maintained, competitive adjustment at home is required. Its achievement is a matter of 'police'. 'Whatever regulations are made with respect to the trade, commerce, agriculture, manufactures of the country are considered as belonging to the police' (Smith 1978, 5). Effective policing entails a strong state, a state where it belongs: over and above the egoistic interests and class struggles, ostensibly not governing in the interest of either but in the interest of the beauty of the well-ordered whole, securing its propriety. Concerning the poor, policing is needed to make the worker accept that 'if he is frugal and industrious, [s/he] may enjoy a greater share of the necessaries and conveniences of life than it is possible for any savage to acquire'. There is thus need, also, for public systems of education and diversion to promote 'the instruction of the people' (Smith 1976a, 10, 723).

In summary, the system of liberty is a practice of good government (Smith 1978, 5–6). Smith does not believe that the invisible hand is capable of integrating society. It does not remove the social impediments to its operation, nor does it create the moral sentiments upon which the conduct between the private interests depends, nor does it resolve the clashes of interest between the classes. It does not create and sustain a system of justice, a monetary standard and a functioning price system. The Smithean state is not a weak night-watchman state. It is a strong state. It is not meant to yield to the social interests. It is not a state of privilege. It is a state of law and as such a moral institution. It secures for the invisible hand that unimpeded order upon which the progress of liberty is said to rest and depend. It eradicates disorder, establishes the rules of justice, facilitates the moral sentiments and restrains the passions, secures the cheapness of provision on the basis of greater labour productivity and instructs the people. As the impartial observer of justice, the state maintains 'the rich in the possession of their wealth against the violence and rapacity of the poor' and it does so for the benefit of the poor (Smith 1978, 338). It is in the poor's self-interest to let wealth trickle up to allow for that improvement of conditions, which only economic growth can bring.

The Smithean state does not compete with the invisible hand as if it were some alternative source of regulative power. The invisible hand has no independent reality. In Smith's political economy, the state is the political form of the invisible hand. It is the predominant power of the system of liberty. The Smithean state is responsible for facilitating the law of private property by removing various institutional and legal impediments, and by confronting those private interests that impede the perfect liberty of the market by advancing their egoistic interests and indeed class interests. It restrains the quarrelsome nature of commercial society, prevents the political assertion of the private interests, quells social unrest, suppresses the class struggle, facilitates the further progress of the common wealth by liberalising intervention and prevents illiberal manifestations of freedom on the basis of a law governed, perfectly civil constitution of social interaction, in which the individuals are free because they are only governed by the law of private property, which for Smith manifests the most developed historical form of Man's natural propensity to truck, barter and exchange. The Smithean state is thus also an ever vigilant state. It polices the conduct of the governed to prevent illiberal, seemingly unnatural and in any case reckless socio-economic behaviours. In the Smithean community of equals, as Marx put it with mocking irony, 'each pays heed to himself only, and no one worries about the rest. And precisely for that reason, either in accordance with the pre-established harmony of things, or under the auspices of an omniscient providence, they all work together to their mutual advantage, for the common wealth and in the common interest' (Marx 1990, 280). Smith's political economy makes clear that the sociability of bourgeois society 'must assume the form of the state and must gain expression as the will of the state, as law' (Marx and Engels 1976, 180).

ORDOLIBERALISM AND THE FORCE OF LAW: ON SOCIAL ORDER

For the ordoliberals, too, free economy cannot be built on pious aspirations. Rather, it rests on the use of honest and organised coercive force.[19] They thus dismiss laissez-faire as an option of government and reject the idea that government intervention entails less liberty. Instead, they call for more liberty by means of state. Laissez-faire describes the wished-for economic conditions. It does not extend to the political sphere. Hayek made this point, arguing that laissez-faire is 'a highly ambiguous and misleading description of the principles on which a liberal policy is based' (Hayek 1944, 84). Laissez-faire is not an 'answer to riots' (Willgerodt and Peacock 1989, 6). Nor is it an answer to majoritarian democratic assemblies that do not impose limits onto themselves (Hayek, cited in Cristi 1998, 168). In sum, laissez-faire is no defence against the political assertion by private powers and social organisations, principally by organised labour, which, they argue, tend to convert the political state of liberty into a state of the vested interests.

In the ordoliberal view, the well-being of capitalism is synonymous with the well-being of the entrepreneur – innovative, energetic, enterprising, competitive, self-reliant, uncomplaining, always ready to adjust to price signals and so on (Eucken 1932, 297). Müller-Armack (1932) speaks about the 'doing' of the entrepreneur, whom he identifies as the embodiment of civilisation. The identification of capitalism with the figure of the entrepreneur means that they conceive of capitalist crisis as a crisis of the entrepreneur. Things are at a stand because the entrepreneur is denied – not just by 'mass man' but also, and importantly so, by a state that gives into and thereby governs for mass man.[20] In the context of the crisis of the Weimar Republic they argued for the rediscovery of the liberal utility of the state to restore to society the enduring vitality, innovative energy and human qualities of the entrepreneur. Rediscovery amounts to an eminently political practice. It entails a process of reasserting the distinction between society and state, rolling the state out of society and, conversely, rolling society out of the state. For the ordoliberals, the strong state is the limited state, that is, a state that has the capacity and power to limit itself to 'the organisation of the market' (Eucken 1989, 45 fn. 2) and that thereby secures 'the possibility of spontaneous action', which characterises the human economy of complete competition (34).[21]

For the sake of the freedom of enterprise, therefore, liberalism cannot and does not demand 'weakness from the state, but only freedom for economic development under state protection', to prevent 'coercion and violence' (Hayek 1972, 66). What is protected by the state is not independent from it. On the contrary, its independence is a function of political action, that is, a political practice of order and law, of depoliticisation and legal regulation. It is its independence from society that allows that state to be a 'strong and neutral guardian of the public interest', of the *bonum commune* of capitalist social relations, asserting 'its authority vis-à-vis the interest groups that press upon the government and clamour for recognition of their particular needs and wants' (Friedrich 1955, 512; Vanberg 2015, 29–30). The free economy is thus a stateless sphere under state protection; that is, the stateless sphere of private conduct amounts to a political practice of socio-economic depoliticisation. It amounts to political practice of social order. The stateless sphere of depoliticised conduct belongs to the state inasmuch as it is the state that determines the order of liberty and secures the liberal character of society in both its structure and the mentality of the economic agents, ensuring the freedom of economic compulsion on the basis of law and order.[22]

Milton Friedman provided a cogent account of capitalist political economy as a political practice.[23] As he put it, 'The organisation of economic activity through voluntary exchange presumes that we have provided, through government, for the maintenance of law and order to prevent coercion of one individual by another, the enforcement of contracts voluntarily entered into, the definition of the meaning of property rights, the interpretation and enforcement of such rights, and the provision of a monetary framework'.

The state has to 'promote competition' and do for the market what the market 'cannot do for itself'. The state, then, is 'essential both as a forum for determining the "rules of the game" and as an umpire to interpret and enforce the rules decided upon', and enforcement is necessary 'on the part of those few who would otherwise not play the game'.[24] The state, he says, is the means through which 'we' set and modify the rules that govern the sociability of the unsocial interest (Friedman 1962, 15, 23, 25, 27, 34). However, what happens when 'they' resist and instead start to rebel?[25]

The ordoliberal idea of economic freedom is essentially based on distrust. There is no freedom without surveillance to ensure that the orderly conduct of self-interested entrepreneurs does not give way to devitalised proletarians, permissiveness, socio-economic politicisation and monopoly pricing or reckless 'greed' or special interest rent-seeking. Freedom is a constantly empowered freedom. It 'requires a market police with strong state authority' (Rüstow 1942, 289) to sustain it. Fundamentally, free economy entails individuals who are not just complying with the rules of the game but do so out of their own free will. Here, too, freedom is defined both by the absence of the state, as a stateless sphere of individual purposes, and by a strong state that plans for that freedom, that is, and paraphrasing Rousseau's dictum about the purposes of education, a political practice that forces a people to be free.

The political character of liberal political economy is brought out well by Franz Böhm. He argues that, for the sake of market liberty, the socialisation of the state by the social forces has to be rejected in favour of the 'etatisation of society' (Böhm 1969, 171). That is, the state not only governs over society, but it also governs in and through society to secure and sustain the will for enterprise in the mentality of the governed. As the independent power of bourgeois society the state governs for the ORDO of a 'human' economy, suppressing the class struggle and containing the natural tendency of capitalism towards proletarianised social structures within the framework of private property, and 'formatting' the will for enterprise in society at large.[26] It would therefore be insufficient to characterise the strength of the ordoliberal state only according to its ability to keep the social interests at bay, securing the liberal utility of government in face of both political pluralism and mass democratic demands for material security. Rather, the strength of the state resides also in its ability to facilitate the entrepreneurial governmentality of society, preventing the politicisation of society by successfully incorporating enterprise competition into the 'psycho-moral forces' of society (Röpke 1942, 68; also Müller-Armack 1978, 328).[27] Incorporation is a matter of social policy. It envisages a society of self-responsible and vitally satisfied entrepreneurs of labour power, which does not ask for collective provisions and protection from competitive pressures. Unlike a devitalised society of proletarian welfare seekers, it gets on with things on its own initiative and for its own sake. The purpose of ordoliberal social policy, of *Vitalpolitik*, is to prevent proletarianisation. It is a politics of moral sentiments, fabrication of entrepreneurial will and surveillance of conduct. For the 'etatisation of society' the independence of political will is precondition.

Anthony Nicholls (1994, 48) and Sibylle Tönnies (2001, 169) see Rüstow's (1963) enunciation of the strong state in 1932 as a landmark in the theory of the social market economy. Rüstow conceives of the strong state in terms laid out by Carl Schmitt's critique of Weimer democracy. The strong state does not make itself available to the 'enemies' of a free labour economy. It maintains the political as the substance of its own independence. It governs society and thus does not let itself be dragged down into society. Only the weak state allows society to govern through the state, which makes the state the prey of the contradictory and antagonistic social interests that latch on to the state to advance their own 'private' interests, carving out privileges and special licences for themselves. Instead of competing on the basis of price, competition changes into impediment competition that, based on access to political power, literally impedes the market process by inserting protectionist defences against competitive pressures, distorting free economy. The distinction between state and society is thus breached with dramatic consequences. The organised power of free economy, that is the state, is literally 'being pulled apart by greedy self-seekers. Each of them takes out a piece of the state's power for himself and exploits it for its own purposes. . . . This phenomenon can best be described by a term used by Carl Schmitt – "pluralism". Indeed, it represents a pluralism of the worst possible kind. The motto for this mentality seems to be the "role of the state as a suitable prey"' (Rüstow 1963, 255; also Röpke 2009, 107). Greedy self-seekers belong to the economic sphere, where they oil the machinery of competition on the basis of clear rules of conduct. However, their political assertions have to be resisted, and capture of the state by the socio-economic interests has to be prevented at all cost for the sake of freedom under the rule of law.

Röpke had already demanded the strong state in 1923, long before the onset of economic crisis. Liberalism, he argued, has to put itself at the 'forefront of the fight for the state' (1959b, 44). Only the state, he says, can guarantee the 'common wealth', and liberalism should not involve itself with defending particular interests. It should always focus on the 'whole', and this whole 'is the state' (45). Eucken, too, demanded the strong state over and above the social interest and class conflicts. In his view, the 'economic state' is a state of total weakness.[28] 'If the state . . . recognises what great dangers have arisen for it as the result of its involvement in the economy and if it can find the strength to free itself from the influence of the masses and once again to distance itself in one way or another from the economic process . . . then the way will have been cleared . . . for a further powerful development of capitalism in a new form'. For the sake of free economy, independence of the political will is of utmost importance (Eucken 1932, 318, also 308). As Foucault put in, in the ordoliberal scheme, 'freedom is never anything other . . . than an actual relation between governors and governed' (Foucault 2008, 63). It manifests a social order of rightful conduct and recognition of that order as a moral obligation and public duty. The stateless sphere of economic conduct rests therefore on the 'complete eradication of all orderlinessess from markets and the elimination of private power from the economy' (Böhm 1937, 150) – the depoliticised society entails the politicised state in its concept. Depoliticisation is an eminently political practice of social order, and ordering.

In distinction, in the early 1930s Müller-Armack did not argue for the depoliticisation of socio-economic relations by means of state. He argued instead for the total politicisation of economic relations as a means of crisis-resolution. In his view then (1932, 110), the 'statification of economic processes' was 'irreversible', and the demand for overcoming the economic state was therefore not realistic.[29] Instead, he demanded the 'complete sovereignty of the state vis-à-vis the individual interests' by means of a 'complete integration of society into the state in order to change the development of the interventionist state' (126) from a collectivist economic state to an economic state of enterprise and competitiveness that governs with the proletarian enemy in clear sight, suppressing the class struggle, incorporating society and organising the freedom of labour. He demanded the total state as the basis for the 'national formation' of all economic and political interests. Its purpose was the freedom of the 'entrepreneur', that is, 'by means of the complete integration of the economic into the state, the state attains room for manoeuvre for the sphere of private initiative which, no longer limiting the political sphere, coincides with the political' (127). He thus defined the Nazi regime as a 'accentuated democracy (Müller-Armack 1933, 34), declared *Mein Kampf* to be a 'fine book' (37) and argued that socio-economic difficulties can be 'resolved only by a strong state' that 'suppresses the class struggle' and that thereby renders effective the free initiative of individuals within the framework of 'decisive rules' (41). He thus endorsed national socialism as creating a new form of democracy, which transcended mass democracy for a leadership democracy that is characterised by a unity of mass movement, national unity and political will. This new democracy of *Volk* and *Führer* mobilised the masses as disciples of a new political order. The new order galvanised a demoralised and devitalised society, reenergising the will for 'ordered' enterprise. Still, the purpose that Müller-Armack ascribes to the total state – the political formation of entrepreneurial freedom and suppression of class struggle – does not differ in substance from the purpose of the strong state ascribed to it by Eucken, Rüstow and Röpke. The distinction, however dramatic in its political assertion, is one of the techniques of power

(Foucault 2008; Haselbach 1991) – the one requires the political organisation of an economic order to secure the freedom of entrepreneurial decision making on the basis of a domesticated labour movement, formatting workers as disciples of order, and the others declare for the forceful depoliticisation of society, formatting workers as self-disciplined entrepreneurs of labour power.

The ordoliberals conceived of the agents of the strong state as modern-day aristocrats of the common good (Rüstow 1963, 257f; see also Eucken 1932, 320). The potential revolt of the masses 'must be counteracted by individual leadership', based on a 'sufficient number of such aristocrats of public spirit. . . . We need businessmen, farmers, and bankers who view the great questions of economic policy unprejudiced by their own immediate and short-run economic interests' (Röpke 1998, 131). These 'secularised saints . . . constitute the true "countervailing power"', providing 'leadership, responsibility, and exemplary defence of the society's guiding norms and values'. This defence 'must be the exalted duty and unchallenged right of a minority that forms and is willingly and respectfully recognised as the apex of a social pyramid hierarchically structured by performance' (130). He calls these experts of the free economy 'a true *nobilitas naturalis* . . . whose authority is . . . readily accepted by all men, an elite deriving its title solely from supreme performance and peerless moral example' (130).[30] Understanding economic development, says Eucken (1932, 320), is very difficult and therefore 'requires robust theoretical instruction' and for the Freiburg-based thinkers it is therefore essential that their advice is sought. As they put it in 1936, 'Man of science by virtue of their profession and position being independent of economic interests, are the only objective, independent advisers capable of providing true insight into the intricate interrelations of economic activity and therefore also providing the basis upon which economic judgements can be made' (Böhm, Eucken and Grossmann-Doerth 1989, 15, 24). Men of science are to support the state to 'take independent decisions based on objective assessment of all relevant facts and designed to serve the common interest' in a free labour economy (Röpke 1998, 141). The freedom to compete is a function of the 'power of the state' to assert the 'real independence of its will' (Eucken 1932, 307, 308) over an uncivilised society of mass demands, 'mass opinion [and] mass emotion' (Röpke 1998, 142).

In the face of a liberal emergency, what is the character of the 'coup de force' (Tönnies 2001, 194) that is required to reassert the independence of the state from society? What needs to be done to restore relations of freedom 'constrained by rules' and tied to the moral values of responsible entrepreneurship (Vanberg 2001, 2)? According to Tönnies, Rüstow's declaration for the strong state in 1932 took its vocabulary from Carl Schmitt but nothing more. Rüstow, she says, did not support Schmitt's politics of dictatorship. In her view, ordoliberalism is a doctrine of freedom and thus also a doctrine against the abuse of freedom by what she calls the social forces. In distinction to Schmitt who, she says, believed in dictatorship as an expression of political authority, Rüstow advocated for dictatorship as a means of establishing a free society (167). In her view, 'ordo-liberalism in the spirit of Rüstow is "free economy – strong state"' (168). In distinction to Tönnies, Rüstow's formulation is in fact similar in tone and conception to Carl Schmitt's declaration for 'sound economy and strong state' in 1932 (Schmitt 1998).

Nicholls (1994, 48) praises Rüstow's strong state as heralding 'the concept of the "Third Way"' as an alternative for freedom beyond laissez-faire and socialism. He recognises, however, that 'Rüstow's call for a strong state in 1932 could have been seen as an appeal for authoritarian rule' (68). Indeed, Rüstow had already done so in 1929, when he called for a dictatorship 'within the bounds of democracy'. This state was to be 'forceful' and 'independent' and was to govern with of 'authority and leadership' (1959, 100). Röpke (1942, 246, 247) defines 'dictatorship within the bounds of democracy' correctly as a commissarial dictatorship, which temporarily suspends the rule of law to restore legitimate authority in the face of an 'extreme emergency', for which he holds responsible those who lack the 'moral stamina' (Röpke 2009, 52) to absorb economic shocks in a disciplined and self-responsible manner.[31]

However, the defence of liberal principles in the hour of need is not enough. In fact, its acuity reveals that the pursuit of liberty had weakened with devastating effect. That is, defence of liberal principles has to be preemptive – the strong state is ever-vigilant, and so properly called a 'security state' (Foucault 2008). Its purpose is the surveillance of individual conduct in a free labour economy. 'Everything which opposes liberalism and proposes state management of the economy thus constitutes an invariant' (Foucault 2008, 115) and in this manner the citizen is both a free entrepreneur and a veritable security risk.[32] The premise of liberal government is that economic 'security is only to be had at a price of constant watchfulness and adaptability and the preparedness of each individual to live courageously and put up with life's insecurities' (Röpke 2002, 198). That is, primarily poverty is not material in character. Rather, for them, it expresses a mode of moral deprivation, that is, a devitalised state of existence that is characterised by the poverty of aspiration. It is a problem of 'vitality, i.e., a non-economic, spiritual problem' (Röpke 2009, 53), which, if left to fester, manifests itself in proletarianised social structures and mass demand for material security. In sum, the strong state of free economy is an ever-vigilant security state. It manifests a latent state of emergency. Its purpose is to prevent illiberal conduct and preempt liberal emergencies. The connection between freedom and surveillance is therefore not incidental. It belongs to the conceptuality of a definite modality of freedom, according to which poverty is not unfreedom (see Joseph and Sumption 1979) but rather an opportunity to do better.

In summary the ordoliberal demand for the strong state is a demand for the limited state. Only the strong state is able to monopolise the legitimate use of violence and limit itself to what is called the political. In this manner the strong state secures economic freedom by depoliticising the social relations, removing 'private power from the economy' (Böhm 1937, 110) and ordering the 'style' of economic conduct (Eucken 1959). For the ordoliberals, the tendency of what they call proletarianisation is inherent in capitalism and, if unchecked, is the cause of social crisis, turmoil and disorder, including 'the pluralistic disintegration of the state' as the indispensable means of liberty (Röpke 1998, 143). Its prevention is an eminently political task. Indeed, 'if liberty is to have a chance of survival and if rules are to be maintained which secure free individual decisions' the state has to act by setting and ensuring the conditions in which the invisible hand can do its work (Willgerodt and Peacock 1989, 6).

CONCLUSION

The Adam Smith who is said to have argued for the autonomy of the economic sphere is quite unlike the Adam Smith who argued that the autonomy of the economy is a political task, comprising the removal of impediments to the market, restraint of the passions of competition within a legal and moral framework and enforcement of the order of freedom to secure the system of perfect liberty in the conduct of society. Without government, Smith argues, liberty descends into 'disorder and bloodshed'. Government civilises society and contains the class antagonism within the limits of private property. Civil society and political state are thus not opposites. Rather, civil society is a political practice of government. For Kant, therefore, the state is a moral institution. It restrains the unsocial interests on the basis of their fundamental sociability. For Smith, and Hegel too, police, public policy, is the premise of liberty. The ordoliberals clearly recognise that in a disunited and antagonistic society, the Leviathan comes first. The political state is the concentrated power of depoliticised exchange relations. It maintains formal exchange equality between all economic agents whatever their circumstances might be, and protects the Rights of private property by guaranteeing and securing its freedoms.

The ordoliberals recognise that the pursuit of liberty takes place under the watchful 'security state', which governs not only over society but, also, through society. Freedom requires the 'etatisation of society' (Böhm 1969, 171) to secure what Röpke (1942, 68) calls its 'psycho-moral forces'. Freedom is a matter for market police, and market policing is a practice of economic freedom – from the constitution of the economic order, enforcement of the laws and rules of the market liberty that sustain the freedom to compete as legal obligation and moral duty, to the achievement of the cheapness of provision and the formation of character. They understand that the system of liberty comprises a class of property-less workers and that class society entails a natural propensity towards proletarianisation. For the ordoliberals, laissez-faire is therefore a dismal doctrine of liberty precisely because it does not comprehend the foundation and dynamic of the free economy. For the ordoliberals, the viability of the free economy is a matter 'beyond supply and demand' (Röpke 1998).[33] In a free labour economy, the political state is the premise of depoliticised market relations between buyers and sellers of labour power. The ordoliberal Smith is the Smith of the moral sentiments and market police, of the laws of justice and empowered entrepreneurship. Compared with the ordoliberal Smith, the Smith of laissez-faire liberalism is a caricature.

In distinction to ordoliberalism, Smith's political economy does not employ the word 'liberalism'. There was no such system to defend. His theory of the system of liberty looked forward to a world that still had to be born. His political economy was a critique of mercantilism, not a political defence of existing social relations.[34] Smith imagined commercial society in critique of mercantilism. In the context of global economy crisis and political turmoil, they asked what is necessary to secure liberty. What needs to be done to achieve an enterprise society of competitive price takers? Their argument that the state is in fact the executive power of liberty is an unacknowledged tribute to Smith's political economy. Unlike Smith, the ordoliberals argue for the preservation of the liberal economic order. They do indeed think in terms of order, and specify the conditions of order and demand the restoration of order. Thinking for the sake of order is thinking against social imaginaries. 'In a conflict between freedom and order, order is the unconditional priority' (Böhm 1937, 101). The founding ordoliberal argument ousts liberality from liberalism and turns towards authoritarianism as a means of liberty.

Writing in the early 1930s, Hermann Heller (2015) characterised the new liberalism as an authoritarian liberalism. With Marcuse (1988), he argued that the authoritarian liberal scheme of social order could not be maintained in democratic form. Indeed, in the ordoliberal view economic crises are crises of democratic excess (Eucken 1932; Rüstow 1932; Müller-Armack 1932). There can thus be no economic crises as such. Rather, economic crises are the consequence of illiberal interventionism. Röpke thus argues that one should 'not speak of a "crisis of capitalism" but of a "crisis of interventionism"' (Röpke 1936, 160). Ordoliberalism recognises the liberal state as the indispensable power of the free economy and identifies economic crisis as the consequence of illiberal interference with the free economy. Economic crises are thus a consequence of the lamentable weakness of a state, which yielded to social demands for protectionism and special favours. In the ordoliberal argument the free economy state is 'the mistress of the economy in its totality as in its parts . . . and the state must master the whole of economic development both intellectually and materially'; it must plan for liberty and competition, and assure itself of the entrepreneurial mentality, of 'the will' for self-responsible enterprise, of the governed (Böhm 1937, 10, 11). They argue that unrestrained by liberal principles, mass democracy weakens the liberal state as planner for competition, as market police, to the point of planned chaos. The following chapter explores the ordoliberal argument about the relationship between democracy and liberty.

NOTES

1. Free economy contains the 'universal propensity to build up monopolies' (Eucken 2004, 31).

2. Böhm (2010) conceives of a competitive exchange society as a private law society. For an account of private law society, see chapter 4.

3. In the words of Hayek (1976, 94–95), 'a functioning market requires a framework of appropriate rules within which the market will operate smoothly'. Their establishment and enforcement is a matter of government because the 'market cannot supply'.

4. On the implications of this point for democratic government, see chapter 3.

5. On these issues in the context of the Eurozone crisis, see chapter 7.

6. I am grateful to David Woodruff for forwarding the web link to Bofinger's paper.

7. For discussion on the innate connection between the force of law and the rule of law, see Walter Benjamin's 'Critique of Violence' (2007) and Carl Schmitt's *Concept of the Political* (1996a). The difference between Benjamin's and Schmitt's conception of the relationship between law and violence stems from their divergent approach to the existing social relations, the one critical in his conception of reality, and the other analytical in defence of the existent relations of rule and power.

8. On the Smithean origin of the orthodox Marxist definition of class, see Clarke (1992b). See also Bonefeld (2011) and the contributions to Dinerstein and Neary (2002).

9. Müller-Armack calls this state of affairs an irenic order. See chapter 5.

10. Müller-Armack is in fact paraphrasing Benjamin Constant's (1998) critique of democratic government. Constant's stance is a regular point of reference in ordoliberal writing.

11. Some might object to the use of bourgeois society in this context and insist on the use of civil society. But recall Hegel's dictum: 'In this society, the individuals are not citoyens, they are bourgeois' (Art. 89 of the *Philosophy of Law of Heidelberg, 1817/18*, first published in 1983. Stuttgart: Klett Cotta). The German for 'civil society' is *Zivilgesellschaft* or *zivile Gesellschaft*, not *bürgerliche Gesellschaft*, which translates as 'bourgeois society'.

12. On the character and dynamic of bourgeois wealth, see Bonefeld (2014) and Postone (1993).

13. On social nature, see Schmidt (2014).

14. In the secondary literature on Smith the political constituent of his political economy is largely ignored. To his benefit Andrew Skinner concludes on Smith's theory of the state in his introduction to the Penguin edition of the *Wealth of Nations*. Yet, he, too, does not expound on Smith's argument that the state is the indispensable power of the system of perfect liberty. The exception to traditional Smith scholarship is Simon Clarke. His account develops Smith's state theory in an insightful manner arguing that 'the purpose of Smith's analysis of the economic system was to define the proper role of the state' (Clarke 1988, 39). I hold that the political state is the historical presupposition and analytical premise of the economic system. This part of the argument draws on Werner Bonefeld, 'Adam Smith and Ordoliberalism: On the Political Form of Market Liberty'. *Review of International* Studies 39(2): 233–250.

15. On this, see Fine's (2002) important book on democracy and the rule of law. See also Pashukanis (1987) and May (2014).

16. Ranciere's critique of police works in a similar manner. As he explains: police denies that struggle has a reality: 'Move along! There is nothing to see here!' (Ranciere 2001, 9).

17. For a discussion of this point in relation to the endorsement of the Big Society by the former British prime minster, David Cameron, see Bonefeld (2015).

18. Hegel recognises the illusory character of what Smith calls the 'liberal reward for labour'. He argues that regardless of the accumulation of wealth bourgeois society is never rich enough to check poverty (see Hegel 1967, 148–150).

19. This formulation derives from Martin Wolf who argued in 2001 that the liberalising success of globalisation cannot be built on 'pious aspirations' but that it rests on 'honest and organized coercive force'.

20. 'Mass-man' is used here with reference to Jose Ortega y Gasset's book *The Revolt of the Masses* (1994). In this account mass man is a menace to liberal society. He is said to live a common life of emotive dissatisfaction and barbaric ignorance. Mass man contrasts with the noble life of the satisfied man who rises above the revolting masses. Jose Ortega y Gasset's account of 'mass-man' is a regular point of reference in ordoliberal depictions of the figure of the proletarian and a proletarianised society. For an account, see chapter 3.

21. Eucken notion of spontaneous action overlaps with Hayek's idea of a spontaneous order (see Streit and Wohlgemuth 2010).

22. The state of freedom 'knows exactly where to draw the line between what does and what does not concern it'. It is not the economy that draws this line. In fact, any such attempt amounts to a 'ruthless exploitation of the state by the mob of vested interests' that need to be fought back by 'a really strong state, a government with the courage to govern' (Röpke 2009, 192).

23. On Friedman's connection with ordoliberal argument, see chapter 1.

24. Röpke (2009, 192) characterises the liberal state as an 'energetic umpire'. It is not the economic interests that determine the conduct of the state. It is rather the state that enforces economic conduct.

25. For Milton Friedman, too, the answer clearly was not to entrust liberty to the providence of the invisible hand. Friedman's support of, and indeed advisory role in,

the Pinochet dictatorship is well known and does not contradict his market-liberal stance.

26. 'Formatted' society is the translation of the German *formiert Gesellschaft*. In the mid-1960s, ordoliberal authors, including the then chancellor Ludwig Erhardt, responded to the first signs of political strife and slack economic growth by arguing for a *formierte Gesellschaft*. Some critics rejected this notion as advocating *Gleichschaltung* – a Nazi policy. *Formierte Gesellschaft* is a total concept (*Gesamtkonzept*). It recognises the mentality for enterprise as a character trait of the free society. See Altmann (1960) and Voegelin (1965). For critique see, among others, Opitz (1965) and Haselbach (1991). For a further discussion of this point see chapter 5 on ordoliberal social policy.

27. Foucault's (1991) term governmentality captures the meaning and supposed reach of ordoliberal social policy well. Government works best when it governs through peoples' heads so that they conduct themselves, seemingly by their own free will.

28. Eucken calls the weak state an economic state because it replaced the machinery of competition and accepted responsibility for the economy and the social consequences of economic development.

29. In this context, the 'statification' of society and the 'etatisation of society' are not the same. The former entails the state as the immediate political organiser of the social relations, and the latter entails the governmentality of social conduct, see the two previous notes, 27 and 28.

30. See also chapter 6 for an argument about the benevolence of economic governance by European bureaucracy.

31. The term commissarial dictatorship is found in Schmitt (2013). In his *Dictatorship* of 1921 he distinguishes between a sovereign dictatorship, which like Lenin's founds a new political economy, and a commissarial dictatorship, which suspends the rule of law in response to a declared state of emergency. The aim of commissarial dictatorship is to re-establish civil society, which had been put under seize by contrarian political forces that, in case of Weimar, demanded welfare provision, full employment and an end to austerity. Commissarial dictatorship suspends the liberal rule of law to preserve it in the long run. For an account, see Bonefeld (2006a).

32. On the connection between freedom and surveillance, see Agnoli (2003). The liberal state entrusts its law-governed and rule-observant citizens to act freely in response to price movements, and keeps them under surveillance to make sure that freedom is not misused for illiberal purposes. In Foucault's succinct formulations, Bentham's Panopticon is 'the very formula of liberal government' (Foucault 2008, 67).

33. The German title of Röpke's *A Human Economy* is *Jenseits von Angebot und Nachfrage*, that is, *Beyond Supply and Demand*. The German title focuses on the state as the political form of market freedom, whereas the English title focuses the liberalising objective of *Ordnungspolitik*.

34. It was not until the early part of the nineteenth century in England that 'liberalisation' became the ideological orthodoxy of a liberalising state (see Clarke 1988, chapter 1).

Chapter 3

Democracy and Freedom: On Authoritarian Liberalism

INTRODUCTION

The previous chapter established that ordoliberalism considers the liberal state as the indispensable power of the free economy and concluded that unfettered by the liberal principle mass democracy weakens the liberal utility of the state with crisis-ridden consequences. In the context of Weimar they demanded a strong state response to overcome the lamentable weakness of the state to govern for the free economy. This chapter examines the ordoliberal argument that the capacity of the state as market police depends on its independence from society, and thus on its strength to neutralise mass democracy. This stance is of key importance for the argument that at its emergence ordoliberalism and authoritarian liberalism cut from the same cloth.

The remainder of the introduction puts the notion of an 'authoritarian liberalism' into a theoretical context to establish analytical links. The term 'authoritarian liberalism' appeared in a 1933 publication by Hermann Heller about the rightist von Papen government of 1932. His account explored Carl Schmitt's 1932 address about 'sound economy and strong state' to a meeting of industrialists (Schmitt 1998) as the theoretical expression of the authoritarian turn in liberal thought. Heller characterised authoritarian liberalism as a demotion of democratic government 'in favour of the dictatorial authority of the state' (Heller 2015, 296; also Marcuse 1988). Schmitt's stance was by and large shared by the founding ordoliberal thinkers (see among others, Tribe 1995).[1] In a nutshell, like Schmitt, the ordoliberals identified mass democracy as a danger to free economy because it emasculates the independence of the state and makes government accountable to the interests of the governed. In Eucken's words, 'Democratisation grants political parties and the masses and the interest groups organised by them a massively increased influence on the government of the state and thus on economic policy as well' (Eucken 1932, 306). As a consequence, 'The power of the state today no longer serves its own will but to a considerable degree the will of the interested parties' (307). Since therefore 'the real independence of its will is missing' (308), government is adrift. The idea that the state has to have its own independent will and make independent decisions is quintessential Schmittean. Röpke, too, writes about the state as an independent power. He demanded a 'moinistic state' that makes 'independent decisions . . . designed to serve the common interest' (Röpke 1998, 141, 142). Röpke's view is equally Schmittean insofar as he argued that mass democracy transformed the liberal state into a 'pluralistic state of democratic practice' (Röpke 1998, 142). Like Schmitt, Röpke (1998, 143) argues that 'any responsible government must examine carefully all the possible means of resisting this pluralistic disintegration of the state'; that is, for the sake of liberty, democratic government has to be 'de-pluralised'.

The ordoliberal endorsement of the state as the independent power of society that acts according to its own will remained a central pre-occupation of market liberalism after the Second World War. For example, at the 1954 meeting of the Mont Pélerin society James Buchanan argued that the 'maintenance of free society may well depend on the removal of certain decisions form majority-voting determination' not least to avert mass pressure for redistribution (cited in Burgin 2012, 118).[2] Similarly, Milton Friedman rejected political liberalism as a soft, self-defeating approach to mass pressures for income redistribution and employment guarantees, arguing that it presents an 'internal threat' that comes from 'men of good intentions and good will who wish to reform us' (Friedman 1962, 200).[3] Hayek's appraisal of the Pinochet dictatorship in Chile as one that 'may be more liberal in its policies than an unlimited democratic assembly' (quoted in Cristi 1998, 168) asserts the authoritarian liberal argument with political gusto and legitimising intent.[4] Indeed, however robust and distinct, his view expressed a common theme of market liberal critique of democratic government in the 1970s. It held that the economic crisis of the 1970s had been brought about by an excess of democracy that had caused the state to become overloaded with economic and social responsibilities, which in their combined effect stifled the economy with crisis-ridden consequences (Brittan 1977). Its crisis diagnoses entailed the prescription for crisis resolution. The economy had to be set free by rolling back the state, reasserting its independence from the influence of particularly the trade unions. Examination of the ordoliberal stance establishes the raison d'etre of these accounts.

The chapter examines the distinction between democracy and liberty and expounds the ordoliberal argument that for the sake of (economic) freedom under the rule of law, mass democracy has to be fettered to liberal principles. The following section explores the meaning of an authoritarian liberalism and develops Schmitt's notion of the strong state. The 'Ordoliberalism and mass democracy' section expounds the ordoliberal critique of mass democracy. The final section, 'Ungovernability and democratic overload', presents the neoliberal account of a crisis of democracy in the 1970s as a more recent manifestation of the market liberal worry about democratic excess. The 'Conclusion' expounds on the seemingly unresolvable tension between democracy and liberty. It establishes connections to the subsequent chapters on competition and economic constitution, social policy and European monetary union, which establishes a market liberal framework for the conduct of democratic government in the member states.[5]

AUTHORITARIAN LIBERALISM: ON SCHMITT AND SOUND ECONOMY

Authoritarian Liberalism

Heller's appraisal of Schmitt's stance detected a 'state of exception', in which government by authoritative decision making replaces parliament as the key institution of the state. In his view, Schmitt favoured an authoritarian state to draw a line of separation between society and state. The independence of the state is fundamental to both, the ability of government to govern and to the 'initiative and free labour power of all economically active people' (Schotte, cited in Heller 2015, 299). In this account, Heller argues, the circumstance that 'nearly 90% of our people' who live off an income barely sufficient for the satisfaction of their needs does not in any way call into question the liberal rule of law. It treats each individual equally whatever their concrete circumstances might be (301). However, assertion of their democratic power imperils the liberal rule of law as the state becomes the target of all manner of demands for social intervention, making it responsible for society at large, from the cradle to the grave. For Schmitt and the ordoliberals, unlimited mass democracy tends towards the development of a state of pure quantity, by which they meant the democratic welfare state of Weimar. The state of pure quantity is at the mercy of a plurality of powerful private interests. It is a totally weak state. It is unable to distinguish between the 'friends' of liberty and its 'enemies' (Schmitt 1985; Müller-Armack 1933, 31; Röpke 1998, 66). Indeed, the weak state does not uphold the liberal rule of law. Rather, law disintegrates into a plurality of contradictory measures that express the social interests in the form of specific legal entitlements to, say, state aid. The liberal equality of everybody before the law thus dissolves into specific legal rights that recognise the political strength of specific social groups and the power of professional and political organisations, including trade unions and political parties. Instead of regulating the conduct of society on the basis of non-directive abstract legal principles, mass society, as it were, 're-feudalises' the liberal rule of law. Government by means of concrete measures is government by concessions to, and in the interest of, a plurality of private powers groups. The state of total quantity is a state of its clients; it secures them against the risks of a free labour economy by welfare guarantees and protectionism.[6] It is a weak state without political quality.[7]

Heller characterised authoritarian liberalism as an attempt at establishing what Schmitt called a state of total quality, that is, a state that asserts itself as the independent power of society and in this manner depoliticises the socio-economic relations, achieving sound economy by securing and sustaining the 'free labour power' of the '90 per cent' who struggle to make a living. This state of total quality successfully claims the monopoly of the legitimate use of violence by asserting itself as the concentrated power of a depoliticised exchange society in which political assertion is illegitimate. Instead, as laid out by the ordoliberals, the individuals compete and exchange with one another in freedom from personal coercion and private power. Each is obliged only to comply with the rule of law. They thus exchange as equals in the eye of the law, the one buying labour power the other selling. Authoritarian liberalism recognises that the political equality of a class of dependent sellers of labour power manifests a danger to the laws of private property, and it therefore demands a strong state that does not become the target for welfare-seeking workers.[8] It recognises the demand for a freedom from want as an affront to liberty and the legitimate Rights (*Rechte*) of private property. It therefore 'defends work as a duty, as the psychological happiness of the people' (von Papen, cited in Heller 2015, 300). As argued by Heller, authoritarian liberalism cherishes the heroism of poverty and service, of sacrifice and discipline, by which the 'disciples' of a free labour economy commit themselves unselfishly to the governing authorities (Schmitt 1934).

Streek's interpretation of Heller's account is both insightful and misleading. He argues that 'Heller understood that Schmitt's "authoritarian state" was in fact the liberal state in its pure form, weak in relation to the capitalist economy but strong in fending off democratic interventions in its operation' (Streek 2015, 361).[9] I agree with the latter and disagree with the former. Streek rightly argues that the 'depoliticised condition of a liberal economy is itself an outcome of politics' (361). It is, says Schmitt, 'a political act in a particularly intense way' (Schmitt 1998, 227). In distinction to Streek, the liberal character of the state does not just rest on restraining democratic intervention into a free labour economy, protecting the relations of private property from market restricting demands for collective provision. It is also defined by its role as 'market police', enabling and facilitating the capitalist economy – capitalist economy does not posit itself as if by force of nature. It posits strife and struggle, and it posits both monopoly pricing and cut-throat competition. Capitalist economy amounts therefore to a political practice of economic order. As Miksch (1947, 9) explains, economic freedom is not a manifestation of some natural propensity as in classical liberalism. Rather, it is a 'political event [*staatliche Veranstaltung*]' (also Böhm 1937, 34). Authoritarian liberalism makes clear that the capacity of the state as the market police depends on its strength to govern for the 'cheapness of provision'.[10]

Sound Economy and Strong State[11]

Carl Schmitt perceived the crisis of the late 1920s/early 1930s as a crisis of political authority.[12] The German revolution of 1918 had transformed liberal parliamentary democracy into a majoritarian mass democracy. Prior to the incursion of mass society into the political system, parliamentary representation was founded on a homogeneity of interests. For Schmitt it had amounted to a democracy of friends, who might squabble about the best way forward but were united by their recognition of what Schmitt refers to as the 'stranger' (1985, 9–11), that is, the socialist labour movement, which had been excluded from political participation as a democratic equal. With the onset of mass democracy, this 'stranger' to liberty and the legitimate Rights of property had gained entry into the political institutions, democratising the system of parliamentary representation and parliamentarising the system of government. Instead of law making by a democracy of liberal friends, law was made by a heterogeneous chamber dominated by mass interests, which held government accountable and demanded conditions. In Schmitt's account Weimar mass democracy exerted not only influence on the conduct of government. It also legislated, subjecting the rule of law to 'mass emotion and mass passion', as Röpke put it (1998, 152). For Schmitt, then, the transformation of liberal democracy into a mass democracy expressed itself in the democratisation of the rule of law, which in its effect eliminated the distinction between legitimate Rights and ordinary law. In fact, majoritarian parliamentary democracy collapsed this distinction. All law thus became ordinary law in the true meaning of the word; that is, it became the common law of a politicised and conflict-ridden mass society. Lacking in transcendental purposes to do with the legitimate Rights of private property, the law became contradictory and fractured into all manner of concrete measures and commands, establishing concrete entitlements and objectives that articulated the conflicting social interests in the form of law. The legitimacy of law no longer derived from the divine Rights of property, king and country. Instead it became bound to the 'rightful' procedure of parliamentary law making and the rule-based rationality of administration.[13] The rationalisation of legitimation belongs to a disenchanted age of mass politics and mass political interference with the established Rights of private property.[14]

Schmitt argued against the mass democratic dethronement of Right. He asserted that the legitimacy of ordinary law is not a matter of rational-legal procedure. Rather it derives from definite extralegal decisions about the fundamental character of a political community. That is, for Schmitt sovereignty does not rest with the liberal rule of law. Rather, sovereign is the one who has the power of authoritative decision to govern either through the rule of law or its suspension in times of emergency. Its suspension is not a matter of law or objective facticity. It is a matter of sovereign judgement and political decision. It is thus a matter of an authoritative decision. In Schmitt's telling phrase the 'sovereign is who decides on the exception' (Schmitt 1985, 5).

For Schmitt the distinction between friend and enemy, this socialist stranger, defines the essence of the political. He rejects the idea of one person, one vote as irrational. It treats enemy and friend as equals, and gives in to the enemy. For Schmitt, democracy works on the condition that it is a democracy of friends. As he put it, 'Every actual democracy rests on the principle that not only are equals equal but unequals will not be treated equally. Democracy requires therefore first homogeneity and second, if the need arises, elimination and eradication of heterogeneity' (Schmitt 1985, 9). Schmitt recognises that for the sake of trade, commerce and exchange, liberalism presupposes depoliticised social relations and that the liberal rule of law provides for the rules of the game in liberty from direct violence and personal coercion. However, 'in the concrete reality of the political no abstract order or norms but always real human groupings and associations rule over the other human groupings and associations' (Schmitt 1996a, 72–73). For Schmitt, Man is neither a neutral nor a humanist category. At its core, it is a social category and above all a political concept, which designates a definite social relationship between friend and enemy. The state is the political form of this relationship. Further, for Schmitt, law is not a neutral category either. It, too, expresses the domination of one group of men over another group of men. It determines the rules of conduct, Right and duty, in a definite social order. Indeed, the rule of law presupposes social order. 'There exists no norm that is applicable to chaos. For a legal order to make sense, a normal situation must exist, and he is sovereign who definitely decides whether this normal situation actually exists' (Schmitt 1985, 13). Order entails the security state. Disorder is not a matter of law. It is a matter of police, of force. Since the rule of law cannot defend itself against a politicised mass society and is instead at risk of being devoured by mass society, and since it also cannot decide whether it applies or not, the decision to uphold the rule of law is not a matter of law, legal argument and adjudication. The rule of law wages no battles and does not fight. The rule of law is not, as it were, a person apart that achieves its own aims. It does not make itself nor suspend itself, nor does it know whether there is order or disorder. Whether society is law-governed is a matter of authoritative judgement about the prevailing conditions of (dis-)order. The state is the institution of social order and legal authority, of order and law. Order is the precondition of law.

All law, as Schmitt (1985, 13) put it, is 'situational' – not as an expression of a shifting balance of democratic majorities. Here the rule of law reflects the 'situation' of shifting parliamentary majorities.[15] For Schmitt, the rule of law is situational in character because its veracity is a matter of authoritative judgement about the conditions of social (dis-)order. Society is either governed by the rule of law or it is not, in which case the situation of the enemy might require government by extralegal means. The state of exception does therefore not govern against the rule of law. Rather, it governs for it. A state of emergency suspends the rule of law so that it may not be damaged by the forces of social disorder. Its suspension is thus a means of preserving it in the long run.[16] In this context Schmitt denounces the tradition of political pluralism and legal positivism as doctrines of vacuous universal claims. That is, they are doctrines based on relative truth. Normative values, he argues, are either absolute and worthwhile fighting for, or they posit nothing at all, mere chitter chatter in the face of the enemy. That is, 'relative truth never gives one the courage to use force and to spill blood' in defence of a definite form of political morality and political authority, Right and rightfulness (Schmitt 1988a, 64).[17]

Liberal emergencies necessitate a state of exception. Necessity knows no law. The law of necessity is the law of violence. The decision to suspend the rule of law is valid because it has been made. For the decision to be valid any doubt in its veracity has to be eliminated by the unleashed power of the exception. By 1930 and especially 1932, in 'the face of the left's attempt to construct the democratic welfare state . . . *just such an emergency is what Schmitt now proposes. . . .* The "quantitative total state" – a weak, social democratic inspired interventionist state – should be replaced by a "qualitative total state" – an alternative brand of interventionism, but one which guarantees authentic state sovereignty and simultaneously manages to provide substantial autonomy to owners of private capital' (Scheuerman 1999, 214–215). For Schmitt, the struggle for a state of pure quality entails the elimination of all forms of social conflict, of 'orderlessness' (Böhm 1937, 150). That is, 'only a strong state can depoliticise, only a strong state can openly and effectively decree that certain activities . . . remain its privilege and as such ought to be administered by it, that other activities belong to the . . . sphere of self-management, and that all the rest be given to the demonian of a free economy' (Schmitt 1998, 226–227).

In summary, Schmitt's conception of the political as the relationship between friend and enemy entails that the state is properly a state on the condition that it recognises the political enemy and conducts itself on the basis of this recognition. That is, 'a democracy [of friends, WB] demonstrates its political power by knowing how to refuse or keep at bay something foreign and unequal that threatens its homogeneity' (Schmitt 1988a, 9). Rossiter's notion that there can be 'no democracy in abnormal times' (1948, 8) does therefore not go as far as Schmitt's. He accepts with Schmitt that abnormal times may require a dictatorship that 'ends the crisis and restores normal times' (Rossiter 1948, 7). Yet, for Schmitt, dictatorship is a latent presence in normal times, too. In its dormant form it manifests itself as an ever vigilant security state that employs all 'technological means, especially military technology' to keep its citizens under surveillance, just in case (Heller 2015, 301). The strong state of a sound economy is armed.

In conclusion, the strong state of sound economy curtails democratic excess, rules society with the identified stranger to sound economy in mind and maintains its independence from society to enforce the rules of order. Freedom either expresses order, or it is order-less. In either case, it is an object of police either to sustain order or to restore order, and the latter expresses the failure of the former. The Schmittean politics of order is about the recognition and containment of the 'stranger' within the limits of the legitimate Rights of private property, of 'sound economy'. Order is the premise of law as Right. As Rossiter (1948, 11) puts it, 'Law is made for the state, not the state for the law'. Indeed, Schmitt supplied the rule of law with an extralegal sovereign who as guarantor of rightful order, may act unbound by the formalism of law. Dictatorship is an exceptional force of order. It dictates the conditions of conduct to the identified enemy.

Authoritarian liberalism recognises that the liberal utility of the state is a function of its independence from society – it is its independence from society that allows its effective operation as a liberal state. The state thus needs to be 'powerful . . . to preserve its own independence' (Rüstow 1942, 276). It is its independence from society that allows the state to be a 'strong and neutral guardian of the public interest' asserting 'its authority vis-à-vis the interest groups that press upon the government and clamour for recognition of their particular needs and wants' (Friedrich 1955, 512). A liberal state that does not defend its independence from mass society will lose its authority to govern and will instead become 'their "prey"' (513). For the sake of liberty, democracy has thus to be fettered to avoid liberal emergencies.

ORDOLIBERALISM AND MASS DEMOCRACY

Peacock and Willgerodt (1989, 6) are right to say that the ordoliberals are 'well aware of the . . . totalitarian tendency of mass democracy' that Hayek talked about in his *Road to Serfdom* of 1944. Echoing Schmitt's warnings about a mass democracy that does not exclude the 'enemy', this stranger to the Rights (*Rechte*) of private property, Röpke (1942, 253) argued that 'everybody knows that democracy can really function properly only when there is a certain minimum of agreement about the essential problems of national life'. Once mass interests take hold, 'democracy necessarily falls victim either to anarchy or collectivism' (246). In any case, a politicised mass society entails 'loss of social integration', diminishes 'differentiation of social status' and leads to increasing 'standardisation and uniformity'. It destroys, he says, 'the vertical coherence of society' and leads to the loss of 'vital satisfaction' (246, 240). At the start of the last century, out of the midst of industrialisation and urbanisation, there arises the figure of the dissatisfied and restless proletarian. A state that yields to proletarian demands for material satisfaction impairs not only the 'economic machinery of market adjustment through prices'. It also enflames the 'menacing dissatisfaction of the workers' (Röpke 1942, 3) further as the passions of the dispossessed are left to fester, potentially on the pain of ruin.

Eucken too identified the 'chaotic force of the masses' as the root cause for the transformation of the liberal state into an 'economic state' of planned chaos (1932, 312). In this line of argument, weak governments sought to appease social discontent by broadening their popular appeal, bending to sectional interests and class-specific demands. Instead of enabling free economy, government intervened into the free play of the market, creating new dislocations which necessitated further interventions, leading to spiral of self-perpetuating interventions (also Hayek 1944). In this climate of market-disabling interventionism, private interest groups came to the fore, lobbying for restraint on competition in order to secure rents or market-distorting privileges for themselves. Böhm (1937, 122) rejects the economic vocabulary for such restraint on competition. Instead of speaking about 'cartels, market regulation or mutual support', he characterises these so-called market-distorting behaviours as acts of '*sabotage* or *complot*.' In sum, weakened by mass democracy the Weimar state also yielded to the demands that derived from a plurality of economic interest groups with the result that it lost 'its force and its authority'. Unable to maintain 'its independence' from the clamour of society, it began 'to succumb to the attacks of pressure groups . . . monopolies and later unionized workers' (Rüstow 1942, 276). The resultant 'economic state', which institutionalised 'concession to vested interests' as a principle of government (Eucken 1932, 318), embodied the power of the masses. As Röpke argued in 1933, the 'current world crisis could never have grown to such proportions . . . if it had not been for the many forces at work to undermine the intellectual and moral foundation of our social system and thereby eventually to cause the collapse of the economic system indissolubly connected with the social system as a whole. . . . [I]t is condemned to waste away if its three cardinal conditions – *reason, peace, and freedom* – are no longer thought desirable by the masses ruthlessly reaching for power' (quoted in Gregg 2014, vii). Weimar democracy, then, had allowed the masses to transform the state into a collectivist interventionist state, and in this manner, 'it was and is the masses under whose increasing pressure . . . the historical structure of the state had been destroyed and the economic state had been erected . . . *whereby the social and the structure of the state decay*' (Eucken 1932, 312). In the ordoliberal argument, the spectre of an irrational mass society looms large.

As pointed out by Müller (2011, 20), '[t]he anxiety about "the masses" was a qualitative, not a quantitative problem. "Mass man" was characterized primarily by what he lacked: the supposed qualities of the good nineteenth century liberal self, above all rationality and self-restraint. Even worse, "mass man" was getting hold of the levers of the state and modern technology, which in turn further homogenized "the masses". The state, "the machine" and "the masses" almost inevitably appeared together as a single threat'. Mass man belonged to an irrational society of mass politicisation, mass culture, mass organisation, mass strike and mass parties, which was both feared and held in contempt. The ordoliberal critique of laissez-faire liberalism as being blind to the social consequences of capitalist development was driven by anxiety about the moral and economic consequences of 'massification' or 'proletarianisation' (Röpke 1942; Rüstow 1942). Röpke thus rejected the 'rotten fruit' of the welfare state (Röpke 1957, 14) as 'the "woodenleg" of a society crippled by its proletariat' (36). Like Rüstow (1942), he scorned the welfare state as an expression of 'mass emotion and mass passion' (Röpke 1998, 152) and saw it as an institution of 'mass man' who 'shirk their own responsibility' (Röpke 1957, 24). It institutionalises the proletarianised social structures and expresses a condition of profound 'devitalisation and loss of personality' (Röpke 2002, 140). This fear of, and contempt for, a proletarianised mass society was most strongly articulated by Ortega y Gasset's *The Revolt of the Masses*, which was a regular point of reference in ordoliberal thinking about the then crisis of capitalist political economy.[18]

Ortega y Gasset's book was first published in 1930. It articulated the liberal-conservative despair about the supposed Decline of the West. Ortega y Gasset argues that 'Europe is suffering from the greatest crisis that can afflict peoples, nations and civilisations' (1994, 11). 'Mass man', he asserts, had replaced 'select man' (15) and transformed the liberal state into a mass state'. 'Mass man' is the common man, an intellectual barbarian, lacking in moral standards, personality and civility. Mass man lacks culture and has no sense of duty or obligation. Respect for private property had gone, and morality vanished. Nothing remained sacred. Mass society demanded material security at all cost, leading to the decline of a liberal order that ostensibly is founded on self-earned private property. Mass man demanded 'freedom from want' and demands to be 'satiated' by the state (Röpke 2002, 245). Eucken explains the anti-capitalist attitude of the masses as a substitution process. As he sees it, mass society is fundamentally secular – it seeks deliverance from misery in the here and now. With the weakening of religion as a means of social cohesion, as articulation of moral duty and as the oracle of deferred satisfaction, 'the ensuing vacuum was filled by a belief in a total, all-encompassing state' (1932, 306), which laissez-faire liberalism had allowed to fall into the hands of social democracy. Indeed, laissez-faire in political life 'gives a free hand to all trouble makers and agitators, thereby condemning itself to death with open eyes, must ultimately reduce "pure democracy" to the defence-less victim of anti-liberalism' (Röpke 2009, 50). Weimar democracy had removed 'the whip of competition' (cf. Eucken 1932) and was 'pulled apart' (Rüstow 1963, 258) by 'totalitarian mass parties' that 'abuse the rules of liberal-parliamentarianism' for the pursuit their own – collectivist – interests and demands (Rüstow 1942, 277).

The Weimar state had yielded thus to mass demands, leading to its transformation into a 'totalitarian state' (Röpke 1942, 4) that replaced 'the democratic sovereign, the market' (254) by 'collectivist tyranny' (248). For the ordoliberals, tyranny is 'rooted in democracy that is unrestricted and not sufficiently balanced by liberalism'. Tyranny ensues not because of the 'liberal principle but because of *its absence*' (Röpke 1942, 248). Tyranny, Röpke argues, 'has always governed with the masses . . . , against the *elite* that carries civilisation on' (248). Mass society appears irresistible: '[a]nybody who is not unlike everybody, who does not think like everybody, runs the risk of being eliminated' (Ortega y Gasset 1994, 18). Mass man breaches the distinction between state and society, imposes mass demands on the state and turns liberal parliamentary institutions into chambers of mass opinion, mass demands and mass politics. Since 'mass man fights against liberal-democracy in order to replace it by illiberal democracy' (Röpke 1969, 97), liberal democracy has to be defended, for the sake of freedom, private property, respect for law and order and Right. Its defence requires the deproletarianisation and depoliticisation of society.

According to Röpke (1942, 3), 'the challenging problem' of a proletarianised mass society is not an economic one but a human one. It is characterised by a lack of vitality and psychological happiness. Mass society is deemed rudderless and easily manipulated. The masses are fundamentally ignorant. They are thus easy prey for illiberal demagogues and street dictators. Liberalism has therefore to fight for mass man and govern the mentality of mass society for the sake of freedom under the liberal rule of law. According to Rüstow, the authentic desire of the unruly masses is not to destroy liberal society or to assemble in protest on street corners in constant defiance to the given situation, seeking salvation by a welfare providing state. Rather, said Rüstow in 1929 (1959, 102), the authentic desire of mass man is to be led and governed, if only they knew whom to follow. He thus calls upon men of honest convictions to lead mass man away from the abyss, for the sake of liberty, common decency and security of private property. In the context of Weimar, the intended transformation of mass democracy into a liberal democracy, which insulates government from direct exposure to mass demands, entailed a Schmittean process of depoliticisation.

Eucken's (1932, 318, 307) call that the liberal state asserts itself to find 'the power' and the 'will' to govern rings with Schmittean intent and purpose. This holds for Röpke, too. He argued that for the sake of liberal order the power of the revolting masses must be countered by 'the revolt of the elite' (Röpke 1998, 130).[19] It must lead, assume the leadership of the state and defend liberalism not only in the hour of need but, rather, preemptively to prevent emergencies from arising in the first place. They therefore argue that liberalism has to be a militant liberalism; liberality or laissez-faire will not do. 'Liberalism', argued Rüstow, 'had not demanded weakness from the state, but only freedom for economic development under state protection'. Such protection 'demands a strong state' (Rüstow 1963, 68). The strong state is a 'state where it belongs; over and above the economy, over and above the interested parties [*Interessenten*]' (258). The point of the strong state is not to ignore the social but to police it so that it does not drift towards a proletarianised mass society and mass democratic tyranny.

In conditions of liberal emergency a 'coup de force' might well be required to protect individual freedom and property. In this case the question arises regarding how to limit dictatorship to liberal purposes, how to keep the Hitlers out, how to make sure that dictatorship is in the name of freedom – like Pinoche's in Chile that Hayek, and Friedman too, found so praiseworthy. According to Friedrich (1968, 580) a benevolent dictator is required: dictatorship needs to be 'in the hand of persons who would understand the nature of the world-revolutionary situation and would appreciate the limits of force in dealing with the conflict of this type'. Yet, 'no democracy' emerges from dictatorship unaltered and some 'dictatorships turned against what it is meant to defend' (Rossiter 1948, 13). There is thus no certainty. As Friedrich (1968, 581) put it, 'How are we to get effective, vigorous governmental action and yet limit the power of governmental bodies so as to forestall the rise of a despotic concentration of power?' For Friedrich this is a 'logical paradox' that can be resolved only in practice. In the face of a liberal emergency, there is no alternative to dictatorial defence of 'freedom'. As Rossiter puts it, 'Into whatever forbidden fields of freedom the necessities of crisis may force the leaders of a constitutional government to go, go they must or permit the destruction of the state and its freedoms' (1948, 290). The freedom to dictate has to be tied to the particular purposes of the 'friends'. For the comfort of friends, the 'enemy' needs to be well defined. The 'prize is freedom' (Friedrich 1968, 581).

UNGOVERNABILITY AND DEMOCRATIC OVERLOAD

During the 1970s, neoliberal interpretations of the then crisis of capitalist accumulation focused either explicitly or implicitly on the crisis of state authority. Fundamentally, the crisis was seen as a crisis of governability, which had come about as a consequence of democratic excess (see Crozier et al. 1975; Buchanan and Wagner 1978). Like in the ordoliberal analyses of the early 1930s, these accounts, too, did not subject the economy to scrutiny nor was there an argument that the roots of the crisis might in any way be economic in origin. The economy was deemed in disarray because of democratic overload, Keynesian interventionism and politicised socio-economic relations that checked liberalising efforts.

Neoliberal commentators thus analysed the economic crisis as a manifestation of either social disorder or democratic overload, or both. Confronted by unrestrained mass democratic demands for collective provision and protection from competition, governments, so ran the argument, conceded ground to mass democratic interests and the so-called special interests, leading to illiberal socio-economic policies, which in its effect led to and reinforced the economic crisis. Mass democratic systems work in favour of short-term policies because politicians have to win (buy) votes at elections (Tullock 1976). Mass democracy thus proved to be a danger to the liberal rule of law because 'it is a system of highly weighted voting under which the special interests have great incentive to promote their own interests at the expense of the general public' (Friedman 1976, 4). Politicians seek re-election and need thus to calculate how to achieve a winning coalition between conflicting social demands, leading not only to short-termism but also to contradictory policies by 'simultaneously taking into account group interests that oppose each other' (Nörr 2010, 185). Instead of liberal interventionism that plans for competition, interventionism was muddled at best, stifling the market forces. There was thus a crisis of liberal interventionism, which expressed the underlying conditions of social disorder. Social disorder had led to a politics of compromise and discretionary policy responses to all kinds of perceived social ills and needs that government attended to with often contradictory policy responses that, lacking in cohesion and direction, led to what von Mises had earlier described as 'planned chaos' (von Mises 1947).

The neoliberal diagnosis of the crisis asserted that an excess of democracy had weakened the liberal resolve of the state. The political parties tried to outbid each other for greater shares on the 'electoral market'. This was seen to have led to the 'expansion of inflationary expectations' on the part of the electorate, which the democratic system encouraged. As Sam Brittan (1976) put it, 'Excessive expectations are generated by the democratic aspects of the system' (97) and 'the temptation to encourage false expectations among the electorate becomes overwhelming to politicians' (105). The basic trouble, according to Brittan, was *the lack of a budget constraint among voters* (104). It seems as if the state lacked the appropriate means of containing mass expectations within the limits of a free society. The open character of the democratic system was said to have failed to curb the 'inappropriate' politicisation of society, with crisis-ridden consequences. In fact, government was said to have become 'a sort of unlimited-liability insurance company, in the business of insuring all persons at all time against every conceivable risk' (King 1976, 12). The entrepreneur, this figure of the market liberal vision of a free society of self-responsible seekers of economic value, was thus denied by protectionist forms of market regulation and by the institutionalisation of a dependency culture that, in the form of the welfare state, punished success, provided for the idle and politicised the social relations. According to Anthony King non-compliance with the rights of private property and rejection of traditional norms of behaviour was rife. As he put it, 'The man dependent on his wife to drive him to work finds increasingly that she refuses to do so' (23). Regardless of what King's specific problems might have been, the general thrust of the argument was that the crisis of the 1970s was caused by the combined effect of politicised social relations, non-compliance with expected norms of behaviour and an unrestrained democratic system that encouraged political parties to outbid each other with welfare state promises. Public policy was thus deemed to be driven by politicised social interests and discretionary in its conduct. Instead of government by rules there was a politics of compromise. Policy was made in response to mass demands and trade union power, neither of which the state was able to ignore. The state, it seemed, had become the hostage of the Fourth Estate or what Röpke (1998; also Ancil 2012) calls proletarianised social structures and mentalities.

The crisis of ungovernability brought the lamentable weakness of the state into sharp focus. It had become entangled with the social interests, lost its independence from society and was at the mercy of an unrestrained democratic system that institutionalised the entrenched power of the masses in a permissive society, leading to illiberal interventionism, planned chaos and economic crisis. For the neoliberals, the 'economic consequences of democracy' (Brittan 1977) are formidable. Indeed, in the neoliberal argument the Keynesian welfare state appeared as the embodiment of the 'servile state' that Hayek (1944, 13) had warned about in his *Road to Serfdom*. Competition has no lobby and no mass support. Nor does it have a 'value in itself. It is not directed towards specific objectives' (Möschel 2003, 284). It is about enterprise and freedom, that is, the freedom to compete and that includes the freedom to work. Competition is entirely dependent on the 'independent will' and 'power' of the state to create and sustain 'competitive order' (Vanberg 2001, 50) in the face of a mass society that does not know who to limit itself to the purposes of a civil society of self-responsible entrepreneurs of what Gary Becker (1993) called human capital.

For the neoliberals, crisis resolution required the liberalisation of the economy from mass 'democratic' interference, curbing the excess of democracy for the sake of liberty, individual autonomy and a culture of enterprise. For the transformation of mass democracy into liberal democracy, the establishment of depoliticised socio-economic relations and the curtailment of the power of the democratic majorities to influence and shape the conduct of public policy are essential. The effort at tying the democratic aspects of the system of government to its liberal foundation is intensely political. It entails the politicisation of the state as the concentrated power of socio-economic depoliticisation. The stateless character of the economy amounts to a political practice of liberalisation. It exposes society to the freedom of (labour) market competition.[20]

CONCLUSION: ON LIBERTY AND DEMOCRACY

The free economy depends on the capacity of the state to sustain a 'competitive order' (Hayek 1949, 111). The chapter argued that market liberals attribute economic crises to the failure of the state to govern decisively for the freedom of competition. In the late 1970s, Hayek rehashed Eucken's (1932, 307) argument from the 1930s according to which the 'expansion of government activities . . . not at all meant a strengthening, but to the contrary, a weakening of the state' and that the power of the state had vanished because it had 'absolutely no unifying thought and will'. In the words of Hayek (1979, 99), 'Democratic government, if nominally omnipotent, becomes as a result of unlimited powers exceedingly weak, the play-ball of all the separate interests it has to satisfy to secure majority support.' In the early 1930s, Eucken had demanded that the state assert itself and do what is needed to be done (1932, 318). Similarly Hayek, and Friedman too, argued that the state asserts its independent will and 'de-pluralises' democracy and contains its excesses, and 'the most fundamental principles of a free society . . . may have to be temporarily sacrificed . . . [to preserve] liberty in the long run' (Hayek 1960, 217). Indeed, according to Hayek, 'a dictatorship may impose limits on itself, and a dictatorship that imposes such limits may be more liberal in its policies than a democratic assembly that knows of no such limits' (Hayek, citied in Cristi 1998, 168 fn. 16). Hayek, as Cristi put it, identified the Pinochet dictatorship in Chile as liberalising. It resolved the excess of democracy, drew a line between society and state, governed for personal freedom and the free economy, liberalised the economy and enabled the economic freedom of entrepreneurial decision making by the owners of private capitals.[21]

Unlimited democracy is neither an answer 'to the hungry hordes of vested interests' (Röpke 2009, 181) nor to politicised socio-economic relations, nor to mass demands for conditions. If then there has to be democracy, it must be 'hedged in by such limitations and safeguards as will prevent liberalism being devoured by democracy' (Röpke 1969, 97). How to hem it in? In the words of Peacock and Willgerodt (1989, 6), 'Those who rely on the rules for liberal decisions, irrespective of the results of these decisions, must answer the question: how can it be guaranteed that these decisions will not destroy the liberal rules'. In a mass democratic setting, the task laid out by Röpke is difficult to achieve. Contemporary ordoliberal writers clearly recognise the unresolvable tension between mass democracy and the system of liberty. Cassel and Rauhut (1999, 21) identify the German political economy as an 'un-purposefully constituted democracy'. It allows 'the collective agents. . . to restrict individual freedoms und thus endanger the economic order of the market'. Yet, a clear proposal for how to address this shortcoming is not forthcoming. Schwarz, too, offers proclamations. He asks himself whether 'a more democratic or a more dictatorial state' is better placed to secure free economy. In his view, for the 'long term interest in political freedom this same freedom has to be restricted in the short term' to sustain the freedom of economic compulsion and its regulation by the free price mechanism. The circumstance that the pursuit of freedom entails the restriction of freedom 'has', he argues, 'long been recognised by ordoliberalism, which holds that both the introduction and maintenance of a social market economy requires a strong government' (Schwarz 1992, 76, 86). Viktor Vanberg offers a most succinct characterisation of the strong state. It is 'as a shorthand for a state that is constrained by a political constitution that prevents government from becoming the target of special-interest rent-seeking' (Vanberg 2015, 31). Clearly, the 'players in the game' need to accept the rules of the game, especially those who 'might systematically do poorly' (Vanberg 1988, 26), and who, one might add, therefore demand employment guarantees and welfare support to make ends meet. Within this zone of conflict, he declares for the strong state as the 'the guardian of competitive order' (Vanberg 2001, 50). These quotations offer a clear demonstration of the issues at stake. They suggest that liberal democracy is not a democracy in which the rule of law is determined by the governed. Rather it is one in which the rule of law sets the framework that determines the scope of democratic activism and the extent of democratic policy making. Yet, how this is to be resolved is not at all clear.[22]

In the wider literature there are some pointers as to how to achieve liberal democracy that is assured to work in the manner outlined by Schumpeter (1950).[23] Hayek's argument that the constitution of liberty must make paramount the distinction between law as command and law as a system of general rules and that the separation of power should provide for proper checks on democratic law making articulates in fact a more or less generalised praxis of juridical oversight over parliamentary law making in liberal democracies. Especially since the Second World War constitutional courts has been granted extraordinary powers of adjudicating on the legitimacy of parliamentary law, subordinating parliamentary law to judicial review, oversight and power of declaring majoritarian law invalid if found to be contrary to the basic values of the constitution (see Agnoli 1990). Hayek also proposed to limit the right to vote to those over the age of 45 and to exclude from voting the unemployed and those members of the public who are either employed by, or financially dependent on, the public sector, including old-age pensioners (Hayek 1979, 447–455). There has also been discussion of unanimity rules for law making to restrict law by simple majorities (Buchanan and Tullock 1962; Brennan and Buchanan 1980; Buchanan and Wagner 1977), and more recently there has been the introduction of, for example, debt ceilings as a constitutional constraint of parliamentary power.[24] Then there has been the trend of weakening democratic oversight over and input into public policy by transfer of policy responsibility to rule-based, extra democratic institutions like central banks that have been provided with independent powers of policy making (Bonefeld and Burnham 1998).[25] Concerning the system of checks and balances, federalism and devolved power arrangements are said to have the potential of putting an effective break on mass democratic influence at the central level, providing protection against big government (see, among others, Riker 1987; Eucken 2004, 323; Röpke 1954). Finally, there is the system of 'interstate federalism' that for Hayek (1939) establishes a supranational framework of individual economic rights, laws and regulations over and above the democratically constituted and governed member states. He endorses this system for its irresistible deregulatory or liberalising dynamic. Indeed, some commentators see Hayek's interstate federalism as blueprint of the European Union (see, for example, Anderson 1997; Streek 2015; Wilkinson 2015; also Bonefeld 2005).

Looking forward to the remaining chapters, after 1933 ordoliberal thought consolidated into two distinct areas of enquiry. The so-called Freiburg school developed an account of the economic constitution of a system of complete competition, while the sociological approach associated with Röpke, Rüstow and also Müller-Armack developed the ordoliberal approach to social policy in the distinctive sense of the term explained previously. The next chapter, chapter 4, examines the ordoliberal argument for complete competition and economic constitution. The ordoliberals do not just endorse complete competition for reasons of economic efficiency. They conceive of it also, and importantly so, as a check on private political power and a means of sustaining depoliticised socio-economic relations. Economic constitution is to keep the principles of free economy outside the sphere of democratic decision making. Chapter 5 explores ordoliberal social policy, which is about the establishment of market enabling social and moral frameworks. The aim of social policy is to achieve deproletarianised social structures as the premise of a self-responsible enterprise society.

Chapters 6 and 7 explore the ordoliberal elements of the European Union. Chapter 6 introduces Röpke's argument for subsidiarity as a constraint on democratic government and Hayek's interstate federalism as a system of 'imposed liberty' (Engel 2003). Chapter 7 analyses the ordoliberal elements of European monetary union in its institutional structure and political organisation. These chapters argue that the European Union federalises the relationship between democracy and liberty. It incorporates democratic government in the member states into a liberal supranational framework. Chapter 8 argues that this incorporation transforms the member states into 'executive states' (Schmitt 1996b) of a European system of liberty.

NOTES

1. In the late 1920s and early 1930s, Schmitt and the ordoliberals fed on each other's analyses; their vocabulary and concepts were interchangeable. After the Second World War, there was great ambiguity towards Schmitt. Hayek, for example, rejected Schmitt in toto, denouncing him as the 'leading Nazi theoretician of totalitarianism (1944, 187) only to acknowledge that Schmitt 'probably understood the character of the developing form of government better than most people' (1979, 194). He accepted Schmitt's distinction between democracy and liberalism and argued that Schmitt's analysis was 'most learned and perceptive' (1960, 485). Hayek accepts that Schmitt's conception of sovereignty – 'sovereign is the one who decides on the exception' (Schmitt 1985, 5) – has 'some plausibility' (Hayek 1979, 125). To the best of my knowledge, the founding ordoliberal thinkers did not distance themselves from Schmitt.

2. For a detailed account, see Kiely (2016) and Biebricher (2015).

3. Political liberalism refers here to the liberalism of social and political equality, democratic inclusion, tolerance, liberality and liberal reformism.

4. In the words of Jean Kirkpatrick (1979), dictators like Pinochet are benevolent. They 'do not disturb the habitual rhythms of work and leisure, habitual places of residence, habitual patterns of family and personal relations. Because the miseries of

traditional life are familiar, they are bearable to ordinary people who, growing up in the society, learn to cope'.

5. The chapter draws in parts on my 'Authoritarian Liberalism: From Schmitt via Ordoliberalism to the Euro', *Critical Sociology*, published online first, 7 August 2016.

6. Schmitt perceives of this development as democratic disorder. On mass democracy and the refeudalisation of law, see especially Böhm (1980b, 258). In Böhm's view once the rule of law expresses the demands of specific social interests, it becomes a law of privilege. It operates in the service of the special interests. The weak state allows the unsocial interests to assert themselves as law making. See also chapter 4.

7. The view that the crisis of the early 1930s amounted to a crisis of govern-ability, which had been brought about by the mass democratic emasculation of the liberal utility of the state, was widely shared. For example, Bernard Baruch, a leading Democrat, had protested against Roosevelt's decision to abandon the gold standard in 1933 by stating that 'it can't be defended except as mob rule. Maybe the country does not know it yet, but I think that we've been in a revolution more drastic [than] the French revolution. The crowd has seized the seat of government and is trying to seize the wealth. Respect for law and order has gone' (quoted in Schlesinger 1958, 202). The gold standard provided for an extra-democratic framework of decision making particularly in the field of monetary and economic policy. It operated akin to a denationalised and entirely depoliticised mechanism for economic adjustments in territorialised labour markets, each competing with the other on the basis of world market price. Its abandonment made monetary policy subject to democratic pres-sures. For Baruch, this 'opening' of policy making to popular pressure led to the seizure of the state by the mob. That is, it allowed for the establishment of New Deal Keynesianism under Roosevelt. On the gold standard, see Eichengreen (1995). See Holloway (1995b) on the coming of New Deal Keynesianism. See chapters 6 and 7 on European monetary union as establishing a supranational monetary standard in the Eurozone countries.

8. I use the phrase 'dependent sellers of labour power' as shorthand. See Röpke (1998, 33) on 'dependent labour' and see Rüstow (2005, 365) for an orthodox defini-tion of social class. For an account see chapter 2.

9. See also Leo Strauss's (1996) rebuke to Schmitt as a closet liberal.

10. 'Cheapness of provision' is Smith's term (Smith 1978, 6). As argued in chapter 2, it entails a comprehensive judgement about the political character, social structure and morality of 'commercial society'.

11. The heading 'Sound State and Strong State' is in reference to Carl Schmitt (1998).

12. Schmitt's analysis of Weimar conditions was shared not only by the founding ordoliberal authors but, also, by thinkers associated with the Frankfurt School, includ-ing Neumann and Kirchheimer. Where Neumann and Kirchheimer differed was in the prescription of crisis resolution (see Haselbach 1991; Tribe 1995; Scheuerman 1996). In distinction to their socialist argument for a democratic welfare state, Schmitt and the ordoliberals identified this socialist resolution as the rotten foundation of Weimar. They argued for an authoritarian response to restore strong government.

13. Schmitt's critique was directed against Kelsen's (2009) pure legal theory, which holds that laws made by parliamentary majorities according to established rules and procedures embody legal legitimacy. Whether they do is a matter of adjudication by juridical authority in the form of a constitutional court. Schmitt rejected this stance as abandoning the political sovereign as the political foundation of definite social relations. For a recent restatement, see Mestmäcker's (2007a) critique of Posner (2003) as a contemporary exposition of a pure theory of law. Kelsen was the outstanding liberal advocate of democratic law making and of democracy as procedural democracy (see Maus 1976). In contemporary debate about the European Union, Habermas (2012) rejects as undemocratic the European Council decision making in response to the euro crisis because it amounted to an assertion of power that was unbound by the formalism of law. See also Wilkinson (2013, 2014).

14. See Weber (2013) on legitimation by legal-rational procedure as characteristic of modernity. In modernity, legitimation is no longer based on traditions and habit and legitimation by charisma is no longer predominant. It adds enchantment to a fundamentally rationalised system of legitimation. Schmitt recognises the dangers of a rationalised mass society and argues for the safeguard of rightful legitimacy by the irrational power of extralegal political authority.

15. The idea that the liberal rule of law is an effect of the prevailing balance of (class) forces belongs to the new left. See, for example, Chantal Mouffe (1999). For critique, see Scheuerman (1996).

16. In the words of Röpke (1942, 146), dictatorship amounts to a 'temporary form of state organisation to restore legitimate authority once the emergency for the state is over'.

17. Röpke (2009, 192) argues similarly for a 'really strong state' that has the 'courage to govern' to achieve and sustain what Schmitt calls 'sound economy'. Like Schmitt, Röpke also warns against a state run 'by the mob of vested interests', which leads to a state of pure quantity, that is, a state that 'acts as a maid of all work' and that therefore 'finally degenerates into a miserable weakling' that lacking in principles has no basic values to defend.

18. See, for example, Eucken (2004, 16–19) and Röpke (2002, 53–59).

19. For the leadership qualities of the elite, see chapter 2.

20. On the politicisation of the British state as the concentrated force of socio-economic depoliticisation during the early Thatcher governments, see Gamble (1988) and Bonefeld (1993).

21. In 1978, in a letter to *The Times*, Hayek wrote 'I have not been able to find a single person even in much maligned Chile who did not agree that personal freedom was much greater under Pinochet than it had been under Allende' (quoted in Farrant et al. 2012, 522).

22. Chapters 6 to 8 explore European monetary union as an institutional means of strengthening the liberal foundation of the democratically constituted member states.

23. According to Schumpeter (1950) liberal democracy is the best system so far invented to secure the peaceful circulation of elites by means of competitive elections. Hayek concurs. Democracy is 'a mere convention making possible a peaceful change of the holders of power' (1979, 4, also 98). See also Hayek (1949, 271).

24. On these efforts see also Biebricher's (2015) insightful contribution. See also Haselbach's (1991, 173–183) assessment of Röpke's (1998, 69) argument that liberal democracy must 'rest on above party agreement with respect to the unchallenged validity of the state's ethical, social and political principles'. On the introduction of debt ceilings as political decision, see Radice (2014).

25. Burnham (2001, 2014) has analysed these developments to amount to a depoliticisation of policy making. Of course, central bank monetary policy is entirely political in character, and the decision to let a technocratic institution conduct monetary policy is a political act. Röpke likens central bank independence as a Bastille of freedom, see chapter 6.

Chapter 4

Economic Constitution and Social Order: On the Freedom of Complete Competition

INTRODUCTION

Ordoliberalism consolidated into two strands of thought after 1933. On the one hand, there is the sociological strand that was developed most strongly by Röpke, Rüstow and also Müller-Armack. Its exploration is the task of the following chapter, chapter 5. This chapter presents the economic account of ordoliberalism that is associated with the Freiburg school, particularly the work of Eucken and Böhm. Its founding texts are Eucken's *Grundlagen der Nationalökonomie* (*Foundations of Economics*) of 1939 (1959) and *Grundsätze der Wirtschaftspolitik* (*Principles of Economic Policy*) of 1952 (2004) and Böhm's *Die Ordnung der Wirschaft* (*The Order of Economy*) of 1937 (1937). These texts organise the political experience of Weimar conditions in the form of an argument about economic constitution, economic order and *Ordnungspolitik*.

The idea of an economic constitution is specific to ordoliberalism.[1] It does not describe the basic characteristics of an evolved economic system. Rather, economic constitution amounts to 'an explicit and uncompromising decision' (Röpke 1982b, 39) about the founding principles of an economic order. For the ordoliberals these principles determine that 'all governmental decisions that might affect the economy should flow from the economic constitution' (Gerber 1994, 47). Economic constitution articulates economic categories as legal norms and designates economic policy as a politics of the constituted economic order. The working properties of an economy and legitimacy of economic policy depend on the character of the legal-institutional frameworks within which economic life takes place. Their regulation is a matter of a politics of order (*Ordnungspolitik*). *Ordnungspolitik* is concerned with the establishment and maintenance of a constituted economic order. In the case of the economic constitution of a free labour economy, *Ordnungspolitik* is about the creation of 'conditions under which the "invisible hand" that Adam Smith had described can be expected to do its work' (Vanberg 2015, 29).

The fusion of legal thought and economic argument is fundamental to the Freiburg school. It conceives of the economic order as a legal order and considers the legal order to amount to a constitutive political decision about economic structure of, and the rules of the game in, a definite social order (see Eucken 1959, 241). Government policy is bound by the economic constitution, which compels it to intervene into the economy to secure the constituted order in economic life as a whole. Gerber (1994, 45) posits the ordoliberal character of political intervention succinctly when he argues that it 'flows from, and is constrained by, the principles embodied in the economic constitution'. Economic constitution is meant to narrow the scope of legitimate parliamentary law making and intervention into the economy. *Ordnungspolitik* manifests thus a constitutionally defined conduct of government – the ordoliberal state operates akin to an economic *Rechtsstaat*, which is a state of legitimate Rights (*Rechte*) through the application of law (*Gesetz*). *Rechtsstaat* means a Rights-based and law-governed state. Indeed, as Gerber (1994, 47) makes clear, '*Ordnungspolitik* represents an adaptation and transfer of ideas from liberal political theory to the economy'. The *Rechtsstaat* idea is fundamental to this adaptation (Eucken 2004, 48–53). For Eucken (2004, 52, 332) *Rechtsstaat* and free economy are interdependent concepts. Concerning the economic constitution of the free economy, its regulative means is what the ordoliberals call 'complete' competition.[2] Competition is rule-based and law-governed. It is also enforceable by law and expresses a legal obligation and public duty (see Böhm 1937; Müller-Armack 1979, 147). Ordoliberalism conceives of competition as a moral responsibility. It is the means of individual freedom and individual autonomy. Indeed, the expectation is that an economic ' "order" . . . which . . . perpetuate[s] individual freedom' (Peacock and Willgerodt 1989, xvi) civilises economic conduct; instead of reckless and irresponsible market behaviour each participant expresses his or her freedom within the constituted framework of economic order (Müller-Armack 1947a, 147). Böhm considers the freedom to compete to bring about a private law society, which recognises the individual as a subject of competition law.[3]

The chapter establishes the ordoliberal argument for economic constitution and expounds the meaning of *Ordnungspolitik*. The first two sections explore the meaning of economic constitution and develop the concept of *Ordnungspolitik* as a political practice of establishing and maintaining economic constitution by dispersing and depoliticising economic power. The final section introduces Böhm's concept of the private law society. The chapter concludes on the ordoliberal characterisation of an economic order of complete competition as a moral order.

ECONOMIC CONSTITUTION
AND THE POLITICS OF ORDER

The notion of an economic constitution derives from what Eucken (1959, 58) calls 'thinking in orders'. He conceives of two fundamental orders, that is, the economic order of a free labour economy, which Eucken refers to as transaction society (*Verkehrsgesellschaft*), and a centrally planned labour economy (*Zentralverwaltungswirtschaft*). In a planned labour economy the conduct of economic policy is determined by entirely different principles to those of a free labour economy, and conversely, in a free labour economy the conduct of economic policy is determined by entirely different principles to those of a planned labour economy. A planned labour economy is centrally directed by economic planners and technocratic decision makers that act according to centrally devised economic development plans. In a transaction society, central planning of economic resources is contrary to its logic. Instead, the economic agents interact with each other based on their own self-interest. No single individual or institution is in overall control of the market processes. Eucken's 'transaction society' comprises a spontaneous order.[4] The market participants are entrepreneurs of economic value, trading and exchanging as equals on undivided and undistorted market that are regulated by competitive price movements. The regulatory rules of market freedom are destructive to the principles of central planning. Similarly, in a transaction society directive interventions into economy process are destructive to the principles of market freedom.

In a market system economic policy is not to direct the economy. Rather, it is to enable it, nudging it along and 'steering' it through liberal intervention (Müller-Armack 1947a, 95; 1960). Thus economic policy has to 'be fully aware of its' constituted objectives 'so that it does not transgress the boundaries which characterize a compatible form of interventionism' (Röpke 1950a, 228). The idea of a 'compatible form of interventionism' is fundamental to the ordoliberal notion of *Ordnungspolitik*. Economic policy is bound by the principles of economic constitution. The ordoliberal argument that state intervention has to be in conformity with the constitutive principles of economic order rejects the idea of a mixed economy, in which the state intervenes either for the system of liberty and against its logic or for the system of central planning and against its logic. *Ordnungspolitik* rejects the very notion of a mixed economy, which combines elements of fundamentally incompatible economic forms of social order. Any such 'intermingling' (Gerber 1994, 42) imperils the capacity of either system to function properly. Instead of intervening in a consistent manner, 'mixed' interventionism follows neither principle of economic order. It thereby becomes muddled and self-contradictory,

creating chaos and disorder which lead to the 'degeneration' of a definite
order, to the point of destruction.

Economic constitution amounts therefore to a 'comprehensive decision
(*Gesamtentscheidung*) concerning the type (*Art*) and form of the processes of
socio-economic cooperation' (Böhm 1933, 106; Eucken 1959, 52). This definition of economic constitution bears a clear resemblance to Carl Schmitt's
argument in his *Constitutional Theory* (see Gerber 1994; Tuori 2015; Tuori
and Tuori 2014, 14). In this work Schmitt defined a constitution as a 'comprehensive decision (*Gesamtentscheidung*) concerning the type (*Art*) and
form of the political unity' (Schmitt 2008a, 75).[5] Schmitt's 'political unity' is
Böhm's 'economic cooperation'. Following Gerber (1994, 45), the economic
constitution 'represents a political decision about the kind of economy a
community wants in the same way that the political constitution represents
a basic decision about the kind of political system a community wants'. The
economic constitution of a free labour economy establishes a clear value
decision about the economic system (Böhm 1933, xiv). Conceived of as a
constituted order, the 'constitutional choice' defines the rules and 'constraints
within which market participants are allowed to pursue their own purposes'
(Vanberg 2015, 28). It determines the type of economic organisation, its principles and basic regulatory rules, and it determines both the scope of legitimate parliamentary law making and the type of political interventionism, and
establishes the kind of conduct that is expected from the economic subjects. It
excludes certain other forms of intervention and conduct as unconstitutional
and incompatible with the defining 'style' of constituted economic system
(Müller-Armack 1976, 279).

The economic constitution of a transaction society does not permit discretionary intervention into the economy. Economic policy is not at the discretion of policy makers. It is to be rule based and law governed.[6] It excludes 'an
economic policy that seeks to improve outcomes *directly*, by way of specific
interventions in the economic process' (Vanberg 2015, 29). Instead, economic policy is to promote and enable the founding constitutional principles
in the conduct of the economic actors. Economic constitution requires that
the conduct of policy, and parliamentary law making too, is in line with basic
principles. In this context, the ordoliberal critique of unlimited democracy
turns into an argument against discretionary policy responses to particular
economic pressures, social demands and mass democratic aspirations. Discretionary economic policies are rejected because they encourage a politics
of compromise, political log-rolling and party political pandering to mass
expectations. Discretionary policy making tends thus to be at variance with
the rules of the game and makes economic policy unpredictable and unprin-
cipled. Interventionism becomes muddled to the detriment of constancy in
economic policy, which for Eucken is a fundamental constitutive principle of

a free market order.[7] Furthermore, disregard for the rules of the game tends to 'refeudalise' the social relations as discretionary policy making tends to privilege arbitrary parliamentary majorities and the lobby of the politically powerful and assertive economic interests.

The ordoliberals argue for an economic constitution as a legally binding decision on the basic principles and rules of economic organisation, social conduct and political power. It establishes the fundamental Rights of economic life. Just like a political constitution, the economic constitution ties the conduct of government, law makers and market participants to the basic principles. Impediments to the constitutional facility of free economy are thus violations of basic principles and Rights, and need to be eradicated for the sake of maintaining the constituted economic order. *Ordnungspolitik* is thus 'needed to establish and . . . maintain an appropriate *economic* constitution', and it is also needed 'to establish and . . . maintain an appropriate *political* constitution' (Vanberg 2015, 31) to safeguard from interference the legal, social, moral and institutional frameworks within which the free economy unfolds. The fusion of law and economics defines the political *Rechtsstaat* as an economic *Rechtsstaat*. It infuses market institutions with juridical authority that express the force of law making violence in normative terms.[8] It also establishes a legal obligation on the part of the market participants to compete, that is, to perform willingly and diligently as self-responsible agents of economic value.[9] In this context, the ordoliberals speak about enterprise (*Wettbewerb*) as a constitutive principle of the free economy (Böhm 1937; Eucken 1959, 52). Fundamentally, the economic constitution determines the economic *Rechtsstaat* as an enterprise state (*Wettbewerbsstaat*).

Originally, the concept of the state as *Rechtsstaat* developed in nineteenth-century Germany as a restraint on the arbitrary power of the sovereign. It established control over the discretionary power of the sovereign by subjecting the conduct of decision-making to the rule of law. In this manner, it tied the sovereign to the legitimate Rights (*Rechte*) of the emerging class of private property owners. The *Rechtsstaat* operates like a 'bulwark against the abuses of power' (Gerber 1994, 47). It civilises the state as a state of law and, also, in and through law. In a *Rechtsstaat*, parliament operates within a constitutional environment that makes parliamentary law making subject to overarching constitutional values. Conflicts between parliamentary law and constitutional law are subject to adjudication by independent judicial bodies. Regarding the ordoliberal account of economic constitution, it restraints parliamentary sovereignty and limits the scope of executive power. Economic interventionism has to flow from the economic constitution, has to conform to the basic values of liberal political economy as set out by the economic constitution and has thus to articulate basic economic values. Economic policy is thus a politics of order. That is, and as by Barry (1989, 115) put it succinctly, 'the state may intervene to preserve the "form" of the economic constitution not the process of the market itself'. Economic constitution thus establishes a framework in support of constancy of policy making. Government by rules requires certain types of policy and excludes alternative types of policy, which are at variance to the constituted rules of the game and thus do not conform to the basic economic principles of a transaction society. Its economic constitution excludes direct political intervention into the economy. Instead, it requires liberal interventionism which does not interfere with a market process based on the system of complete competition because it is by definition 'consistent with that system', enabling its operation and eliminating impediments to market freedom (Gerber 1994, 47). As a consequence, the scope of parliamentary law making narrows to the pursuit of sound money and open markets, guarantees of private property and freedom of contract, a regime of legal liability and fiscal discipline and a functioning price system. The economic constitution of a transaction society makes parliamentary law making both 'simple and realistic' (Eucken 2004, 298) and limits the conduct of government towards the achievement of conditions of complete competition on all markets, including the labour market.

The economic constitution of a transaction society entails that 'every type of "competition of impediment"' by the powerful private interests 'must be forbidden' (Eucken 2004, 267) and eradicated (Böhm 1937, 15). What is necessary, argues Eucken (2004, 255), is a 'positive economic constitutional policy . . . , which aims at developing the market form of complete competition and thereby fulfils the basic principle' of a transaction society. The concept of complete competition is the cornerstone of ordoliberal thought. Regarding the state, it holds that 'the realisation of a system of prices . . . is the criterion of every economic (policy) measure' (Eucken 2004, 254). For the economic actors, it holds that 'no firm in a market has power to coerce other firms in that market' (Gerber 1994, 43). In conditions of complete competition the economic relations are entirely depoliticised because 'the subjection of man to man' has 'stopped' since all market participants are equally exposed to the dynamic of market competition, regardless of the inequality in property and social position (Böhm 2010, 173). Not only is the economic constitution of complete competition 'the most genial instrument of emasculating power' (Böhm 1961, 22). It is also an order that 'is invisible' (Röpke 1942, 6) and is thus beyond the influence of private power. The invisible order of free economy is governed solely by the free price mechanism.

In Röpke's view, complete competition is the organisational form of true democracy and the free price mechanism its non-political ballot box (see Röpke 1959b, 76). For Böhm (1980a, 89), too, it is the 'most ideal form of democracy' in that it manifests a 'daily and hourly' unfolding of 'plebescitarian democra[tic]' market decisions. Indeed, the 'free price mechanism is the indispensable instrument of [coordination]' (Müller-Armack 1955, 83) by the 'democratic sovereign, the market' (Röpke 1942, 254). There is individual freedom precisely to the extent that there is complete competition. In this freedom the individual is a moral person and the moral person is the entrepreneur who takes full responsibility for his or her life circumstances and acts accordingly in good times and bad times, too. The entrepreneur engages in competition as an autonomous individual who endowed with the Rights of property seeks gratification by means of voluntary exchanges on free markets. Free markets are governed by the principles of scarcity, private property, freedom of contract and exchange between equal legal subjects, each pursuing his or her own self-interested ends as equals and in liberty from direct coercion. The harmonious order of private property is premised on the condition that everybody is accountable only to themselves.

The free economy is thus seen as the organisational form of individual freedom. It is an order of self-responsible participants and autonomous decision makers. Their social cooperation is established by an impersonal 'signalling system', the free price mechanism. It tells consumers and producers alike what to buy and sell, and where to invest and withdraw. Market government by the free price mechanism is premised on monetary stability to permit its effective operation as a 'calculating machine' (Eucken 1989, 28) that informs sellers and buyers, consumers and producers, of the degree of scarcity in the whole economy. As such a 'scarcity gauge' (29) it sustains the seemingly automatic, non-coerced coordination and balancing of the interests of millions and millions of people, each partaking in a 'continuous consumer plebiscite' (Röpke 1989, 76). Prices, says Röpke (1987, 17), 'are orders by the market to producers and consumers to expand or to restrict.' The free economy is thus endorsed as a particular 'social instrument' that allows for the spontaneous communication and free cooperation between self-interested and self-responsible participants who make contracts with each other by their own free will and according to their own purpose, and in doing so they all work together in the common interest.

The strong state is also a constitutive principle of a liberal economic constitution (Eucken 2004, 337). It has to hold out against monopolies, politicised social relations, party politics and lobby by powerful economic interests, including trade union power. The depoliticisation of the socio-economic relations is a constitutive principle of a free labour economy. Next to the state, there cannot be any other claim for or concentration of political power. The strong state is a constitutive principle because it is the power of the fundamental sociability of the unsocial interests.[10] The role of the state is to civilise the conduct of self-interest, removing market impediments that, say, protect certain participants from exposure to market pressures, and create conditions under which market regulation by the free price mechanism can take place.

That is, under no circumstances should the money supply 'be subjected to political manipulation' (Feld, Köhler and Nientiedt 2015, 52). Instead, it has to take the form of a 'rational automatism' that adjusts economic expectations according to agreed-upon rules to the signals of competitive price movements (Eucken 2004, 263). Automaticity is a political act. The willingness, say, to price oneself into employment presupposes not only the acceptance of competition as a moral obligation. It also presupposes that there is 'a functioning price system of complete competition' (254), the establishment of which is a constitutive necessity in a transaction society. The constitutive principles of the free economy amount thus to a politics of order, *Ordnungspolitik*. Its objective is to secure the constitutive principles of the free economy, including the stability of the monetary system, fiscal discipline, undivided and undistorted markets, the guarantee and enforcement of private property rights, freedom of contract, acceptance of (unlimited) liability for the consequences of non-coerced transaction decisions, complete competition on all markets, including labour markets, and steadiness, consistency and reliability of economic policy in support of entrepreneurial decision making (Eucken 1959, 26, 52; 2004, 254–291).

These constitutive principles entail definite regulative principles of liberal interventionism. These principles flow from the economic constitution and are bound by its basic value decisions. The constitutive principle of a stable monetary system entails the regulative principle of achieving monetary conditions in which money has value.[11] Especially the monetary system and the credit system require constant attention to secure the effectiveness of 'price competition' (Eucken 2004, 337). The establishment of a functioning price system does not entail an attempt at price fixing. Rather, it entails the control of inflation. Further, for the sake of price stability, the objective of economy policy cannot be the creation of aggregate demand by deficit spending. Demand-side interventionism associated with Keynesianism is rejected as market distorting in its effect. Nor can it be the achievement of full employment or the protection of specific commodity markets and industries. In Foucault's (2008, 139) succinct formulation, 'whatever the rate of unemployment . . . you must absolutely not intervene directly or in the first place on unemployment, as if full employment should be a political idea. . . . What is to be saved, first of all and above all, is the stability of prices'. A policy of full employment is contrary to the constitutive principles of the free economy; debt and inflation erode social cooperation by price signals; manipulation of money undermines the standard of exchange and tampers with the measure of labour productivity. Currency devaluation amounts to perverse labour market policy (Feld 2012). Policies that are meant to advance complete competition 'would have little effect . . . if firms could act in concert in setting prices or determining output or if firms with economic power could use that power to foreclose opportunities for competition'; or if trade unions had the power to politicise the labour market relations and demand wages and conditions (Gerber 1994, 48).[12]

For the sake of the free economy, no 'benefits will be granted to any vested interest however politically strong they might be' (Nicholls 1994, 8). Finally, the constitutive principle of unlimited liability holds that freedom of decision making comes with moral responsibility for the outcomes of those decisions. 'Unlimited liability' belongs to the concept of an enterprise society (Eucken 1959, 242). The relations of complete competition do not involve the state as a public insurance company for the hazard of private risk-taking. Any such insurance, it is argued, is an incentive for irresponsible risk-taking and an encouragement for 'rent seeking' by the powerful private actors (Eucken 2004, 282). Personal liability is a most important constitutive principle of free economy.[13] It holds the market participants accountable for the adverse consequences of their decisions; it is meant to moralise them. Freedom entails responsibility. It may change the assessment of risk and restrain reckless risk-taking. Eucken therefore insists that 'liability is not only a precondition of the economic order of complete competition but in general for a society in which freedom and self-determination prevail' (2004, 285). In a free society, individuals make decision for and by themselves, and they are thus self-responsible for the outcomes of their decisions.[14] In a free market society the state is the public authority of self-responsible enterprise competition. It does not intervene on behalf of the indebted and bankrupt, the unemployed and underpaid. It guarantees the Rights of private property and intervenes for the sake of sound money, sustaining the price mechanism as the calculating machine of economic pain and pleasure.[15] In this manner, the ordoliberal state really is a planner for competition by the free price mechanism, as Balogh (1950) argued. It exercises political power not as a counterweight to the freedom of competition but, rather, as the mainspring of competition as a legal obligation, individual responsibility and public duty. Instead of directing the conduct of the economic agents, it establishes the constitutive framework for the economy as a whole and intervenes on 'the frame', enforcing and, if need be, reforming the rules of conduct.[16]

For the ordoliberals, therefore, 'order means the regulation of freedom' (Eucken 2004, 179). On the one hand, it entails quite reasonably the provision of legal security for economic decision making. Legal security is the necessary condition 'of individual planning in a market society and safeguard against arbitrary practices', by either political authority or powerful market participants (Mestmäcker 2007a, 42). It assures them that law is not subject to manipulation and that it is dependable and knowable (see also Hayek 1979). On the other hand, it also entails that 'for both the state and for individuals, the economy must be a game: a set of regulated activities' that are determined by a 'set of rules which determine the way in which each must play a game whose outcome is not known to anyone' (Foucault 2008, 173). For the politics of freedom the dispersion of economic power is fundamental (Eucken 2004, 334). Failure to meet this requirement will lead, as Eucken put it, to the 'neo-feudal loss of political authority' (334).[17] If there is unemployment, government must not intervene in a direct manner. It must plan by the free price mechanism, enabling the unemployed to price themselves into employment.

In summary, the ordoliberal concept of economic constitution holds the same validity as the concept of political constitution. It mandates adherence, establishes the framework for legitimate economic activity and lays down the principles of conduct for the whole political economy. The Freiburg school emphasises the need for an 'integrated policy perspective' (*Ganzheitsbetrachtung*). In this conception each policy area is a constituent of liberal political economy. Each constituent has a meaning and significance only in and through the whole. Social policy, say, is thus distinct only as a constituent of liberal political economy, and its conduct is defined by its contribution to the system of complete competition as whole. 'All principles – the constitutive as well as regulative – belong together. To the extent that economic policy is consistently based on them, a competitive order will be created and made operational. Every principle receives its meaning only in the context of the general blueprint (*Bauplan*) of the competitive order' (Eucken 2004, 204). *Ordnungspolitik* is thus not at all restricted to economic policy. It is rather about the achievement of a consistent conduct of government in all policy areas. It is as much about what needs to be done as it is about what needs to be avoided. In the free economy the freedom to compete is paramount. Its conduct requires clear rules and enforcement of the rules decided upon. It also requires entrepreneurial will and stamina.[18]

COMPLETE COMPETITION VERSUS PRIVATE POWER: ON *ORDNUNGSPOLITIK*

Complete competition is the 'economic instrument of negating power' (Nörr 2003, 306). Assertion of private power is detrimental to the liberal foundation of society. *Ordnungspolitik* is about the replacement of private power by market power. Paraphrasing Kant's dictum of freedom, Man is free if he needs to obey no person but solely the market democracy of demand and supply (cf. Böhm 1980a, 89).[19] Competition law is the regulative means of *Ordnungspolitik*. It is meant to disperse private economic power for the sake of a freedom of economic compulsion.

Ordoliberalism accepts that the tendency towards monopoly is innate to the logic of competition (Eucken 2004, 31; Röpke 1950a, 143; Müller-Armack

1978, 326). Indeed, monopoly is an 'understandable' reaction against potentially loss-making market pressures (Eucken 2004, 237). Eucken therefore argues that 'laissez faire and complete competition should not be confused' (191). Laissez-faire leaves free economy at the mercy of the private interests that, instead of adjusting to market pressures by their own free will, distort the free price mechanism by monopoly pricing and market closure. Since therefore competition and freedom of contract 'can abolish themselves' (Peukert 2010, 120; Eucken 2004, 31, 55), a strong state is required that acts 'with severity and impartiality' (Röpke 1942, 5) to ensure that the 'freedom of contract [is] not . . . used for contracts that restrict or eliminate freedom of contract' (Eucken 2004, 278). As Gerber (1994, 47) puts it, for the ordoliberals, the experience of Weimar translated into a demand for the 'elimination of monopolies', cartels and economic syndicates. The means of 'elimination' is the establishment of a system of complete competition. In case of unavoidable natural or public monopolies, their regulation has to be market based as if there were complete competition.

Initially, the Chicago school shared the ordoliberal critique of monopoly as the great enemy of liberal political economy.[20] However, in the post-war period the Chicago school developed a more optimistic view about the effect of monopolies on prices arguing that the power of the market will ultimately prevail and bring monopolies to heel. Monopoly power was thus seen as a transitory phenomenon that will be eroded by the market forces themselves.[21] In distinction the ordoliberal argument holds that the economic system needs 'to be consciously shaped' (Eucken 2004, 106) by all manner of rules and regulations to prevent economic distortions by market closing assertions of private power. The ordoliberal definition of market closure is far reaching. Not only does it include the banning of cartels and syndicates. It also aims at the decentralisation of industry and proliferation of medium-scale production units.[22] In addition, Eucken demands that 'loyalty rebates, exclusive contracts, and aggressive low pricing against outsiders with the aim to deter or destroy must be forbidden' (Eucken 2004, 267). Moreover, he demands the abolition of modern patent law, trade mark laws and suggestive advertisements (269). The areas in which restrictive practices are acceptable include 'the work of women and children, regulation of the length of the working day, protection against accidents and by means of industrial inspection a protection of workers' (267). For Eucken (1952, 36) 'the problem of economic power can never be solved by further concentration of power, in the form of cartels or monopolies'. Nor can the solution be found in 'a policy of laissez faire which permits misuse of the freedom of contract to destroy freedom' (Eucken 1952, 37; 2004, 26). He argues that the 'problem of economic power can only be solved by an intelligent co-ordination of all economic and legal policy. . . . Any single measure of economic policy should, if it is to be successful, be regarded as part of a policy designed and to establish and maintain economic order as a whole' (Eucken 1952, 54). The system of complete competition therefore 'requires . . . servicing, above all legal safeguards' to ensure that the economic agents do 'not destroy it into an anti-market direction' (Müller-Armack 1978, 326). That is, and as pointed out by Foucault (2008, 133) it requires an 'active and extremely vigilant policy'. It is, as Eucken saw it, 'not enough to realise certain principles of law and for the rest leave the development of the economic order to itself' (Eucken 2004, 373). Rather the economic has to be consciously steered to curb the 'universal propensity to build up monopolies'. This propensity is 'a *fact*' of free economy, '*which has to be accounted for in any economic policy*' (Eucken 2004, 31, 55; also Böhm 1973, 39). Thus sustaining complete competition might in fact require as 'many economic interventions as in a policy of planning'. Indeed, the 'freer the market', the 'more rules' are needed to sustain the freedom of competition in the conduct of its participants (Miksch 1947, 133, 327). The quantity of state intervention is not an issue. What is at issue is its purpose and objective, its specific (political) quality. *Ordnungspolitik* sustains free economy by curbing the innate logic of competition towards monopoly power and closure of markets by discriminatory practices. It submits the market participants to the power of the market and establishes the 'co-ordination between autonomous but not self-sufficient individuals' by means of market prices (Böhm 2010, 169, 176).[23]

Ptak (2004) has argued that the ordoliberal critique of economic power undermines the essence of competition, which is a manifestation of economic power. Marbach (1965, 25) argued likewise: competition 'amounts to a modification of a given structure of power'. Eucken's (2004) notion of complete competition is ambiguous. He speaks about the elimination of economic power and defines complete competition as a mechanism 'which leads to the equilibrium of the economic process' (Eucken 2004, 198). However, Eucken did not argue for the suspension of price competition. Rather, he argues for it and conceives of it as the means of economic freedom. Eucken is not a visionary of economic powerlessness and imponderable conditions of competitive equilibria. The ordoliberals do not therefore argue that markets have to be regulated in order to minimise market power.[24] Rather, markets have to be regulated to minimise – eliminate – the assertion of *private* economic power on them (Böhm 1960). Private power tends to close markets and impair the workings of the price mechanism, '[reducing] the freedom of the many in favour of the domination by the few in the economic system' (Streit and Wohlgemuth 2010, 226). This is indeed Eucken's justification of the benefits of complete competition. It 'surrenders each one to the control of the market, deprives him of power, forces him to increase his work, necessitates constant adaptations, and by the means of bankruptcy has unpleasant means of coercion' (Eucken 2004, 237).[25] Market power checks private power, and the prospect of bankruptcy checks irresponsible risk-taking. As Böhm (1960, 162) clarifies, the issue of complete competition that he and Eucken 'focused together was. . . the issue of private power in a free society'. Complete competition is not an economic end in itself. Rather, it is to prevent the assertion of private power on the working of the free price mechanism (Eucken 2004, 67). Indeed, the surrender of the individuals to the movement of the free price mechanism 'is a public duty to which the entrepreneurs [have] to submit' for the sake of a well-ordered society (Müller-Armack 1979, 147; Böhm 1937, 102; also Müller-Armack 1978, 326). Competition is to be performance based, not power based. Nor should the economic agents compete against each other for access to policy makers and influence on policy. They should compete on the basis of price competitiveness alone.

The ordoliberal notion of complete competition is distinct. It is not the same as perfect or pure competition, which is the designated character of competition in neoclassical economics. In this account, competition is perfect on the condition that no participant has the power to determine prices; that is, competition is perfect when it is at its greatest possible level. Eucken's notion of complete conception is not just about the absence of price determination by private power. At its core, it is about the 'absence of *coercive* power' (Möschel 1989, 157 fn. 16, emphasis mine). It is a means of economic *freedom*. Complete competition is as much a social category as an economic one. Above all, as an instrument and safeguard of individual autonomy, it is a moral category. It presupposes depoliticised social relations and entails autonomous individuals who exchange with other and recognise each other in this exchange as moral subjects. Complete competition is thus not just a matter of competition law. Fundamentally, it is a matter of social policy. Core to Eucken's notion of complete competition is a moral question of what it means to be human.[26] Foucault (2008, 120) captures this insight well when he argues that in ordoliberalism 'competition is an essence. Competition is an *eidos* [an intuition of essence; as opposed to an empirical fact, WB]. Competition is a principle of formalisation'. It validates, reinforces and enacts individual freedom and human autonomy in depoliticised conditions of social interaction.[27]

The distinctively social and moral character of complete competition is perhaps best explained by looking at the consequences of incomplete competition, which for the ordoliberals are formidable. Following Eucken (2004, 224) it leads to the 'formation of autonomous power-blocs in industry, agriculture and the labour force', which, together with 'the particularly dangerous instability of the monetary order', undermine 'the rationality of the economic processes, leading to depression, unemployment and undersupplied markets.' These outcomes 'trigger' strong demands for 'central economic planning' that, if left unchecked, lead to the development of an economic state of planned chaos, that is, the Keynesian economic welfare state. The 'elimination of these demands' for economic planning is fundamental to the achievement of a free labour economy. Elimination is, however, 'only possible on the condition that the premises on which they arise are changed fundamentally'. For Eucken, the deterioration of liberal capitalism is caused by the formation of social power blocs and entrenched class relations. The trade unions monopolise the supply of labour (44) to which the employers react, leading, he argues, to the division of society into classes and the politicisation (*Vermachtung*) of the labour market (18).

Once the state asserts itself as a 'mediator' in the ensuing 'class struggles' the free labour economy changes towards the system of 'central planning' (Eucken 2004, 214, also 244). In fact, any assertion of private power however slight 'can in its effect' transform a liberal social order into a centrally planned economy (221). Assertion of private power undermines the social equilibrium of an open society and disfigurers its entrepreneurial participants into petitioners for, say, state aid and employment guarantees. That is, it transforms the freedom of competition and regulation of expectations by price movements into the freedom of the social forces to coerce government to intervene directly on their behalf to the detriment of a free and open society. Here, the private interests compete against each other in order to impose their 'real or putative interests' onto the state demanding 'subsidies, price guaranties, higher wages, import tariffs, nationalisation, etc.' (18). The assertion of this private power is counteracted by the assertion of that private power, and 'the probable result would be inefficiency, confusion and, ultimately, economic chaos' (Gerber 1994, 47). In condition of chaos, political interventionism does not satisfy any interest in particular. On the contrary it deepens social resentment and intensifies the struggle for privileged access to policy makers. Inasmuch as 'the interest groups determine state policy, . . . the state becomes dependent on the balance of the social forces' (Eucken 2004, 328) to the detriment of social harmony and freedom under the rule of law. In fact the rule of law transforms into a law of privileges. 'The torrent of personal interests' (Röpke, cited in Lenel 1989, 22) not only leads to the capture of the state by powerful vested interests. It also 'refeudalises' the social relations (see Böhm 2010) with the consequence that the state of law is supplanted by a state of clients. In Röpke's (1936, 163) telling phrase, 'It is not the state that is "corporative" but the corporation that is "statable"'. For the ordoliberals the 'statable' assertion of private power is the political effect of the 'refeudalisation of society' (Böhm 1980b, 258; see also Eucken 1952, 45; 2004, 357f; Rüstow 1942). In 'refeudalised' society the 'populace confuses its freedom with its power' (Röpke 1950b, 23). Concerning the argument about complete competition, what is at stake is therefore not economic efficiency and competitive effectiveness as such. Rather, what is at stake is a free society, which is the bedrock of a free market order characterised by equivalence exchange relations between self-responsible entrepreneurs of economic value.

A free labour economy is not a natural order that is somewhat 'independent of the extra-economic framework of moral, political, legal and institutional conditions' (Röpke 1942, 68). It is a politically constituted and sustained social order. Its formation is a matter of *Ordnungspolitik*. *Ordnungspolitik* has to sustain the liberal rule of law as a '*privilege-free*, non-discriminating constitutional order' (Vanberg 2015, 29). It is a politics of sustained competition for the sake of depoliticised social relations, individual autonomy, entrepreneurial freedom and social enterprise. The precondition of a free labour economy is that 'the state should under no account be allowed to confer privileges' (Böhm 2010, 174). It has to resist the influence of private power groups and disperse private power. For the sake of civil society, *Ordnungspolitik* has to 'eliminate the independence of the sectional interests and force them to become *instruments* of a competitive order' (Eucken 2004, 327, emphasis mine). For the Freiburg school, therefore, complete competition is not primarily a 'means to achieve economic goals like growth and efficiency. It is mainly advocated as a procedure to curb the power of economic agents and organizations. Economic power, in turn, is regarded as evil not only because it cripples the price mechanism and its allocative potential, but also, and primarily, because it allows infringements on the liberty of others which is regarded the fundamental preconditions of moral behaviour' (Streit and Wohlgemuth 2000, 231). Economic freedom does not create moral behaviour. It is, however, premised on it.[28] Since the 'granting of freedom might well become a danger for freedom, if it allows the creation of private power' (Eucken 2004, 53), *Ordnungspolitik* protects the freedom of self-interest from itself, discourages immoral behaviour and disciplines recklessness through a regime of full legal liability. In the ordoliberal scheme, complete competition is a means of achieving a civil society that is 'reigned by sovereign consumers' (Engel 2003, 430). Complete competition, as Foucault pointed out, 'can only appear if it is produced . . . by an active governmentality' (2008, 121) and that is one which transcends the unsocial interests, overcomes the fractured character of society and resolves the class-divided character of capitalist society on the basis of an overarching moral-legal code (see Böhm 1937, 21; Röpke 1942, 6). It submits every single market participant to the power of the market, whatever their specific interests might be and regardless of their inequality in property. The ordoliberal defence of freedom should therefore not be identified with liberality or laissez-faire. Rather, it is freedom in the name of order and through order. That is, freedom is right only 'within the framework of order' (Böhm 1937, 101). *Ordnungspolitik* is the politics of ordered freedom.

THE PRIVATE LAW SOCIETY: ON PRIVATE
AUTONOMY AND FREE ASSOCIATION

The concept of the private law society focuses the freedom of competition on the conduct of autonomous market individuals. The private law society is the counter-expression to a mass society of welfare entitlements. Its logic is Smithean: with the state securing the rules of the game and creating conditions of complete competition the individuals are authorised to pursue their own self-interest as equals before the law. They pursue their own self-interest by interacting with each other as subjects of law. Every single market participant is endowed with equal economic rights and moral duties. Although they are independent from each other, they are also obliged to each other. Their relations with each are mediated by contracts. In the private law society, no individual is able to define and pursue the collective good. Rather, individual decision making is compelled by the price mechanism, which coordinates 'the partial plan of all participants on the basis of decisions which are made by these participants' (Böhm 2010, 170).[29] In Böhm's argument private autonomy expresses itself in the form of a spontaneous market order of individual sellers and buyers, each assured of their duties and rights vis-à-vis each other. For Böhm the free economy manifests itself as an association of freedom, equality, utility, property and market-mediated connectivity.

Böhm likens the private law society to Marx's notion of a communist society arguing that it is an 'association, in which the free development of each is the condition for the free development of all' (Böhm 2010, 171).[30] In fact, according to Böhm, 'this quotation . . . could serve as the leading principle for private law society and its market economy' (171 fn. 20).[31] In this argument, liberalism did not emancipate the individual from society. Rather, it changed society from a feudal society of privileges into a society of 'free and equal members' (Nörr 2010, 158) who pursue their own self-interests as equals before the law. In the private law society 'each member enjoys the social permission to act as an entrepreneur' (Böhm 2010, 174) and thus 'to plan and implement their own economic decisions by relying only on prices and legal rules' (Mestmäcker 2007a, 22). The abolition of feudal privilege established thus a society in which there is 'only one legal status for all and only a single competent authority governing human plans and actions, namely private autonomy' (Böhm 2010, 162). Freedom of property and contract are guaranteed by public authority. Each individual is endowed with equal rights and secures his or her interests by means of exchange, buying and selling on competitive markets, including labour markets. Society manifests all manner of contractual relationships between exchange-positing individuals who make independent decisions on the basis of non-discriminatory rules and according to an objective standard of prices. Their decisions transform into public virtues by means of an invisible hand that manifests the sociability of their price-taking behaviour in the form of an economic calculus of consumer preferences (Eucken 2004, 263).

In the free association of a spontaneous market order, 'the individual is bound to his state through the medium of the private law society' (Böhm 2010, 166). The freedom of contract entails the state as the independent power of the individual economic rights. Instead of privileges, the state sets equal rights; instead of relations of will and power, the state sets relations of law; instead of despotism, the state concentrates coercion as law and order; instead of relations of conflict and social struggle, the state sets contractual relations of social interaction. The state thus civilises the conduct of freedom and moralises the spontaneous market order in the form of a private law society. Each participant is not only governed by law. He or she is also a moral person. That is, each individual embodies the rights and responsibilities of the laws of private property and bestows them with a consciousness and a will. In a private law society, the individual is an independent agent of free association. He or she is free to obey only the rule of law and to adjust to competitive price movements as a self-responsible entrepreneur. The private law society recognises the individual property owner as an abstract citizen. It treats rich and poor as equals. Assertion of private power, including monopoly power, social power blocs and class power, is detrimental to its sociability and civility. The establishment of 'power groups' within society, 'which would make it possible for others, individually or as a group, to be subjugated and exploited' (Böhm 2010, 176), is contrary to its logic. Complete competition is a necessity of free association since it 'permanently endangers and often actually erodes economic power' (Engel 2003, 431).[32] For the sake of freedom, private autonomy and individual economic rights, it checks the assertion of the special interests that seek dispensation from competitive pressures by, say, a politics of full employment and comprehensive forms of welfare support. For the individuals, free association in the spontaneous market order is a moral duty.

The purpose of all legal rules in a private law society is legal equality.[33] Its safeguard requires organised force. 'A private law society cannot function without authority' (Böhm 2010, 167; also Mestmäcker 2007a, 22). It achieves 'order' on the basis of a 'set of legal rules' that regulate 'a society of essentially self-reliant decision makers whose actions are controlled and coordinated by market competition' (Streit and Wohlgemuth 2010, 226). In a private law society there can thus be no specific laws that deal with particular issues and intervene in a directive manner. Any such law contains its own concrete purpose and thus discriminates between discernible purposes. Law has to be abstract to avoid the award of privileges. By abstracting from concrete purposes, law recognises the equality of individuals as autonomous decision makers, each endowed with the same rights and each equally empowered to act 'as an entrepreneur' whatever their concrete conditions and purposes might be (Böhm 2010, 174).[34] In 'the private law system . . . people are not supplied with a prescription of the behaviour expected from them *vis-à-vis* innumerable known and unknown members of society with equal rights. Moreover, people are expected to guess and find out for themselves that attitude that is in each case correct or expedient, that is to say they individually adjust, as it were, to the constellation of the outside world by taking their bearings form the social data known to them' (167–168). Each member of the private law society is thus equally endowed with negative economic rights. The unemployed is as empowered as the owner of great wealth to act on the permission of enterprise.

In conclusion, Böhm recognises the market individual as a price-taking subject that acts according to a 'certain concrete order, Law and order' (Foucault 2008, 174). As such it is also a subject of *Ordnungspolitik*. *Ordnungspolitik* resolves around competition law to prevent the 'degeneration of the competitive process' (Gerber 1994, 50). Any such degeneration puts a private law society in jeopardy. Competition law articulates the principles of a private law society. The 'ordnungspolitical' necessity of competition law recognises the social pressures that threaten to derail it. For the sake of a private law society, political authority is needed since 'experience has shown that the protection of competition is neglected if it is subject to a discretionary political decision' (Möschel 1989, 288).[35] Freedom of contract can be used either in compliance with the rule of law or in violation of it, in which case it has 'no private autonomy, no legitimacy of economic acting or non-acting' (Nörr 2010, 160). As Tuori (2015, 134) puts it, the economic constitution 'imposes an interpretative duty not merely in public but also, and even primarily, in private law. . . . Private law institutions are instruments for realization of a constitutional *Gesamtentscheidung*. . . . Together the public and the private law elements produce a "*herrschaftsfreie* [depoliticised] order of social cooperation, a market economy governed by performance based competition"' (quoting Böhm 1933, 124; see also Böhm 2010, 169–170). A *herrschaftsfreie* social order, free association, amounts to an entirely depoliticised social order that is one from which 'all orderlinessess [has been eradicated]' and from which 'private power [has been eliminated]' (Böhm 1937, 150). In this 'powerless' social order, what counts is performance-based competition, not the kind of 'impediment-based competition' by cartels and powerful labour unions, which in Böhm's account sabotage 'free association' to the detriment of a free society.

CONCLUSION: ORDO AND THE MORALITY OF COMPETITION

The ordoliberal conception of ordered competition recognises the freedom to compete as a moral obligation and public duty. The chapter argued that in ordoliberalism, competition is more than just an economic 'instrument'. Most importantly, it is a means of freedom and individual autonomy, and the foundation of Böhm's idea of free association as a spontaneous order of private initiative and coordination of social cooperation through price movements. Eucken therefore sees it as the fundamental means of the 'god-willed order' of a 'universal human form of life' (Eucken 2004, 176, 321). Since, however, this order of life does not come about 'just like that' (360), it needs to be constructed and sustained by order of state. The liberal state is therefore a moral institution. In creates and maintains the 'god-willed order' of private property and 'moralises' the conduct of the owners of private property. In distinction to a planned labour economy, in which 'Man becomes a tiny part in the anonymous, state-run economic machine' (Eucken 1989, 35), a free labour economy manifests the 'essence of man' in the structure of society (Eucken 1959, 239).

Not every social order constitutes an ORDO (Böhm 1950, xvi). A planned economy manifests a definite order of political economy; however, it does not amount to an ORDO. In the ordoliberal argument a planned economy defies the essence of Man. The Keynesian democratic welfare state is also not an ORDO because it is a 'muddled' system of mixed socio-economic principles. Furthermore, the competitive order of laissez-faire liberalism might also not manifest an ORDO for the simple reason that it presumes free economy as a natural thing and assumes that, unless the state interferes, economic freedom will come about spontaneously as if by the magic of invisible market forces. For the ordoliberals free economy 'is not a given of nature' (Foucault 2008, 120). Rather, it is the sustained result of a 'policy towards the organisation of the market', of *Ordnungspolitik* (Eucken 1989, 45 fn. 2). Ordoliberal economic policy intervenes into the economy not arbitrarily or in a discretionary manner, conceding privileges to the powerful economic interests. Rather, the objectives of economic policy are 'clearly identified in economic clauses in a written constitution' (45) that establishes the price-taking autonomy of freely associated entrepreneurs as the basic social value decision about the character of economic life in social market economy. 'Without the possibility of spontaneous action, man [is] not a "human being"' (34). The human essence has to appear. According to Eucken, it appears in the form of an economic order that 'accords with reason'. He calls this accord an ORDO. ORDO combines the essence of Man with the world of things (Eucken 1959, 239). ORDO manifests a harmonious order of individual price taking that is enacted and guaranteed by means of complete competition. The combination is political in its construction and requires the independent power of the state for its maintenance.

Eucken develops his argument with reference to Kant's moral philosophy. Freedom is the condition of morality, and the denial of freedom is immoral and spells tyranny (Eucken 2004, 176).[36] Kant's categorical imperative principle holds that Man is a purpose and not a means. In Eucken's (2004, 126) view, a centrally planned economy makes Man a means. It is the institutional manifestation of self-imposed immaturity. It is thus a state of immorality, which defies the god-willed order of free competition and regulation of economic behaviour by impersonal price movements (Eucken 2004, 53). With reference to Kant, Eucken therefore argues that 'it is the responsibility of the state to find a *form*', which guarantees the sociability of the unsocial interests and which provides for the 'greatest possible opportunity for the free development of individual capacities'.[37] He rejects the 'absolute freedom of the natural condition', that is, in this context, cutthroat competition and unrestrained greed. Freedom 'should be constrained by statutes, through which, on the one hand the individual is protected against the discretion of others and through which the free activity of the many individuals in competition with each other should support [the progress] of society' (Eucken 2004, 360). In the words of Franz Böhm, the sociability of competition manifests a certain 'type of order' which he likens to a 'scored social symphony' (1937, 93). Everybody conducts himself or herself freely in harmony with a civil constitution that moralises the unsocial interests, eliminating 'conflict. . . as far as possible' (188).[38] The order of freedom compels the individuals to accept their place in society and follow society's moral code akin to an orchestra that follows 'the musical score'.[39] Disharmony is not permitted, and dissonance forces the state to act. Indeed, the much-praised autonomy of the individual is in fact 'limited in scope [*begrenzter Ermessungsspielraum*]'. In reality the individuals 'do not possess autonomy'. They are not permitted to act freely according to their own desires. Autonomy is law-governed and rule-based. That is, it is governed by the order of society and expressed in accord with that order (Böhm 1950, xlvi). Without exception everybody is to sing from the same hymn-sheet, whether endowed with independent means or compelled to work for their supper.

In the ordoliberal scheme, competition law is the means of ORDO. It compels individual autonomy and permits the economic agents to endow free economy with an independent will, sustaining their so-called 'free association'. In summary, 'ORDO is INRI from a political economy viewpoint, and full competition the cornerstone in methodological, ethical, moral and social respects' (Peukert 2010, 119). Complete competition disperses economic power as every economic agent 'possesses a small portion of power'. In this manner 'the problem of economic power is . . . practically non-existent' (Eucken 2004, 250). Whatever the inequality in property, in this society of ordered freedom everybody is exposed to the dynamics of market order and everybody has therefore the permission and moral duty to act according to his or her essence, that is, to compete. Fundamentally, *Ordnungspolitik* amounts to a social policy.

NOTES

1. It has metamorphosed since into the school of constitutional economics. See Buchanan (1990), Buchanan and Tullock (1962), and Brennan and Buchanan (2000). See also Vanberg (1988, 2001, 2002) and Feld and Köhler (2011). Kerber and Vanberg (2001, 53) define economic constitution as a political instrument that 'defines the rules of the game under which economic activities can be carried out in the respective jurisdiction'. This definition falls short. It says, correctly, that the economic constitution sets out the *rules of the game* under which social and economic life is to be played out. The institution that sets them out is the state. In the context of ordoliberal anxiety about state capture by private interests and democratic excess, economic constitution is also meant to restraint policy making on the basis of binding rules. The authoritative 'decision' about the economic constitution establishes a normative framework to parliamentary law making. It recognises the liberal rights, quintessentially the Rights of private property, as establishing the ground rules for the conduct of government.

2. The German term is *vollständige Konkurrenz*. I follow Gerber (1994, 1998) in translating this term as 'complete competition' to distinguish it from neoclassical notions of 'perfect' or 'full' competition. In neoclassical economics perfect competition is the economic category of optimum market efficiency. Complete competition is not just a category of economic effectiveness. Most importantly, it is also a moral category of a well-ordered political economy. Ordoliberalism conceives of complete competition as a means of individual freedom and moral conduct. Competition is as much a moral category as an economic one.

3. Böhm developed this concept in 'Private Law Society and Market Economy', originally published in 1966. Translations are available in Peacock and Willgerodt (eds.) (1989) and Koslowski (2010). Elements of the concept can also be found in Böhm (1937, 11, 53, 56). See also Eucken (2004, 365) on the order of enterprise (*Wettbewerbsordnung*).

4. This is Hayek's (1944) concept. The terms transaction society and spontaneous order are congruent. See Streit and Wohlgemuth (2010).

5. Translation amended. The English language version of Schmitt's work translates *Gesamteintscheidung* as complete decision. Böhm (1933, 107) explicitly refers to Schmitt, arguing that 'from the constitutional law perspective the system of commercial freedom is a constitution of economic life in the positive sense. . . in the same sense as Carl Schmitt has called the constitution an overall decision on the kind and form of political unity'.

6. On rules and discretion in ordoliberal thought, see also White (2017).

7. This was discussed previously in chapter 2. On the constitutive principles of the free market, see Eucken (2004, 254–289).

8. On the rule of law as a civilised manifestation of political power, of force and violence, see chapter 3.

9. On this, see also Davies (2015). Davies distinguishes between an ordoliberal juridification of economic institutions and juridical rationalisation of economic behaviour that for him defines Chicago neoliberalism. However, the distinction is

not one of principle. It is one of emphasis. The ordoliberals stress both. The order of competition entails the formalisation of society as an enterprise society and the juridification of economic institutions, rights and obligations. 'Economic structure' and 'economic behaviour' belong to the same reality of economic order.

10. On this, see chapter 2 on Kant's argument for a civil constitution.

11. In the language of Margaret Thatcher, 'you cannot spend what you have not earned'. On this, see Bonefeld (1993).

12. See chapter 5 for the implications of this point for ordoliberal social policy.

13. See also chapters 6 and 7. European monetary union rejects risk sharing. On this, see also Varoufakis (2013).

14. On liability and the ordoliberal limits to Eurozone crisis resolution, see Siems and Schnyder (2014) and chapter 7.

15. Jevons (William Stanley Jevons, *The Theory of Political Economy* [London 1888]; http://www.econlib.org/library/YPDBooks/Jevons/jvnPE.html [accessed 4 February 2013]) conceived of the relationship between economic benefit and economic cost in terms of a relationship between pleasure and pain, which crudely put involved the pain of spending money in relation to the pleasure of purchasing a commodity. He therefore defined value in subjective terms as utility: the utility of a commodity accords value to it as an expression of pleasure over pain.

16. Ordoliberal social policy does not just intervene on the framework conditions. It intervenes also into mentality of the governed, see chapter 5.

17. The German original reads: 'Jede Festigung der Machtgruppen verstärkt die neufeudale Autoritätsminderung des Staates'.

18. See chapter 5 on ordoliberal social policy as a regulative principle also of the economic constitution of a free labour economy.

19. Kant says that man is free if he only has to obey the law. For an application of Kant's dictum as moral legitimation of a spontaneous market order, see Hayek (1944, 58) and Eucken (2004, 176).

20. See especially the work of Simons (1948).

21. See, for example, Director and Levi (1956). For a critical account, see van Horn and Mirowski (2009) and van Horn (2011). Nevertheless, the distinction between the Chicago free market approach and the state-centric Freiburg approach to market competition and monopoly is one of emphasis, not substance. As Hans Willgerodt (1986, 55) put it, 'In reality there exists only a difference in emphasis, and opportunities for an academic and political division of labour'.

22. See the debate about the German *Mittelstand* as the backbone of its economy. Glasman's (1996) account of ordoliberalism feeds on this idea.

23. The conventional view that the ordoliberal argument for restraint competition means less competition, see for example Sheppard and Leitner (2010), is entirely at odds with ordoliberal doctrine.

24. Siems and Schnyder (2014) misconceive the ordoliberal critique of private power as a critique of market power.

25. Profit is thus deemed to be the reward for entrepreneurship. As Röpke (2009, 105–106) makes clear: 'Under the rule of profit, the entrepreneur who adapts himself, receives form the market an acknowledgment to that effect in the form of a bonus. . .

the entrepreneur who does not fit in is penalised by the market. . . the economic system is governed by the fear of bankruptcy' – and profitable adaption to the dynamic of the market is thus a means of avoiding bankruptcy.

26. For detailed discussion of complete competition as a moral institution see 'ORDO and the Morality of Competition, see below. The remainder of this part and the following account, 'The Private Law Society', explore the moral premises of complete competition. The Conclusion, 'ORDO and the Morality of Competiton, draws this together.

27. In Foucault *vollständige* competition is also translated as 'pure' competition (see, for example, Foucault 2008, 121), which is the alternate term of perfect competition. Nörr (2010) translates it as 'effective' competition. Although *vollständige* competition overlaps with the neoclassical prescription of competition, it is nevertheless distinct. Its distinction is founded on a moral argument, which upholds the ideal of an absence of private economic power and coercive force. *Vollständige* competition is the economic category of the liberal idea of negative rights as the social condition of individual autonomy, economic liberty, and freedom of price.

28. On this, see also Bonefeld (2013) and Ronge (2015). See also chapter 2 for an account of the moral sentiments in Smith's political economy.

29. This is Böhm's formulation of Hayek's spontaneous order.

30. See Marx and Engels (1996, 35).

31. He might as easily have quoted from Marx's depiction of the buying and selling of labour power as a 'very Eden of the innate rights of man. It is the exclusive realm of Freedom, Equality, Property and Bentham. Freedom, because both buyer and seller . . . are determined only by their own free will. They contract as free persons, who are equal before the law. Their contract is the final result in which their joint will finds a common legal expression. Equality, because each enters into relation with the other . . . and they exchange equivalent for equivalent. Property, because each disposes only of what is his own. And Bentham, because each looks only to his own advantage. The only force bringing them together, and putting them into relation with each other, is the selfishness, the gain and the private interest of each' (Marx 1990, 280).

32. The task of 'compelling enterprises to act in the public interest is assigned to market competition and, by extension, to the legislature, who should protect competition from restraints created by enterprises' and powerful labour unions (Mestmäcker 1993, 71).

33. Hayek went furthest in developing this notion in his *Law, Legislation and Liberty*. He quotes Kant in support of this view of society as a law-governed spontaneous order: 'The law leaves it to everybody's voluntary will which purpose he pursues with his conduct' (1979, 113 fn. 26). The quotation is from Kant's *Foundation of the Metaphysics of Morals*.

34. Hayek's (1944, 1979) argument that individual liberty requires the rule of law to be abstract in character and Böhm's private law society are cut from the same cloth. Hayek (1944, 78) illustrates the liberal utility of the abstract rule of law with reference to the highway code: it does not tell anybody where to go, on which road to travel and makes no reference to particular purposes. Everybody can go wherever

they want as long as they obey the highway code, which tells the drivers in advance what the state will do if they disobey the traffic rules. Röpke had already made this same point using a similar illustration in his *Gesellschaftskrise* of 1942 (see Röpke 2009, 185–186). See also Dardot and Laval (2013, 143). With good reason they see Hayek as a follower of Böhm.

35. Competition policy is law-based and law-governed. It is thus not a matter of discretionary law making. Nor should its enforcement be a matter of discretionary political judgement. Eucken calls for enforcement by an independent and quasi-judicial technocratic body that wields real political power. He calls for the establishment of independent monopoly office, which, he says, 'is as indispensable as the highest court' (Eucken 2004, 294). On the (West-)German cartel office and its significance as a blueprint for the European Monopolies and Merges Commission, see Gerber (1998).

36. As does Hayek, see, for example Hayek (1944, 84; 1979, 113).

37. On this point, see chapter 2, "From Kant to Hegel".

38. Müller-Armack's characterisation of social market economy as an irenic order cuts from the same cloth. Irenic order is one in which social strife, economic conflict and the struggle to make ends meet make way for a society in which 'competition is a public duty to which entrepreneurs [have] to submit' and indeed do so willingly and on their own initiative (Müller-Armack, 1979, 147). On market economy as an irenic order, see Müller-Armack (1976, 300) and chapter 5 on social policy.

39. See also Röpke (2009, 185): 'There is an order of the integrated whole . . . and the order of the varied detail. . . . The former causes all musicians in a concert to play in time, the latter sees to it that they all play different parts.'

Chapter 5

Social Policy: From the Class Society to the Enterprise Society

INTRODUCTION

The sociological account of ordoliberalism is associated with the work of Wilhelm Röpke, Alexander Rüstow and Alfred Müller-Armack. It would, however, be wrong to draw a sharp line of differentiation between this account and Freiburg school thinking about economic constitution and *Ordnungspolitik*. As the previous chapter set out, the Freiburg school interprets the economic constitution in terms of a comprehensive decision (*Gesamtentscheidung*) about the fundamental character of liberal political economy, which is founded on the completeness of performance-based competition. Complete competition unfolds not only within a robust legal and institutional framework. It also unfolds within performance enhancing social and moral frameworks. Indeed, for Walter Eucken *Ordnungspolitik* is social policy. As he put it, 'Social policy should not be regarded as an appendage of economic policy but should rather be seen as the essence of economic policy.' Indeed, it is 'identical with the politics of economic order or the politics of economic constitutionalism [*Wirtschaftsverfassungspolitik*]' (Eucken 2004, 313). The relations of complete competition presume the existence of a definite socio-moral order. As Böhm (1937, 11) put it succinctly, nothing is worse than a condition in which the capacity of the free price mechanism to regulate the coordination of, and adjustment between, individual preferences is undermined by 'the will of the participants [who] rebel against that movement'. The formatting of this will defines the ordoliberal purpose of social policy.

For ordoliberalism the viability of free economy is a matter beyond demand and supply. Markets do not generate the entrepreneurial morality and coherence of social structure upon which their conduct depends. On the contrary, they tend to erode their moral and social preconditions. The

ordoliberals understand that capitalism has a 'natural tendency towards proletarianisation' (Röpke 2009, 218). Since therefore economic freedom might
turn the 'proletariat into a problem', the premise of economic freedom is the
'deproletarianisation' of society (52). Their conception of proletarianisation is specific. They define the proletarian as a property-less wage labourer
and reject the idea that the proletarian condition is material in character.
Instead, they perceive it as an immaterial condition. It results from the effect
of 'urbanisation and massification' and the barracks discipline of industrial
work. Working-class discontent can thus not be overcome by higher wages
and achievement of welfare security. Rather, proletarianisation amounts to
problem of 'vitality, i.e., a non-economic, spiritual problem' (Röpke 2009,
53; Rüstow 2009, 71). They thus conceive of social policy as a *Vitalpolitik*,
that is, a politics of life or, in the words of Foucault (2008), a biopolitics. It
is to enable the vitality of the property-less to meet the challenges of a free
labour economy in the self-responsible manner of the entrepreneur (Rüstow
1963, 2005, 2009). As they see it, vitally satisfied workers cope with wage
pressures, adjusting to adverse market conditions and perilous working conditions in a robust and entirely responsible manner because they have the
courage to get on with things (Rüstow 2009, 73–74).

Vitalpolitik is about the transformation of recalcitrant proletarians into
willing and self-responsible entrepreneurs of labour power. It is tasked with
penetrating the mental make-up of workers to embed the 'psycho-moral
forces' of enterprise into the mentality of the governed (Röpke 1942, 68; also
Müller-Armack 1976, 198). Instead of asking for welfare support, workers have
to learn to accept economic risk akin to an entrepreneur who sees opportunities
when misfortune strikes. Ordoliberal social policy is thus to secure for the free
economy that very entrepreneurial vitality that 'market and competition . . .
constantly strain . . . , draw upon . . . , and consume' (Röpke 1998, 126). Peacock and Willgerodt (1989, 9) capture the essence of ordoliberal social policy
well when they characterise it as 'medication' that is administered to help the
market 'organism to self-regulate'. Röpke and Rüstow thus conceive of *Vitalpolitik* as a politics of human economy – the fabrication of Man and formation
of character define the ordoliberal purpose of deproletarianisation.

The chapter is divided into two sections and a conclusion. First, it introduces the ordoliberal critique of collectivist responses to pressing social
problems and expounds its rejection of the welfare state as an illiberal
manifestation of 'a degenerated capitalist system' (Röpke 2009, 15). Second,
it expounds the social character of market economy in three steps, which
explores the ordoliberal notion that social policy is first and foremost about
the achievement of economic growth; establishes the ordoliberal account of
human community as an organic counter-world to the harsh reality of market competition; and finally, assesses the ordoliberal argument for a popular

capitalism based on widespread property ownership. The conclusion argues that *Vitalpolitik* is based on distrust. It recognises the entrepreneur as a potential security risk. In the final instance, social policy combines with surveillance under an ever-vigilant 'security state'.

'IN UNISON WITH THE SOCIALISTS
WE REJECT CAPITALISM'[1]

Capitalism and Proletarianisation: Beyond Laissez-faire

Sociological ordoliberalism denounces the capitalism of the inter-war years as a 'degenerate form of the market economy'. It had reduced liberal society to 'something entirely unnatural'. Its 'pathological [degeneration]' (Röpke 2009, 117, 119; also Müller-Armack 1981c, 453) had to do with the politicisation of the capitalist class relations that posited the owners of great wealth, privilege and power against dispossessed labourers, creating an unpalatable 'massification' of society, which in cohorts with 'diseased democracy' became uncivilised in its conduct to the point of depression (Röpke 2009, 52; also Eucken 2004, 46; Rüstow 2005, 353ff). Ordoliberalism recognises the proletariat as the 'uprooted class of the population which is dependent on the constant utilization of its productive power'. The 'class which we call the proletariat' is a capitalist phenomenon (Röpke 2002, 116).[2] This class struggles to make ends meet. The effort at deproletarianisation has to recognise the socio-economic foundation of this struggle in the property-less character of the proletariat. Given that the ordoliberals perceive of proletarianisation as a problem of personality, deproletarianisation amounts to an attempt at transforming a proletarian personality into personality of private property.

The ordoliberal critique of capitalism as a class system based on dependent labour relations amounts fundamentally to a critique of socialism. Laissez-faire liberalism is the medium of critique. They charge capitalism with destroying 'the substance of binding forces inherited from history and [of placing] the individual in often painfully felt isolation' (Müller-Armack 1979, 152), denounce laissez-faire liberalism as the 'theology' of degenerate capitalist system (Rüstow 1942, 271), accept that socialism offers an understandable critique of capitalist misery (Rüstow 2005, 365) and condemn socialism as the culmination of capitalist misery. The 'sociological blindness' (Röpke 2009, 52) of laissez-faire liberalism is total. It assumed 'that the market mechanism supplies morally and socially justifiable solutions if left to its own devices' (Müller-Armack 1978, 329) and turned a blind eye to the 'problems lying in the obscurity of sociology' (Rüstow 1942, 265). Its ignorance 'turned the proletariat into a problem' (Röpke 2009, 52). Proletarianised social structures express the destruction of a civilisation based on the human quality of the entrepreneur. In its stead there emerged what the intellectual conservative Ferrero (1963) called 'a quantitative civilisation', which reduces 'qualitative greatness to . . . nothing but numbers, and since quantity can only be toppled by ever greater quantity, the intoxication with size will in the end exceed all bounds' (Röpke 2009, 67). Socialism, they say, is both a rebellion against the cult of pure quantity and its 'climax' (Röpke 2009, 15). In short, the ordoliberals identify capitalism with proletarianisation and argue that it nurtures socialism as its false alternative. Instead of overcoming capitalist proletarianisation, socialism declares for the complete proletarianisation of society.[3] It stands for the universalisation of the proletarian way of life and is therefore the culmination of capitalism's 'spiritual collectivisation', 'cult of the colossal', 'quantitative civilisation' and ethical abandonment of what it means to be human to an artificial and unnatural life of mechanised processes characterised by social engineering and technocratic planning.[4]

Röpke characterises the proletarian condition as one of total estrangement. It 'means nothing less than that human beings have got into a highly danger-ous sociological and anthropological state which is characterised by lack of property, lack of reserves of every kind. . . by economic servitude, uprooting, massed living quarters, militarization of work, by estrangement from nature and by the mechanisation of productive activity; in short, by a general devi-talisation and loss of personality' (Röpke 2002, 140). The capitalist concen-tration of wealth and the emergence of giant enterprises makes 'a large part of the population dependent, urbanized cogs in the industrial-commercial hierar-chy' (Röpke 2009, 15), rendering life 'shallow, uniform, derivative, herdlike, and tritely mediocre' (54).[5] The proletarian is prised 'out of the fabric of true community' (Röpke 1998, 57; also Müller-Armack 1981a, 58, 260), lives a 'mechanical life' (Rüstow 2005, 353), lacks entrepreneurial stamina and conviction and does not possess the requisite ethical commitments to succeed (see Müller-Armack 1981a, 260; Eucken 1989, 34). The proletarian is thus somebody who has lost the moral capacity to act as a civilised member of a private law society and 'accept responsibility' (Röpke 2002, 192) for his or her own circumstances and prospects.

Proletarianised social structures exhibit therefore 'a remarkable *loss of social integration*'. Social disintegration is 'brought about by the general atomisation of society, the individualisation . . . and the increasing standardi-sation and uniformity that are destroying the vertical coherence of society, the emancipation from natural bonds and community, the uprooted character of modern urban existence with its extreme changeability and anonymity ("nomadisation") and the progressive displacement of spontaneous order and coherence by organisation and regimentation'. Then there is the 'equally remarkable *loss of vital satisfaction* brought about by the devitalising influence of these conditions of work and life imposed by the urban-industrial existence and environment' (Röpke 1942, 240). Finally, there is the 'machine technology, the manner of its application, the forms shortsightedly favoured in factory organisation' that makes 'proletarianization the fate of the masses' (Röpke 2009, 14). In a system based on 'private ownership of the means of production' (Röpke 1998, 97), the masses are 'characterised by economic and social dependence, a rootless, tenemented life, where men are strangers to nature and overwhelmed by the dreariness of work' (Röpke 2009, 14). The proletariat is a consequence of capitalist industrialisation (Eucken 2004, 46), and antagonistic to the noble and refined values of citizenship and human community. In fact these values are 'alien, if not repulsive, to proletarianized mass society' (Röpke 1998, 99). Indeed, 'the dehumanizing impact of individualisation and uprooting of populations' (Röpke 1957, 36) explains the 'radical dissatisfaction and unrest of the working classes', which they identify as the fundamental cause of the crisis-ridden disruption of the 'economic machinery' during the inter-war period (Röpke 1942, 3; Eucken 1932; Rüstow 1963; Müller-Armack 1932). Indeed, a crisis of liberal political economy cannot 'be understood except as the manifestation of a world which has been proletarianised and largely deprived of its regulatory forces and the appropriate psychological atmosphere of security, continuity, confidence, and balanced judgements' (Röpke 1942, 4).

Although the freedom to compete is an essential human condition (Eucken 1989, 34), it is also a socially destructive force. It not only 'appeals solely to selfishness', it also '[continuously increases] the property-less masses' (Röpke 2002, 149; also Rüstow 1942, 272) who struggle to make ends meet, and who therefore demand welfare support and other forms of collective provision and protection from labour market pressures, such as employment guarantees, to secure basic needs. For the sake of competition, liberalism has to understand its limits. That is, competition can 'neither improve the moral of individuals nor assist social integration' (Rüstow 1942, 272; 2009, 27; Eucken 2004, 323). It 'nibbles away the substance of historical forces of cohesion' (Müller-Armack 1978, 327), and leads to the 'disease . . . [of] collectivisation' and 'crisis of the economic system' (Röpke 2009, 9, 18). In short, 'Men cannot bear, without excessive harm to themselves and society, the constant mental, nervous and moral tension which is forced upon them by an economic system dominated by supply and demand. Nor can they withstand the insecurity and instability of the living conditions which such a system entails' (119). One should not 'demand more from competition than it can give' (181). Economic freedom is a function of a moral society. Since the 'market and competition are far from generating their moral prerequisites autonomously . . . [t]hese prerequisites must be furnished from outside' (Röpke 1998, 126). In distinction to the unbending trust of laissez-faire liberalism in the magic of invisible principles, one has to look 'outside the market for that integration which was lacking within it' (Röpke 1942, 272). Social policy – *Vitalpolitik* – is a necessity in the social market economy.

The Welfare State and 'Pocket Money'

In the ordoliberal argument the prospects of free economy revolve around the workers' question. For the sake of the free economy, the 'true' determination of this question is therefore of vital importance. As argued earlier, ordoliberalism perceives of proletarianisation as fundamentally 'a psychological condition' (Müller-Armack 1981a, 261), which 'neither higher wages nor cinemas can cure' (Röpke 1942, 3; Rüstow 1942). That is, 'working class problems are . . . problems of personality' (Röpke 2009, 223). Workers are 'too depressed by their proletarian status to help themselves' (Röpke 1957, 23). For the sake of the free economy they need to be helped to prevent its collapse 'into a social dust bowl' (Röpke 2009, 223).

The ordoliberals reject the welfare state as an inadequate means of support. Indeed, it is the false answer to the 'the workers' question' because it 'consolidates proletarisanization' (Röpke 2009, 224). Although the proletarian struggle for material security expresses an elementary human desire, the very attempt at trying to organize it is the 'surest way. . . of coming to grief' (Röpke 2002, 198).[6] The struggle for material security in the here and now subverts both the religious idea of deferred satisfaction and the liberal idea of self-earned property. Instead, it identifies the state as 'a secular God', which came to be seen as the 'great fiction by which everybody wants to enrich themselves at the expense of everybody else' (Röpke 2009, 164; also Müller-Armack 1981c, 556; Eucken 1932, 305).[7] The welfare state institutionalises this 'fiction' as the governing principle of a proletarianised society. It makes a 'cult of the standard of living', which, says Röpke (1998, 109), manifests the 'degradation of man' in that it makes society 'hesitant and cowardly' (also Rüstow 2009, 136; Eucken 2004, 137). The 'cult of the standard of living' is as dangerous as the seductive idea of a freedom from want (Röpke 1998, 109). Freedom from want, the achievement of minimum standards of material security, undermines the 'real freedom' of entrepreneurial decision making. There is no such thing as a 'freedom without risk' (Rüstow 2009, 143). Indeed, its very idea amounts to a 'disorder of spiritual perception of almost pathological nature, a misjudgement of the true scale of vital values' (Röpke 1998, 109). In fact, the proletarian demand for a freedom from want is deemed 'alien to everything vital'. It leads 'to an artificiality of life which man is by nature not fitted to withstand for any length of time' (Röpke 1998, 109; 2009, 52, 119). The demand for material security represents thus a dangerous proletarian craze. Indeed, 'freedom from want' is 'a demagogic misuse of the word "freedom"' in that it means the 'absence of something disagreeable, rather like freedom from pain. . . . How can this be on par with genuine "freedom" as one of the supreme moral concepts, the opposite of compulsion by others, as it is meant in the phrases freedom of person, freedom of opinion, and other rights of liberty without which we cannot conceive of truly ethical behavior. A prisoner enjoys complete "freedom from want" but he would rightly feel taunted if we were to hold this up to him as true and enviable freedom' (Röpke 1998, 172). Indeed, the welfare state enslaves workers to the state (see Eucken 2004, 193, 314). 'Like the worker who is enslaved to the state, the slave had not to fear unemployment' (Rüstow 2009, 140). Freedom from want 'robs us of true freedom in the name of the false' (Röpke 1998, 173). It denies true freedom by detracting from the entrepreneurial spirit of society – innovative, energetic, enterprising, competitive, risk-taking, self-reliant, self-responsible, eternally mobile, always ready to adjust to price signals and so on (see Eucken 1932, 297).

Röpke characterises the welfare state as a 'pumping system of the Leviathan' (Röpke 1957, 20). As the institutionalized manifestation of unrestrained 'mass opinion, mass claims, mass emotion, and mass passion', which is 'directed . . . against property, law, social differentiation, tradition, continuity, and common interest' (Röpke 1998, 152), it allows "mass-produced" men to shirk their own responsibility (Röpke 1957, 24). Progress, they declare, should not be measured by the establishment of a 'pocket money state' that disempowers the individuals to assume responsibility for their own life (Röpke 1998, 158; Rüstow 2009, 142). Rather, it should be measured by what the masses can do for themselves 'out of their own resources and on their own responsibility' (Röpke 1957, 22). Nevertheless, the proletarian demand for material security is a real one. It is 'created by the market' (Röpke 1998, 10). If unfettered, competition – this necessity of human freedom – entails the 'survival of the fittest' (Röpke 2009, 164). In this struggle workers cannot succeed. They cannot 'withstand the insecurity and instability of the living conditions which [this entails]' (119) and they will thus struggle for welfare support and employment guarantees.

Since they identify the proletarian problem as a problem of vitality, it cannot be resolved by meddling 'with the free price mechanism' (Müller-Armack 1976, 132). In fact, any such meddling is contrary to the logic of a free labour economy. Instead of resolving the proletarian condition, it would make matters worse. Its resolution has to be in conformity with the logic of a free labour economy. The workers are 'devitalised' because they are not possessed by the 'ethic and spirit of the bourgeois' (Campbell 2002, xvi). True welfare policy transforms proletarianised workers into personalities of private property (see Rüstow 2005, 111). Instead of welfare provision, it releases workers from imprisonment in the welfare state,[8] empowering them as citizens, who conduct themselves in accordance with the laws of private property and achieve human distinction as entrepreneurs of labour power. In fact, says Müller-Armack (1976, 182), the proletarian masses 'long' for this kind of social policy. As he put it, welfare provision and policies of full employment are 'repugnant to the workers' own sense of freedom'. True welfare policy recognises this longing for freedom and thus relieves workers from the fear of freedom (see Müller-Armack 1981b, 92). It does not give in to a proletarianised society. Rather, it deproletarianises society and (re-)establishes its civility. Behind working-class demands for guaranteed employment and material security there exists, they say, the much deeper human desire to enter the 'civitas' (Röpke 2002, 95) of a human economy, in which individuals relish their freedom as self-responsible and self-reliant entrepreneurs of their own life circumstances. Vitally satisfied workers do not ask for handouts. They help themselves and others when the going gets tough and adjust to market pressures willingly and on their own initiative.

The real alternative to 'a deeply unhappy' mass society (Röpke 1998, 57) and its socialist offspring is (social) market economy, which they proclaim as a human economy. In distinction to a capitalist society characterised by strife and conflict, greed and struggle, avoidance of performance competition and welfare dependency, and in distinction to what they reject as socialism's irresponsible ideas about social equality and material security, 'our programme is in this respect . . . anti-capitalistic. . . . Our first objective – [complete] competition – far from being conservative has a thoroughly revolutionary character' (Röpke 2002, 27). The attainment of vitally satisfied workers in social market economy is the ordoliberal alternative to both laissez-faire liberalism and the Keynesian democratic welfare state.

VITALITY AND ENTERPRISE

Ordoliberal sociological writing hardly ever refers to capitalism, except in negative terms. Terminologically it draws a sharp distinction between capitalism and social market economy. Capitalism is identified with the turmoil of the inter-war period and rejected as the 'calamitous aberrations' and 'deformed' manifestation of an entirely unsocial market society. In this writing, the term capitalism is synonymous with monopoly power, proletarian hardship, economic crisis, political turmoil and class struggle. It is, says Müller-Armack (1981b, 181), a profoundly 'emotion laden' term. It distorts the true character of a free labour economy, which they call a 'social market economy'. The attribute 'social' is meant to distinguish the market economy from capitalism. The attribute social does not derive its meaning from ideas of social justice as a collective good. Rather, it alludes to the unsocial charac-ter of 'Weimar' capitalism and suggests a new beginning for liberal economy. The characterisation of post-war capitalism as a social market economy projects a new liberal market benevolence. The new liberalism speaks about vitally satisfied workers, couches social policy as a *Vitalpolitik* and identifies the class-divided social individual as an entrepreneurial multitude. Indeed, even the term competition was effected by these terminological efforts at distancing post-war capitalism from its pre-war experience. Sociological liberalism replaced the term competition by terms like 'race' [*Wettlauf*] or 'enterprise' [*Wettbewerb*], comparing it to an athletic performance or a sport's event of truly Olympian quality.[9] Participation is everything; nobody is excluded; cheating is disallowed and special favours are not offered to anybody. In this new economy what matter are the 'quality, sincerity, eter-nity, nobility, human scale, and simple beauty' of performance competition (Röpke 1950a, 194).

Ordoliberal social policy is law-governed and rule-based. It is not discre-tionary in character. Social policy is not meant to be an expedient or pragmatic means of dealing with particular social issues, hardships, or socio-political pressures. Ordoliberal social policy does not intervene at particular points in the social structure. Any such intervention is potentially detrimental to the coherence of economic order as a whole. In the words of the former (West) German Minister of Economics, Ludwig Erhard, a social market economy ceases 'to flourish if the spiritual attitude on which it is based – that is the readiness to assume the responsibility for one's fate and to participate in hon-est and free competition – is undermined by seemingly social measures in neighbouring fields', that is, the employment and welfare policy objectives that characterise the Keynesian welfare state (Erhard 1958, 184).

Social policy has to be 'conducted from the perspective of economic order' (Eucken 2004, 313) and in support of that order. Whether welfare support is required is therefore not a matter of political judgement about a given social situation. Rather, this judgement needs to be made in the context of a *Gesamtentscheidung* (comprehensive decision) about the character of politi-cal economy (Müller-Armack 1976, 236). Naturally, says Röpke, nobody 'ought to be allowed to starve' but he continues, 'it does not follow from this, in order that everybody should be satiated, the State must guarantee this' (2002, 245). The really weak and helpless need to be supported to prevent destitution; a system of poor relief and assistance to the unemployed is not to be argued with, financial support to help those who help themselves, includ-ing (re)training programmes, is a good thing; and philanthropic support and voluntary assistance is entirely welcomed. Nevertheless, public provision has to be conducted in conformity with the economic constitution of a free labour economy, enabling performance competition on competitive labour markets. It should neither 'undermine the willingness to work' nor 'add to the rigidity . . . and . . . also to the instability of our economic system' (Röpke 1936, 210, 211; Eucken 2004, 314).[10] However, as recognised by Barry, even here there is danger: 'A government dependent on public opinion, and particularly a democracy, will not be able to confine such attempts to supplement the market to the mitigation of the lot of the poorest' (Barry 1989, 142). What is therefore required is a social policy that does 'away with the proletariat itself', 'eliminating' it (Röpke 2009, 225).

Since a proletarianised mass society is one which is 'largely deprived of its regulatory forces and the appropriate psychological atmosphere of security, continuity, confidence and balanced judgements' (Röpke 1942, 4), the effort of deproletarianisation has to '[influence] the psychology' of workers (Böhm 1937, 117). In the post-war period Müller-Armack initially identified this effort as comprising the 're-christianization of our culture' ostensibly in order 'to prevent its imminent collapse' (1981c, 496; also Rüstow 2009). Yet, in the context of the so-called West-German economic miracle, he argued that the economic system itself creates the ideological glue that holds society together. It offered a new kind of national mythology rooted in the idea of an economic miracle as the founding myth of the new (West-)German Republic (see Haselbach 1994). Röpke was critical about the psychological effect of the economic miracle and legitimation of the market economy by economic results. He feared the further erosion of traditional-conservative values, of family and community, by an increasingly materialistic and consumerist mass society that demands its due. With Rüstow (2005, 357), he argued for a peasant-based social mentality and advocated the re-rooting of workers in small-scale communities like, say, garden cities, to prevent proletarian 'enmassment' in urban centres.[11] Ruralised living conditions would give workers a peasant-like resilience and attitude to life, which would secure 'the independence and autonomy of [the workers'] whole existence; their roots in home, property, environment, family and occupation, the personal character and the tradition of their work' (Röpke 2002, 140). Röpke's social philosophy stands out for its combination of the romantic ideas of a long-lost peasant life with the virtues of individualism. His account accentuates the ordoliberal opposition to an ostensibly responsibility sapping welfare state with conservative appeal.

The objective of ordoliberal social policy, of *Vitalpolitik*, is perhaps best summarised in Röpke (1950a, 182): 'We need to eliminate the proletariat as a class defined by short-term wage-income. In its stead we have to create a new class of workers who are endowed with property and assets, and who are rooted in nature and community, self-responsible and able to sustain themselves by their own labour, and who thus become mature citizens of a society of free humanity'. The following subsections examine these points starting with an argument about the social market economy.

The Social Market Economy[12]

Ordoliberal social policy combines the virtues of the market individual with the eighteenth-century ideas of a harmonious social order. The point about this 'combination' is to instil in people the 'self-discipline . . . honesty, fairness, chivalry, moderation, public spirit, respect for human dignity, firm ethical norms' that they 'must possess before they go to market and compete with each other' (Röpke 1998, 125). Müller-Armack articulates the purpose of ordoliberal social policy succinctly when he writes that competitiveness 'requires . . . incorporation into a total life style' (1978, 328). Its pursuit comprises the establishment of 'the bourgeois total order' (Röpke 1998, 99), which incorporates economy, society, politics, morality, personality, governmentality and myth into a seamless order of social being, from the institutions of social life to the mush of the soul. The market economy entails the formation of character to permit individuals to partake in the market economy, which, says Müller-Armack (1976, 300; 1981b, 131), manifests a distinct 'social style' of being. It combines individual 'self-reliance, independence, and responsibility' (Müller-Armack 1976, 279) with the 'market form of complete competition' (cf. Eucken 1959). It fell to Müller-Armack (1947c) to provide the social style of complete competition with a catchy slogan. He called it 'social market economy'.

The attribute 'social' did not meet with unanimous approval. Hayek was the most vocal. His critique of the word 'social' in the 'social market economy' warned about the kind of misperception that sees ordoliberalism to advocate a socially just alternative to market liberalism. For Hayek, it was unclear what the adjective 'social' was supposed to denote (see Hayek 1976) and he rejected it as a 'weasel word' (Hayek 2013, 114) that allows the idea of 'social justice' to take hold. The demand for 'social justice' is a 'dishonest insinuation' (Hayek 1960, 97). It operates akin to a 'Trojan Horse through which totalitarianism has entered' (136). He thus rejects it as useful to the organised social interests that demand social justice to advance their own special interests as the universal interest. Indeed, the demand for social justice seemingly proclaims for a 'freedom from want' that Röpke and his colleagues despised. The freedom to compete and the freedom from want belong to different forms of society: the one is free, the other proletarianised. Not only is 'government-organized mass relief . . . the crutch of a society crippled by proletarianism and enmassment'. As pointed out earlier, it also entails the most 'dangerous and seductive' enunciation of tyranny (Röpke 1998, 155, 172). The significance of the term 'social' in the conception of the social market economy does therefore not refer to a policy of social justice associated with a Keynesian welfare state. Rather, the decisive term in social market economy is 'market'.

Ptak (2004, 47) makes clear that for Müller-Armack the adjective 'social' stands for a sustained effort at achieving the most effective functioning of a free market economy, founded on competition.[13] The social market economy holds that economic prosperity 'is only to be had at the price of constant watchfulness and adaptability and the preparedness of each individual to live courageously and put up with life's insecurities' (Röpke 2002, 198). They thus argue that the free market is in itself 'social' (Müller-Armack 1976, 253). Foucault's comment on ordo-liberal social policy is succinct: for the social market economy there 'can be only one true and fundamental social policy: economic growth' (2008, 144). Indeed, it is its 'social content' (Müller-Armack 1976, 253). Only the 'total mobilisation of the economic forces allows us to hope for social improvements, which achieve real social progress by means of increased productivity' (Müller-Armack 1981b, 79). The free market is social because it 'stimulates production and increases output, leading to greater demand for labour' (Müller-Armack 1976, 253), which will eventually trigger the (in)famous trickle-down effect, spreading wealth to the downtrodden (Müller-Armack 1976, 179; Böhm 1937, 11).[14] In addition, increases in labour productivity tend to reduce prices, which make commodities affordable to workers, who benefit as consumers. According to Eucken (1952, 67), such market-facilitating social policy makes a 'policy of full-employment' unnecessary, since the expansion of the market absorbs available labour into employment. A proper 'social policy' facilitates a 'competitive economic order' (Müller-Armack 1976, 239) that gives 'workers a far greater choice and therefore greater freedom' (Nicholls 1994, 324). It also makes the poor wealthier in the long run as wealth trickles down, rendering 'other forms of social welfare superfluous' (Nicholls 1994, 325). The most important objective, then, of ordo-liberal social policy is to unfetter the 'productive forces of society' (Böhm 1937, 11) to 'encourage economic growth' (Müller-Armack 1989, 85). Social policy has therefore to support 'the initiatives of employers' to 'increase the productivity of their employees who have to regain interest in their work' (Müller-Armack 1981b, 72) so as to achieve the full potential of a free labour economy, ostensibly for the sake of the workers.[15]

In summary, the market economy is social in character on the conditions that it transforms recalcitrant proletarians into willing participants in market freedom and establishes an order of 'achievement' that makes demands for welfare support redundant. The 'social' element of the market economy has therefore a distinct meaning: it is premised on economic growth, connects market freedom with individual responsibility, sets out to reconcile workers with the law of private property and delivers society from proletarianised social structures, promoting enterprise as a character trait.

Deproletarianisation: Community and Nature

Since the status of the worker is characterised by dependency on the vagaries of the labour market, the capacity to absorb shocks is thin. The ordoliberals recognise this and argue for alternative ways of securing access to the means of subsistence without entering into collective welfare arrangements. Since the proletarian condition is one of dispossession, workers have to have access to independent means of subsistence outside the market to maintain themselves as vitally satisfied citizens within economic freedom. The 'misery of "capitalism" is not that some have capital but that others have not, and for that reason are proletarianised' (Röpke 1942, 263). As proletarians, workers are not able to 'accumulate individual property', and dependency on wage income alone is a source of discontent that explains their class struggle.

Deproletarianisation amounts thus to a policy of 'restoring small property ownership' (Campbell 2002, xvi) to the worker who 'must in all circumstances be divested of his chief material characteristic, viz., his unpropertied state' of being. Workers have to be enabled to 'rent garden plots' or, better still, own 'a house and arable ground' as a precondition for 'attaining a degree of relative independence and security, that awareness of kinship and tradition which only property can give' (Röpke 2009, 221). For the sake of social peace, workers have to have access to market-independent means of subsistence to enhance their capacity to make ends meet by their own effort and initiative. Röpke does not endorse proletarian self-help by means of a 'cash in hand' black market economy. He advocates the transformation of proletarians into vitally satisfied individuals who resist, say, the populist tide of commercialism and materialism for a holistic approach to living sensibly and responsibly in small-scale communities, helping themselves and others.[16] Re-rooted in natural forms of community, by which they understand the nuclear family situated in a small 'parochial community', extends to workers a particular 'human warmth', which is indispensable for securing their human anthropological condition (Röpke 1957, 41). Family and community are said to decongest and decentralise the concentration of proletarian spaces in big cities and thus support the effort in 'anchoring human beings in self-provisionment [*sic*] and property' . . . , thus achieving an inner regeneration of the nation' (Röpke 2002, 221). The 'cold' society of economic freedom and performance competition on congested labour markets is to be sustained by a 'warm' community of de-commodified forms of social interaction and neighbourliness (see Rüstow 2005, 357–360).[17]

The proposal to 're-root' workers in 'decongested' and 'ruralised' communities, garden cities and the like envisages as ideal decentralised communities of artisans, small traders and craft workers and family farmers. These forms of life and work are the most 'important sectors of non-proletarian existence' (Röpke 2009, 218). In these ruralised communities workers are enabled to obtain a part of their sustenance by working for themselves once they have exited the factory gate, including vegetable production in 'allotment gardens' (224; also Rüstow 2009, 57–58). These forms of non-proletarian existence provide for an appropriate 'anthropological framework' (Röpke 2002, 32) for a human economy. They establish 'closer relations to the soil and . . . the place of work' (Röpke 2009, 221; Rüstow 2009, 58). Human scale is all important. It is 'indispensable for the salvation of a free economic and social system' and 'will enable [the nation] to withstand even the severest shocks without panic or distress' (Röpke 2002, 34, 221). 'Demassification of society' and establishment of 'smaller units of production and settlements' will afford workers greater independence from the labour market pressures. These 'sociologically healthy forms of life and work' (Röpke 2009, 162) are expected to make them more resilient when faced with economic downturns and prevent them from asking for the 'rotten fruit of the welfare state' (Röpke 1957, 14; Rüstow 2005, 365; 2009, 65). They thus conceive of deproletarianisation in quasi-feudal terms. Workers are to work for an employer during the waged part of the working day, and for themselves during the remainder of the day, once they have exited the factory gate, be it the gate of manufacturing or the service industry. Vitally satisfied workers obtain a part of their sustenance from their own non-commodified labour of agricultural self-provisioning, and from neighbourly support networks and community assistance. In order to meet the challenges of the 'cold society' (Rüstow 2005, 365; 2009, 65) of economic price and factor competitiveness with entrepreneurial resolve and cunning, 'neighbourly love' is of the essence. It renders 'the brutal effect on individuals tolerable' (Röpke 2002, 202).

The intended outcome of the effort in decentralisation, decongestion, ruralisation and neighbourliness is the achievement of a 'real and fundamental alternation of the economic cellular structure' (Röpke 2002, 211; also Müller-Armack 1976, 235).[18] In distinction to 'mass living' it provides for social life on a human scale. Röpke's (1998) attack on rationalism – invariably labelled econonism (a heartless philosophy of numbers, reduction of life to economic quantity and economic calculation), materialism (a graceless life, living for material satisfaction alone) and also utilitarianism (the cold rationality of economic action) – is more apparent than real.[19] The 'naturalisation' of the proletariat in small-scale communities is not the purpose of *Vitalpolitik*. Its purpose is to restore and sustain what Ancil (2012) calls deproletarianised (labour) markets. 'Naturalisation' is a means towards a market liberal end. The point about 'decentralism' is to disperse modern mass society into an atomised landscape of constant commuters and gardeners.

The argument that workers should be given a 'firm anchorage, namely property, the warmth of the community, natural surroundings and the family'

(Röpke 2002, 140; Rüstow 2005, 365; 2009, 65), and also Müller-Armack's endorsement of Christian values after 1945 do not subscribe to ideals of social solidarity and collective purpose.[20] These ideals are absent from ordoliberalism. Indeed, they belong to the 'false' society of illiberal meddling into the free price mechanism. Müller-Armack's mythical ideas of Nation and *Volk*, which he advocated in the 1930s, also do not subscribe to forms of national solidarity, however perverted in content, form and manifestation. Rather, he conceives of them as (opportune) a means of securing economic performance and supporting the leadership role of employers (see Müller-Armack 1981b, 72).[21]

Proletarians and Private Property as a Social Right

Ordoliberalism endorses property ownership as a social right and conceives of it as a means of deproletarianisation. By connecting 'human beings and private property . . . competition [becomes] socially effective' (Müller-Armack 1976, 133, 246). Property ownership is said to instil a certain philosophy of life and establish a particular social and moral universe that makes citizens out of proletarians 'in the truest and noblest sense . . . making them real members of the "civitas"' (Röpke 2002, 95). In this context Röpke speaks about the 'restoration of property for the masses' (156) suggesting, rightly, on the one hand, that capitalist property rights are based on the expropriation of communal property, creating a mass of property-less workers, and wrongly, on the other, that social market economy restores ownership of the means of production to workers.[22] As Rüstow points out, the 'misery of capitalism' has nothing to do with the private ownership of the means of production (Rüstow 2005, 75). Rather it has to do with the circumstance that the majority of the population does not own any capital, and is thus proletarianised – the proletarian lacks 'that awareness of kinship and tradition which only property can give' (Röpke 2009, 178, 221). By spreading property, say for example wider share ownership or home ownership, workers become 'really free' and are thus able 'to consider economic liberty as a matter of course' (178). In this manner, social market economy removes 'from socialism its most fertile soil' (95). There is, says Röpke (2002, 159), one such thing as a 'social "right"' and that is the ' "right" of property'. For the ordoliberals, it is the foundation of human economy. As such, it is a mainspring of vitalised social relations (Rüstow 1942) and, as I argue here, a disciplinary force.

Let us, says Röpke (1950b, 153), 'put *economic freedom on the firm foundation of mass property ownership, of one's house, and one's workshop and garden*'. However, rooting workers in ruralised subsistence work does not empower them as a stakeholder of free economy, transforming a proletarian personality into a personality of private property. For this the worker must 'be able to acquire freely disposable funds and become a "small capitalist", possibly by being given the opportunity of acquiring stocks' or have a 'share in the profits' (153).[23] Then there are the 'beneficial activities of saving banks, mutual building societies, co-operatives', which social policy has to promote in order to 'do away with that leading characteristic of the proletariat, namely lack of property' (Röpke 2002, 156). Ownership of capitalised property instils the 'mentality of privacy, independence, self-reliance, freedom, and dignity'. With ownership comes responsibility, and with responsibility comes a 'particular social and moral universe', for which 'the word "bourgeois" imposes itself' (Röpke 1998, 98). Money, says Röpke (1950b, 252), 'is coined freedom'.[24] *Vitalpolitik* is to make this freedom effective as a character trait of deproletarianised workers who as small-scale property owners enter the 'caritas of responsible brotherhood' (Röpke 1964, 87).[25] The proposed civitas of coined freedom is to harness the 'whole network of social relationships' on the basis of common moral values: 'individual effort and responsibility, absolute norms and values, independence based on ownership, prudence and daring, calculation and savings, responsibility for planning one's own life, proper coherence with the community, family feeling, a sense of tradition and the succession of generations combined with an open-minded view of the present and the future, proper tension between individual and community, firm moral discipline, respect for the value of money, the courage to grapple on one's own with life and its uncertainties, a sense of the natural order of things, and a firm scale of values' (Röpke 1964, 87). As a 'counterweight to labour dependency' (Röpke 2002, 241), a property owning democracy facilitates enterprise. For what, as Foucault (2008, 148) put it, is 'private property if not an enterprise'? What, he asks, is home ownership 'if not an enterprise', 'an investment, a commodity, something for profit, for exchange?' Property is social propriety. It is the foundation of exchange, enterprise and individual responsibility. It is governed by the laws and rules of what Böhm (2010) calls a 'private law society', in which economic success, profit, is a reward that derives from the avoidance of bankruptcy (see Röpke 2009, 105–106). That is, for the working-class proprietors of mortgage debt, private property does not glow as golden as it is made out to be. By analogy with the idea that poverty is not unfreedom (see Joseph and Sumption 1979), exposure to crippling private debt, foreclosure and homelessness is not unfreedom either; it is a market outcome that requires a courageous entrepreneurial response, on the pain of ruin. Röpke's human economy recognises only one form of poverty, and that is poverty of aspiration.

Debt and Discipline

In the ordoliberal scheme, debt has no place in a human economy. They demand sound money and fiscal discipline, which are constitutive principles of economic constitution. Workers are not meant to meet subsistence needs by working and helping themselves and others in small-scale communities. At the same time, however, they also speak about the diffusion of share ownership and partaking of workers as investors in stock markets to make the laws of coined freedom manifest in the mentality of the governed. Indeed, if money is coined freedom, then private debt is an investment into future earnings, into future freedom. It is a promissory note of freedom to come. However, private indebtedness does not reveal entrepreneurial networks of human community; on the contrary, it cripples its owners and destroys communities. Private debt is probably a far greater force of deproletarianisation than the savers' morality, which expects the delivery of a golden goose on judgement day. Private debt privatises the debtor, impoverishes the future in the present and acts as a powerful restraint on working-class solidarity. That is, the diffusion of private property entangles society in the laws of private property, including its laws of bankruptcy and personal liability. Ordoliberal social policy is therefore not really about the spreading of coined freedom. It is about the acceptance of coined freedom on the pain of ruin and default (see Eucken 2004, 237). In ordoliberal political economy, the free price mechanism is the calculating machine of economic freedom, and when the chips are down, society has to accept life's misadventures with 'firm moral discipline', inner strength and 'the courage to grapple on one's own with life and its uncertainties' (Röpke 1998, 98). The meddling state is no alternative to the implosion of private consumer debt. The meddling state is the weak state, one that embodies the moral decay of a society that has lost its capacity to help itself.[26]

The enterprise society of vitally satisfied workers is confronted by the paradox that the law of coined freedom depends on income generation, that is, on the exertion of productive labour in an ever-expanding and always restless, and indeed crisis-prone, economy. The bottom line of human economy is therefore price competitiveness based on increased labour productivity. As discussed earlier, the social content of ordoliberal social policy is economic growth. It is the foundation of popular capitalism. In its essence, says Campbell (2002, xvi), the ordoliberal effort at deproletarianisation is 'an attempt to socially nurture the ethic and spirit of the bourgeois'. It is a 'plea for embourgeoisement' (Quinn 1998, xvii). For this plea to be heard, the free economy has to grow to absorb workers into employment and capitalise on popular investments, including pension funds and annuities, so that the infamous trickle-down effect, this liberal reward of labour, appears in reach. For Müller-Armack (1976, 179, 198), the trickle-down effect of wealth is the raison d'être of social market economy – time and time again, it requires a real breakthrough in labour productivity to sustain the promissory note of future affluence. Ordoliberalism is about this future for which it strives in an ever-renewed present. This future present requires vitally satisfied workers who get on with things and absorb risks in willing compliance with the rules of the game.

CONCLUSION: HUMAN ECONOMY, VITALITY AND SURVEILLANCE

Vitally satisfied individuals are not reliant on welfare support. They rather engage in market freedom in pursuit of their own individual interests. In the face of the natural tendency towards proletarianisation, propertied workers are said to perform much more keenly and willingly as entrepreneurs. They will perceive poverty ownership as an incentive to do better, see unemployment as an opportunity for employment, price themselves into jobs willingly and on their own initiative and meet a part of their subsistence needs by working for themselves and others in neighbourly communities. Vitally satisfied workers are those who take their life into their own hands, get on with things, live courageously and put up with life's insecurities and risks and fit in extra hours of independent work to meet subsistence needs. For the ordoliberals, unemployed workers are fundamentally entrepreneurs in transit, from one form of employment to another. *Vitalpolitik* is about the transformation and multiplication of the social fabric into competitive enterprises (Müller-Armack 1976, 235) and acceptance of competition as a public duty and moral obligation.

Müller-Amarck (1976, 300) thus characterised social market economy as an irenic order, an ORDO, in which social strife, economic conflict and the struggle to make ends meet make way for a society at peace with itself. In irenic order, 'competition is a public duty to which [the] entrepreneurs' submit themselves willingly and on their own initiative (Müller-Armack 1979, 147). He conceives of market economy as the very idea of 'social peace (irenics), partnership and cooperation instead of class struggles, wars, strikes which destroy wealth' (Klincewicz 2010, 223). Society becomes one in the noble figure of the entrepreneur, who competes without greed or despair ostensibly in accordance with his or her assumed human nature and on the basis of a law-governed and rule-based structure of social interaction. The irenic integration of economy, society, politics, morality and personality is seamless (Müller-Armack 1976, 297). It establishes a social order, in which human nature and the order of things conform to each other and thus become one in the form of a social market economy that is both total and human, transcendent and real (1976, 300; 1981b, 131). Man, says Röpke (1998, 89), does not live by 'radio, automobiles, and refrigerators alone, but by the whole unpurchasable world beyond the market and turnover figures, the world of dignity, beauty, poetry, grace, chivalry, love and friendship, the world of community, variety of life, freedom, and fullness of personality'. The dignity of labour and the freedom to compete epitomise a graceful and dutiful life beyond the demands for material security; it recognises, within its inner physiology, the Rights of private property as legitimate Rights of a 'god-willed' order.[27]

The *movens* of irenic order is *Vitalpolitik*. It governs for free economy by establishing the social and ethical frameworks that secure social cohesion and integration and maintain the vitality of the entrepreneur. It shapes the requisite 'psycho-moral forces' that the individuals need to have in order to compete with each other. In this manner it curbs the passions of unsocial greed and restrains the natural tendency towards proletarianisation. *Vitalpolitik* is about the fabrication of law-governed entrepreneurial personalities. It is to eliminate a proletarian consciousness that, says Röpke (1998, 109), is taken in by the 'cult of the standard of living'. It is about committing the social individuals to the (self-)responsible pursuit of economic freedom. Social policy aims thus at making society to 'approximate as closely as possible to the ideal of complete competition' (Rath 1998, 68). Rath's point is worth considering: social policy is intended to make reality in the image of its idea. Free economy 'requires a subject' that enforces its order and ensures that its participants behave 'in a disciplined manner' (Eucken 2004, 197). This subject 'can only be the state' (Rüstow 2009, 192). It is the subject of order and discipline. On the one hand, free markets are endorsed as moral institutions – they 'moralise us' (Quinn 1998, xx). On the other hand, 'markets do not generate moral norms: they presume them' (ibid.). Moreover, they also consume and destroy them. Their 'dependence upon moral reserves' (Röpke 1998, 129) entails the state as a moralising force, that is, as the subject of moralisation (Müller-Armack 1976, 177; 1981a, 263). In summary of this point, free markets moralise us by means of state.

Ordoliberal social policy is therefore more than just a policy towards society. Fundamentally, it governs through society, shaping its inner physiology. It is a means of securing free economy in the mentality of the governed. As a policy that is about the 'formation of character' it is more than just a policy 'of society' or towards society. Fundamentally, it is also a policy in and through society. It is to redress the '*vanishing sense of responsibility*' and ensure the 'advantage of freedom' in the 'spontaneous adaptability' of a people (Röpke 2002, 95) who, without having direct access to the means of subsistence, recognise their moral obligation to '[navigate] on the sea of the market' in a calm and responsible manner (Röpke 1998, 255). Economic freedom is not an economic product. It is a political practice of a *Vitalpolitik* – a politics of life. Economic freedom is a constantly empowered freedom. For the ordoliberals there is as much economic freedom as there are individuals willing to be free.

Fundamentally, then, free economy is defined both by the absence of the state, as a stateless sphere of economic freedom, and by the strong, market policing state that moralises the conduct of the free. *Ordnungspolitik* does therefore not only intervene in the framework of society. It, also, governs through the inner recesses of society. Freedom not only depends on political authority; it is also a manifestation of that same authority in the entrepreneurial conduct of the market participants. For the sake of freedom, there can be only one conduct, that is, the conduct of performance competition which characterises 'an economic order ruled by free prices' (Röpke 1998, 5). Its establishment 'must be supported, managed, and "ordered" by a vigilant internal policy of social interventionism' to ensure a freedom of spontaneous action in the mentality and the conduct of the governed (Foucault 1997, 97).

The effort at deproletarianisation – *Vitalpolitik* – is a Sisyphean undertaking. It is meant to contain what cannot be contained, that is, the 'natural tendency towards proletarianization' (Röpke 2009, 218). Sociological ordoliberalism recognises proletarianisation as innate to the capitalist social relations. Nature cannot be done away with. It can only be harnessed. That is, the free economy 'must be conquered anew each day' (Röpke 1998, 27). The ordoliberal idea of economic freedom is therefore essentially based on distrust. There is no freedom without surveillance to ensure that the orderly conduct of self-interested entrepreneurs does not give way to a proletarian personality that lacks the 'moral stamina' (Röpke 2009, 52) to absorb economic shocks. The defence of liberal principles in the hour of need is not enough. As laid out in chapter 2, liberal emergencies manifest a crisis of interventionism. For the sake of free economy, the liberal state has thus to be an ever-vigilant 'security state' (Foucault 2008; Hirsch 1991).

The ordoliberal purposes of social policy raise the issue about the institutional organisation of liberal governmentality in mass democracies. The following chapters about the European Union explore the ordoliberal elements of monetary union, especially. They argue that the supranational structures of European economic governance fetter the democratically constituted member states to a liberal market foundation. Indeed, they show that monetary union institutionalises a deregulatory dynamic towards free enterprise, transforming the member states into executive states of the supranational relations of law, market and money.

NOTES

1. The quotation is from Rüstow (2005, 365).
2. For a detailed account, see chapter 2.
3. As Röpke puts it, 'Socialism, as the expression of anti-capitalist mass rebellion, is nothing but a reaction imperilling everything' (2009, 19).

4. Weber argued likewise. In his view, socialism is the further rationalisation of the iron cage of instrumental rationality. It amounts to a *Rationalisierungssozialismus* (Weber 1994a).

5. Barry picks up on this asserting that proletarianised workers are 'too stupid. . . to internalise those moral rules which is essential to follow if the market society is to be maintained' (Barry 1989, 119).

6. The Weimar welfare state apart, one other target of their critique is Roosevelt's New Deal and the Beveridge Report of 1944, which established the welfare state in post-war Britain. They inveigh against it as the manifestation of a 'proletarianized' society. It can, says Röpke (2002, 147), 'only be understood from the highly patho-logical character of the English social structure'.

7. Röpke is quoting from Frederic Bastiat, *The Law* (1850), available at http://oll.libertyfund.org/titles/78, accessed 11 February 2016.

8. This point was very much emphasised by Giddens (1998) in his endorsement of New Labour.

9. In contemporary German thought, ordoliberal phraseology is most pervasive. The usage of its vocabulary includes thinkers of the political left like, for example, Joachim Hirsch (1995), who conceived of the state in conditions of globalisation as a *Wettbewerbsstaat* – an enterprise state. In Anglo-Saxon scholarship, the preferred term was 'competition state' (Cerny 1997).

10. The phrase 'workfare state' comes to mind to capture this. The phrase was coined by Bob Jessop in the early 1990 (Jessop 1993). It was to distinguish the neo-liberal welfare state from its Keynesian precursor.

11. On (urban) space as a battleground, see Charnock (2014).

12. This part draws on Bonefeld (2013).

13. On this, see also Watrin (2010).

14. On the 'trickle-down effect' in Smith's political economy, see chapter 2.

15. On this, see also the account about Adam Smith in chapter 2.

16. This is the basis for Peukert's (2009) claim that Röpke is a founding thinker of modern conservative ecological thought.

17. Although the distinction between community (*Gemeinschaft*) and society (*Gesellschaft*), which goes back to Hegel and was popularised by Ferdinant Tönnies (2001), is central to modern liberal-conservativism, it also belongs to the political left. See, for example Habermas's distinction between life world and system world, which doubles society up into society as the sphere of rational action governed by an unassail-able economic system logic and a life world characterised by communicative action.

18. According to Haselbach (1991, 18) ordoliberal social policy is contradictory. It favours a return to a traditional society as the condition of restructuring capitalist society. However regressive, in the ordoliberal scheme traditionalism is a means, not an end.

19. See Rüstow (2005, 374) and Röpke (1998, 89, 107–109).

20. Maurice Glasman (1996) thinks that ordoliberalism is a theory of social soli-darity and, in support of this view, quotes at length from the writings of Popes Leo XIII and Pius XII. His sincere advocacy of Catholic social theory is not shared by the ordoliberals, including Müller-Armack whose post-war endorsement of Christian values was instrumental. Ptak (2007, 42) refers to his effort at metaphysical resource

management as 'ideologisation'. See also Haselbach (1991). On the Popes' contributions to economic thinking, see Hunt (2003). On the importance of Catholic ideas of subsidiarity – God helps those who help themselves – in ordoliberal thought, see Manow (2001).

21. On this, see Haselbach (1991). Christian Watrin (2010, 213) correctly defines Müller-Armack's contribution as a consistent attempt at finding ways to secure market economy: 'Starting from a realistic view of man and recognising the all-pervasiveness of ignorance of human affairs, he looked for institutions with the help of which economic-policy making could be based on "Ordnungspolitik", that is the design of carefully considered rules which fit together and which minimise conflict among the participants to the economic game'. The design includes the ideological formation of society, from the mythical ideas of nation, *Volk* and movement to the myth of Christian values and economic miracles.

22. Since Smith, private property in the means of production characterises the master class. The term master class derives from Smith. He refers to the holders of stock as masters. In ordoliberal thinking restoration of property to workers is to transform their outlook on life. It does not make them masters.

23. Samuel Brittan (1984, 1986) argued similarly, advocating the spreading of private property as a means of creating a property-owning democracy, which he saw to result from the Thatcher governments' privatisation programme. By the early 1990, the property-owning democracy transformed into a property-owning democracy of private debt, especially mortgage debt. This transformation in no way contradicted the attempt at using the market as a restraint on working-class solidarity. On debt, individualisation and social discipline, see Bonefeld (1995), Karacimen (2014), Soederberg (2014) and Lazzarato (2012).

24. The individuals carry their bond with society in their pocket, says Marx (1973, 157). On this, see Bonefeld (2006b).

25. Human economy thus inverts Brecht's imperative 'bread first, moral later' to 'morals first, so that bread may trickle down later'. See his *Dreigroschen Oper*. Oscar Wilde captured the sentiments of the caritas of responsible brotherhood well when he wrote in *The Importance of Being Earnest*: 'if the lower orders don't set us a good example, what on earth is the use of them? They seem, as a class, to have absolutely no sense of moral responsibility.' What Wilde talked about in irony, Röpke conceives of as a human economy.

26. For discussion see chapters 2 and 3. In the British context, David Cameron's enunciation of a Big Society is a more recent example of asserting the power of the state in order to make society stronger in conditions of austerity. On the Big Society, see Norman (2010). For assessment, see Bonefeld (2015).

27. 'God-willed' is Eucken's characterisation of the integrated order of things and Man. See Eucken (2004, 176). See also chapter 4.

Chapter 6

Europe and the Idea of Subsidiarity: On the Elements of Ordoliberalism

INTRODUCTION

The approach to this and the following chapters represents a gear change. Rather than working through the, in any case, fragmentary character of ordoliberal writings about European economic constitution, they explore the elements of ordoliberalism in the European monetary union through the prism of *Ordnungspolitik*.[1] This introduction contextualises both chapters against the background of contemporary debate about an ordoliberal Europe.

The ordoliberal elements of the European economic constitution can perhaps be summarised best with these quotations from Walter Hallstein, Christoph Engel and Wilhelm Röpke:

> A free market economy is a basic principle of the Treaty of Rome. Such a liberal economic system . . . does not exclude state intervention. On the contrary, it presupposes that the state provides a framework for the operation of such a system; for only an appropriate framework allows each section of the economy to exercise its freedom of action, in fact compels it to exercise that freedom. (Hallstein 1972, 110)[2]
>
> A market economy is not a vaccination against [the democratic] disease. . . . Even if the [Member] States have not succeeded in setting up a proper economic constitution internally, one is imposed on them from the outside. The Member States come under a regime of imposed liberty. (Engel 2003, 431)[3]
>
> To diminish national sovereignty is most emphatically one of the urgent needs of our time. But the excess of sovereignty should be abolished instead of being transferred to a higher political and geographical unit. (Röpke 1955, 250)

Ordoliberal Ascriptions and Eurozone Crisis

During the Eurozone crisis, attempts at crisis resolution were criticised either for their doctrinaire pursuit of ordoliberal ideas (Blyth 2013) or for neglect of ordoliberal principles (Feld, Köhler and Nientiedt 2015). Ordoliberal commentators identified design faults at the heart of the monetary union. In their view the rules of the monetary union lacked credibility, which made them vulnerable to exploitation, encouraged reckless risk-taking, permitted free-riding and allowed those member states that were reluctant to restructure their lagging labour markets to beggar their more productive and competitive neighbours. They thus argue that some member states were either not fully committed towards the euro as an external anchor for market liberal restructuring of domestic labour relations or lacked the capacity for liberal interventionism. Their membership in the euro is destabilising and imperils the monetary union (Sinn 2014).[4]

For the ordoliberals, the euro was to be a stateless currency. It was to be based on clear rules of conduct and credible means of enforcement. In the monetary union member governments have to pay their debts in money they no longer create and regulate. However, the expectation that the monetary union would therefore have a disciplining effect on fiscal policy in member states turned out to be misconceived. In spite of the provisions of the Stability and Growth Pact (1996), which institutionalised fiscal discipline as corollary of monetary stability, it is argued that Greece and the other Southern European member states – Italy, Spain and Portugal – ignored fiscal rules, took on debt and deferred economic restructuring (Sinn 2014). Their ability to do so is seen as a major design fault of the monetary union (Feld 2012). Instead of 'imposing liberty' on member states who had 'not succeeded in setting up a proper economic constitution internally' (Engel 2013), they opted to free ride the system (Sinn 2014).[5] Furthermore, the monetary union lacked credible rule-based insolvency provisions. According to Feld (2012), their absence encouraged banks to take unnecessary risks on the expectation of bailout.[6] Indeed, once the banks were exposed, money was poured into the European banking sector to prevent its collapse. Reckless risks taken by banks went thus unpunished, at the expense of taxpayers. A further fault of the monetary union as designed at Maastricht was therefore also that it did not establish a regime of full legal liability. Instead, the monetary union established the propensity for moral hazard. In this argument the monetary union thus encouraged free-riding and risk-taking without responsibility. Finally, the rules governing the institutions of the monetary union, the ECB in particular, were not as robust as they should have been. Indeed, the ECB responded to the euro crisis by violating statutory requirements, politicising monetary policy and accepting liability for insolvent banks. It also assumed a European fiscal

competence, which included support for debt-stricken governments, especially Greece, through the purchasing of effectively untradeable government
bonds on favourable conditions (Sinn 2014; Feld 2012). According to Feld,
Köhler and Nientiedt (2015, 61), 'Germany may have followed ordoliberal
thinking rather too little than too much.' In their view the German government reacted 'pragmatically' to the Eurozone crisis and in so doing eschewed
ordoliberal principles, leading to the surrender of a 'de-politicised' monetary
union and establishing the prospects of a 'risk-sharing union', in which the
fiscally strong state came under the obligation to support fiscally weak states
through transfer of payments.

For the critics, ordoliberalism is an entirely villainous presence at the
heart of Europe. Mark Blyth (2013, 141) associates German ordoliberalism
with austerity, which he rejects as a dangerous idea. In his view, 'Germany's
response to the crisis, and the crisis itself, both spring from the same ordoliberal instruction sheet'. For Bulmer (2014, 1244), Germany's ordoliberal
approach to the euro crisis signalled a dramatic change in German policy.
It 'has trumped pro-Europeanism' as Germany's predominant approach
to European integration in times gone by. With its ordoliberal approach,
Germany is now said to assert hegemonic power in Europe, projecting its
domestic policy agenda and national interest onto the Eurozone (Bulmer and
Joseph 2016; also Hildebrand 2015). Instead of Europeanism, we now have
a German Europe (Beck 2013). As laid out in the introduction to the book,
the new Europe is seen to display an 'ordoliberal iron cage' (Ryner 2015).[7]

According to these critics the ordoliberal character of the monetary union
has stifled economic growth in the Eurozone, particularly in the weaker
member states, who have been left in desolate conditions. The monetary
union is indeed a union of sound money and supply-side economics. That is,
in conditions of sound money and undistorted market conditions, economic
behaviour is expected to adjust to price signals and when the chips are down,
sellers of labour power will have to respond by moderating wage demands.
By pricing themselves into employment the foundations are laid for economic
growth and prosperity in the long run. The critics reject this as market funda-
mentalism, which in practice is said to have led to the global financial crisis
of 2008 (see Stiglitz 2016). For the critics, the monetary union has therefore
to become a union for employment and growth. In place of fiscal austerity
and monetary discipline, European economic policy should encourage a
wage-based recovery and growth should be employment-led. In this view,
the ordoliberal character of the monetary union prevents a much-needed
Keynesian economic stimuli in the Eurozone (see, for example, Varoufakis
2013; Flassbeck and Lapavistas 2015; Stockhammer 2016). For this reason,
the monetary union has also to become a fiscal union to allow for redistribution of wealth in support of a consumption-led recovery, particularly in the

debt-stricken member states. In place of an ordoliberal Europe, the critics demand a Keynesian Europe, institutionalising demand-side economics at a European level. For the critics, the resolution to the euro crisis is therefore also hampered by design faults of monetary union. That is, monetary union not just prevents Keynesian economic policy responses to economic crisis. In fact, it institutionalises an 'anti-Keynesian' market fundamentalist dynamic at the heart of the Eurozone. The liberal-economic market design of monetary union thus punishes struggling member states who have lost the power to devalue and who are not supported by a system of fiscal compensation and equalisation. Institutional safeguards to stop the economic malaise are conspicuous by their absence – on the demand-side. Indeed, monetary union encourages liberal interventionism as the preferred means of economic restructuring and development.

The anti-Keynesian design of monetary union is not a design fault. It was intended and has been reinforced in the course of the Eurozone crisis (see chapter 7). Monetary union was intended as an external market liberal anchor in support of government initiatives to improve economic performance through enhanced competitiveness. In monetary union, governments are no longer able to adjust their economies to world market conditions by currency devaluation and are no longer meant to support economic activity by deficit spending. Instead, monetary union supports the efforts of government to liberalise labour relations and deregulate labour markets.

Ordoliberalism is indeed a statement about the construction and maintenance of a social order founded on complete competition. In this order, the market participants are endowed with negative economic rights, and they are expected to compete with each other on the basis of a civil constitution that lays down the rules of conduct. Economic competition is to be performance based. It argues for the exposure of all market participants to the free price mechanism, and it requires that every market participant adjust to market conditions by their own free will. Ordoliberalism rejects competition for access to political power, be it for political influence on policy, rent seeking or other privileges like state aid. It therefore argues that the independence of the state from the social interests is a condition of the free economy. The state should govern for the system of liberty, not the special interests. Ordoliberalism argues for liberal interventionism and warns against specific interventions into the economy in pursuit of concrete economic outcomes, such as full employment. It identifies the state as the executive power of the system of liberty, as market police. In this role, the state is a 'planner for competition' (Hayek 1944). The argument for the independence of the state from society and for independent decision making vis-à-vis the social interests entails the further argument about how to strengthen and safeguard the liberal utility of the state in mass democracy. The final three chapters of the book argue that the European Union incorporates the liberal state in its role as market police. Monetary union integrates the liberal-democratic member states as executive states of European law, money and market. In this context, the notion of Europe as an 'ordoliberal iron cage' (Ryner 2015) is most suggestive concerning the character of the European economic governance. Nevertheless, the conception of Europe as a bureaucratic apparatus of technical regulation by unelected experts who process policy in a disenchanted world of instrumental rationality falls short. Europe is not an ordoliberal administrative apparatus. It is a political creation and amounts to a sustained political practice and decision making by executive agreement. During the Eurozone crisis, the political character and predominance of executive decision making were well understood by those critics who analysed the response to the crisis as a replacement of law-based politics by emergency politics on the part of the European Council (White 2015; also Habermas 2012; Jörges and Weimer 2014).

The following subsection establishes brief analytical pointers about the ordoliberal elements of the European Union to focus the subsequent discussions in this chapter and those that follow.

Subsidiarity and Liberty: On the Ordoliberal Elements of the European Union

The processes of European integration have been characterised by 'inbuilt distrust of both popular and parliamentary sovereignty' (Müller 2014, 251).[8] According to Müller-Armack – 'probably the most influential German at Brussels' in the 1950s (Moss 2000, 258)[9] – the economic community of Europe was founded 'on law over and above its constitutive political entities' (Müller-Armack 1971, 162). It was thus constructed as a 'law-based order committed to guaranteeing economic freedoms and protecting competition' (Jörges 2005, 461). By establishing individual economic rights over and above the member states, their parliamentary systems of democratic law making have been placed into a supranational framework of stateless law and (negative) economic rights belonging to individuals (Everson 1995). European law is directly applicable in member states and superior to national law made by democratic assembly.

In this manner, the legal framework of the European Union does appear to provide an institutional resolution to the market liberal argument that recognises mass democracy as a 'pathological form of government'. Its institutional structure suggests the curtailment of mass democracy to supranational fetters of law, market and money. At its core, curtailment has to do with restricting the 'set of considered issues' that come before a democratic assembly (Riker 1982, 2), narrowing the scope of legitimate law making and restricting interventionism to liberal interventionism (cf. Hayek 1944; Röpke 2009, 187; Rüstow 1942, 289; 1963, 253).[10] 'We are therefore of the view', says Müller-Armack (1981b, 103), that European integration 'is only possible on a market-economic basis'. That is, the ordo of European integration does not permit a political union. Nor does it permit a mass democratic union, in which parliamentary majorities make law and hold government accountable. In Röpke's dramatic prose, 'Europe is the unity of diversity and centralist organisation entails the treason and the rape of Europe, also in the economic field' (Röpke 2000, 12).[11] Lars Feld is less dramatic in his rejection of political union. 'European unification has its limitations' (Feld 2012, 404). Political union and fiscal union, too, are contrary to the ordoliberal idea of a European market order. European *Ordnungspolitik* rests on the principle of subsidiarity. It combines supranational law, money and market with decentralised decision making by territorialised economic agents that compete with each other as individual price-takers each endowed with 'Europeanised' abstract economic rights.[12]

In the Europe Union policy decisions are made by councils of national executives, and the member states have the sovereignty of politics, implementing EU policy. In the words of Vivien Schmidt (2006, 33), 'while the EU has *policy without politics, the member states end up with politics without policy*'. Schmidt's notion, however insightful, is potentially misleading. Her account implies that member states 'end up with' a politics that they would not have chosen had they been able to determine policy by themselves as independent democratic states (see also Scheuerman 2016: 199). The member states appear thus to lose out from the arrangements that they themselves entered into. Schmidt seems thus to suggest that the European Union forces the member states into 'retreat'. In distinction, I hold that the European *Ordnungspolitik* provides a supranational anchor for the domestic pursuit of market freedom. Europe integrates the democratic member states into a seemingly depoliticised system of supranational governance. Conceived of as what Röpke calls a '*price* and *market* community' (Röpke 2002, 230) it locks-in mass democratic arrangements and aspirations.[13] Therefore, European integration does not in any way limit the state as 'society's [independent] power' (Marx 1987, 438). On the contrary it strengthens the independent power of the state. In fact, it is entirely dependent upon the capacity of the state to enforce the agreed-upon rules of the game by its own independent will, that is, without 'excessive democratic' meddling.[14] What Europe is therefore integrating is the role of the state in establishing and sustaining the market liberal framework within which economic competition takes place.[15] In the European Union, the member states become executive states (*Regierungsstaaten*) of a Europeanised system of liberty.

Chapter Structures

This remainder of this chapter restates key ordoliberal concerns to elaborate the elements of an ordoliberal European Union in the following section. It then introduces Hayek's proposal for an interstate federalism, which is key to the (ordo-)liberal idea of Europe as a *Stabilitätsgemeinschaft* – a community of (economic) stability.[16]

The following chapter, chapter 7, explores the political character of the euro as a stateless currency. It analyses the elements of ordoliberalism in European monetary union. For European *Ordnungspolitik* the principle of subsidiarity is fundamental – for the sake of complete competition, it separates the conducts of labour market policy, fiscal policy and monetary policy into distinct domains of governance. The coherence of European governance is dependent upon the political practice in the member states as executive states of European money.

The final chapter, chapter 8, recasts the book's argument to establish the meaning of the executive state in theoretical perspective and analysis of the European Union.

ELEMENTS OF ORDER: ON EUROPE

I have argued that for the ordoliberals, civil society is the society of economic liberty. The determination of the proper role of the liberal state rests on this conception of society. The state 'is to provide the institutions necessary for a "society of private law", namely, private law and [competition] law' (Engel 2003, 430). In a private law society, autonomous individuals pursue their interests independently from each other and organise their cooperation with each other under legal rules that regulate the manner of their interaction in competitive exchange relations. Market prices provide signals for individual preference calculations. In this manner a private law society constitutes itself as a competitive order. Market processes are thus seen as ongoing referenda of market citizens, establishing an ostensibly democratic machinery based on consumer preferences. Money is held to be the 'democratic means of guiding the economy' (Röpke 1998, 226). The state is to ensure the proper functioning of this order through competition law, creating and sustaining undivided and undistorted markets, and sound monetary policy, establishing an effective guide for market adjustment. The free economy is a function of monetary stability, fiscal tightness, freedom of contract, constancy of socio-economic policy and conditions of complete competition on all markets, including labour markets. The guarantee and enforcement of private property rights is paramount. Lastly, economic freedom combines with the acceptance of legal responsibility for non-coerced decision making on the part of the market participants (Eucken 1959, 26, 52; 2004, 254–291).[17] The state should under no circumstances confer privileges to economic agents. Rather, politics is to be law-governed and policy rule-based. These rules 'require it [the state] in certain types of problem situations to take, or abstain from taking certain types of actions' (Vanberg 2015, 32). In the face of powerful lobbies and trade union power, it is important that the market participants do not obtain benefits from violating the rules of the game. In this argument, government is the weak link. It is 'in the nature of things' that it is 'constantly faced with a considerable temptation to meet the contradictory demands of many pressure groups' and organised social interests (Böhm 2010, 166). That is, since 'competition has no lobby' (Böhm) the state has to be strong to sustain competitive (labour) markets in the face of powerful demands for special consideration and treatment.

For the sake of complete competition the 'inviolability of money' (Röpke 1998, 220; Eucken 2004, 54) is most important. The money supply and the value of currency should under no circumstances be subject to political manipulations (see Eucken 2004, 263). State and society have thus to be kept apart; one governs for economic freedom and plans for the regulation of that freedom by the free price mechanism, the other acts in freedom from political meddling and interference, and adjusts its preference calculations according to price signals.[18] A most basic ordoliberal principle of *Ordnungspolitik* is therefore the 'separation of powers between the state and groups in society' so that neither is able 'to make itself master and the other servant' (Möschel 2003, 293). In this argument, majoritarian democracy inclines towards state coercion because it tends to weaken money and destroy the monetary system.[19] For the sake of short-term electoral success, politicians 'pump small amounts of money into the economy [and] . . . protect national industries from global competition', thus violating core principles of free economy (Engel 2003, 430). Furthermore, democracy tends to weaken the power of money to regulate the natural price of labour power by conceding to trade unions (Rüstow 1959, 58–59; also Eucken 2004, 48, 255). The stability and liberal efficacy of free economy is a matter of stable money. Inflation destroys it. 'Hardly any government ever possesses absolute power over money without misusing it for inflation, and in our case of mass democracy the probability of such misuse is greater than ever before' (Röpke 1998, 195). Sound money is the gold standard of economic liberty. It is therefore 'essential to keep money out of politics' (196) and establish a monetary system that is independent from government 'arbitrariness' (195). That is, 'debt creation [is] not to be used as a regulative instrument of public finance, trade policy [is] not to be used to bring the current account of balance of payments into equilibrium, exchange rate [is] not to be maintained to improve national competitiveness, inflation [is] not a method of attaining full employment; competition policy [is] not to be used as a counter cyclical devise or as a way of protecting particular sectors and big business from modernisation, etc.' (Willgerodt and Peacock 1989, 9). Locking government into an international currency system removes money from political meddling. Better still is the creation of a common currency, which 'provides money that government cannot create', nor regulate or manipulate (Sievert 1993, 14). In this case, the conduct of government would in effect be framed by a community of stateless money.[20]

In the ordoliberal argument the anti-thesis to the 'collectivist state . . . is not democracy . . . but rather the liberal principle' (Röpke 2009, 85). It begs the question about the institutional arrangements that need to be made to restrict mass democracy to the pursuit of *Ordnungspolitik*. In Röpke's words, 'A solution must be found to the problem of how the executive can gain in strength and independence' (1998, 148) in order to halt the 'ruthless exploitation of the state by the mob of vested interests' (2009, 102). Maintaining the value of money presupposes not only 'a really strong state, a government with the courage to govern' (102). It also requires a particular organisation of the state to preempt democratic encroachment on the 'real independence' of state power (Eucken 1932, 308). That is to say, if indeed there has to be democracy, it has to be 'balanced and diluted by "non-political spheres", "corps intermediares" (Monetesquieu), liberalism, federalism, self-administration, and aristocratism' (Röpke 2009, 85). The pursuit of liberty entails government not only by checks and balances. It also entails the conduct of policy by independent technocratic institutions that operate at one remove from social-democratic pressures. It further entails administration of the affairs of state by competent elites that oversee the economic machinery on a quasi-judicial basis and who act in recognition of what is necessary for the safeguard of liberty (see Dardot and Laval 2013, 72–73).[21]

Central bank independence from democratic accountability and political interference is one such institutional device.[22] According to Röpke (2009, 196) 'independent central banks' are '*Bastilles* of liberty'. They must be populated and governed by technical experts who conduct monetary policy solely on the basis of economic insight and rule-based requirements.[23] They must also be defended against mass Man – this figure of 'eternal Jacobins' that is always ready to raze the defences of liberty 'to the ground' for the sake of central economic planning for welfare security (Röpke 1998, 226, 227). In this argument the balance between market economy and majority rule is 'struck inside' the national state (van Gerven 2003, 437). However, since 'market economy is not a vaccination against [the democratic] disease' (Engel 2003, 431) the establishment of binding international or supranational structures of law and money is a potentially better alternative to achieve a 'balance and dilute' (Röpke 2009, 85) the excess of democracy at the national level. Such an establishment would help the member states that have not succeeded in 'setting up a proper economic constitution internally', with the support of a seemingly external anchor (Engel 2003, 431). Röpke (1998, 8) views federalism as a potentially powerful defence 'against the flood of modern mass democracy'. It 'diminishes national sovereignty' for as long as the excess of sovereignty is not transferred to a higher authority (Röpke 1955, 250). Any such transfer is a danger to the system of liberty because it tends to create a 'collectivist form of economic organisation (bloc economy)' (2002, 231).[24] In these arrangements the despised 'economic state' of Keynesian interventionism (Eucken 1932, 2004) is 'transferred from the national level to the international level. It would mean the yet stronger and more inescapable domination of the planners, statisticians, and econometricians, the centralising power of an international planning bureaucracy, international economic intervention, and all the rest of it . . . , creating a giant European organisation' (Röpke 1998, 243, 245). Röpke rejects centralisation as non-European (244, 245) and argues that federalism and collectivism are incompatible (2000, 230). For him a 'genuine federation' is a 'community of price, market and settlement' without a controlling and directing centre (231).

The federal system that Röpke has in mind is the opposite of a political union. In fact, it is an interstate system in which sovereignty is shared between the no-longer fully sovereign member states and depoliticised and deterritorialised structures of economic governance, of money, law and market. Within this system of international relations between states of diminished sovereignty, each member state is tied to the other by common market rules and requirements, commitments and obligations based on international treaties. Wilkinson judges the purpose of this linkage well. He says that it amounts to a '[f]raternity through commerce', which appears as the 'triumphant culmination of Benjamin Constant's project of modern liberty' (Wilkinson 2013, 353). Constant's demand for liberty over social democracy is a constant reference in ordoliberal thought; that is, the state cannot have enough power within its own sphere whereas outside its sphere it should have no power at all. The independence of the political 'will' – a will for liberty – is the prerequisite for the independence of the 'economic will' that is 'formed by the democracy of consumers' (Röpke 2009, 102). In a mass democracy all kinds of 'admixtures' are therefore needed to sustain the independence of the state from the governed, including 'hierarchical leadership . . . heteronomous balancing factors, traditionalism . . . federalism, self-administration and aristocratism' (Röpke 2009, 85, 102).[25] Interstate federalism is a potential means of transforming 'unlimited democracy' and its 'collectivist state' into a liberal democracy and its free economy (Röpke 2009, 85). In the ordoliberal argument the essence of liberal democracy resides in the 'autonomy of the nation' (Röpke 2009, 101).[26] In terms laid out by Rüstow (1963) and Schmitt (1998), Röpke (2009, 102) argues that 'one cannot render a worse service to democracy than to identify it with the complicated and corrupt parlour game of democracy degenerated into pluralism'. Thus the 'real nature of democracy' resides in the 'autonomy of the nation' that transcends its quarrelsome character and unsocial disquietude and that instead presents itself in the independent 'will of the state' as the sovereign embodiment of the national interest (Röpke 2009, 102; Eucken 1932, 308). At its core, liberal democracy is government by a democratically elected executive that governs 'independently from group interests' and with 'inflexible will', asserting 'its dignity as a representative of the community' (Röpke 2009, 102). As noted by Dardot and Laval (2013, 73), 'the people' may 'nominate who will lead, not say what must be done'. In this argument the creation of a common market with institutional safeguards based on law secures the conduct of national democracy with liberalising fetters. The 'pact for Europe' is indeed a pact without demos.[27] It 'owes its existence to the efforts of political elites' (Habermas 2015, 3), who, according to Röpke and Müller-Armack too, personify the autonomy of the national interest and endow the structures of supranational law and money with a consciousness and a will.

In analogy to Marx's argument that 'democracy is the truth of monarchy; monarchy is not the truth of democracy' (Marx 1975, 29), democracy is the truth of the European Union and the European Union is not the truth of democracy. Against the much-lamented democratic deficit of the European Union, which on a closer inspection is understood rather as a deficit in legitimacy (MaCartney 2014), MacCormick (1999), Müller (2014) and Streek (2015), among others, make clear that the European Union was not meant to be democratically constituted. The legitimacy of the European Union was to derive from its 'guarantees of economic freedom' (Mestmäcker 2007b, 3). The Union advances legal equality and secures extra-state civil rights and economic rights, liberal rights par excellence, belonging to individuals. According to Mestmäcker (2003) and Hallstein (1972), Europe made good on Böhm's observation that competition is without lobby. The common market institutionalises the freedom to compete as liberal right. As MacCormick (1999, 126) makes clear, the 'de-coupling' of legal equality from the democratic sovereign secures the liberal utility of the rule of law much better 'than all-purpose sovereignty ever did'. He recognises that the combination between the no-longer fully sovereign states of Europe and the still-not-sovereign Union 'seems the enemy of popular sovereignty'. Nevertheless, it expresses the wisdom of the liberal rule of law because it establishes a decisive framework for democratic sovereignty in member states (MacCormick 1995, 102).[28] Democratic law making by majoritarian parliamentary assemblies at the national level does not coexist with negative economic rights at the Union level. European law is superior to law made by parliamentary majorities in member states. It organises the common market, enables negative economic rights and checks mass democratic intrusion into the operation of the free market. It thus restrains the scope of democratic activism by policing the boundaries of the free market, 'even against democratic institutions whose proposed intervention is not based upon market considerations' (Everson 1995, 138; also Jörges 2005; Habermas 2012).[29]

The European system of economic governance does not replace the political state. On the contrary, 'what the community is integrating is the role of the state in establishing the framework within which economic activity takes place' (Hallstein 1972, 28). The lucid prophet of the liberalising dynamic of a system of interstate federalism was Hayek.

HAYEK AND THE IDEA OF A *STABILITÄTSGEMEINSCHAFT*

In the 1930s Hayek advocated that national states should combine to create a federal interstate system. He endorsed it as a means of encouraging competitiveness, against a national politics of economic protectionism. In his view the system would undercut the power of 'special interests' to subject the national state to commit to material concessions in the form of welfare state guarantees, a politics of full employment and inflationary demand management. It would support the depoliticisation of economic relations and de-democratisation of liberal government and establish a law-based system of negative economic rights. By removing restrictions on the movement of capital, labour and commodities and by creating 'common rules of law, a uniform monetary system, and common control of communications' (Hayek 1939, 255), the scope for government intervention would become much narrower, benefiting free economy. Instead of illiberal political interference into the economy, interstate federalism would strengthen the liberal utility of state.[30]

Hayek also endorsed interstate federalism as a means of curbing democratic excess. Instead of giving in to mass democratic aspirations for a freedom from want, it would place society under a regime of imposed liberty, which would unleash a dynamic of deregulation and liberalisation. Since the 'Union becomes one single market, and prices in its different parts will differ only by the costs of transport . . . [a]ny change in any part of the Union in the conditions of production of any commodity . . . will affect prices everywhere' (Hayek 1939, 258–259). In order to maintain employment, and in the absence of a national currency, competitive adjustment by means of greater labour productivity would become irresistible. Individual states would thus lose the capacity to 'assist particular industries' and 'monopolistic organisations of individual industries will cease' (259) and 'national organisations', whether trade-unions, cartels, or professional associations, will lose their monopolistic position (261). The Union would be united by a uniform monetary system, and 'monetary policy would have to be federal and not a state matter' (260). Since this Union is not a political union, collective forms of '[p]lanning, or central direction of economic activity' would be 'limited to the extent to which agreement on such a common scale of values can be obtained or enforced' from the federated states' (264). He presents interstate federalism as the 'consistent development of the liberal point of view' (271) and pro-claims it as the means of returning to liberalism the 'common ground' that had been taken away from it as a result of mass democracy incursion into the system of liberty after the First World War (271). For Hayek interstate fed-eralism would make the national state leaner, guaranteeing 'individual free-dom' and preventing 'overload' and inflationary demand-management (271).

For Hayek interstate federalism would thus provide 'a rational framework within which individual initiative will have the largest possible scope' (268). Nothing would stand in the way to what, today, is termed economic liber-alisation, including labour market deregulation, labour flexibilisation and marketisation of public provision, including welfare, health and education. As Hayek saw it, 'Even such legislation as the limitation of working hours or compulsory unemployment insurance, or the protection of amenities, will be viewed in a different light in rich and poor regions and may in the former actually harm and rouse violent opposition from the kind of people who in the richer regions demand it and profit from it' (263). In fact, competitive pressures might be such that 'even such legislation as the restriction of child labour or of working hours becomes difficult to carry out for the individual state'. Adjustment of national competitiveness to world market conditions by currency manipulation would no longer be possible. Adjustment would have to be achieved from the more productive employment of the 'methods of production' within the individual states (260).

Within a supranational union, then, individual states 'will not be able to pursue an independent monetary policy' (Hayek 1939, 259). Politicians, he suggests, are always governing with the next election in mind. This perverts even those committed to free economy to give in to 'popular pressures', leading to the politicisation of economic relations and democratic overload, thereby impeding free economy and weakening money, and thus harming the capacity of the invisible hand to regulate the spontaneous actions of the market participants and impairing the system of liberty with potentially tyrannical effect. Furthermore, monetary policy always requires an element of judgement and thus discretion that government might abuse to retain legiti-macy. A supranational operation of monetary policy, with an independent bank removed from domestic considerations, would thus insulate economic policy making in member states from distorting pressures on policy since they could no longer effect money. Instead, economic policy would have to be conducted within a sound monetary framework. Monetary policy would be rule-based and out of reach of parliamentary majorities, government officials and meddling politicians. The independence, then, of monetary policy from democratic influence would accord its conduct a quasi-judicial status. In short, domestic politics would be anchored in a supranational policy regime that, in the view of Müller-Armack (1971), came into being with the European Economic Community, which for him created a European *Stabilitätsgemeinschaft*, a community of economic stability.

Müller-Armack's *Stabilitätsgemeinschaft* is a law-based and rule-governed community of economic freedom. It establishes market relations and regulative media over and above the federated states, and guarantees the constancy of economic policy whatever the democratic majorities and ideological preferences of government in the member states might be. *Stabilitätsgemeinschaft* institutionalises the constitutive principles of free economy. It is a community of *Ordnungspolitik*. In its later incarnation of monetary union, *Stabilitätsgemeinschaft* establishes a system of complete competition facilitating labour market adjustment in member states based principally on enhanced labour productivity, labour mobility and wage flexibility. It also establishes the need for fiscal austerity since the member states would not be able to spend money that they no longer create and regulate, reinforcing the need to achieve and maintain economic competitiveness as a condition of the fiscal state. In fact, member states would come under an obligation to achieve competitive labour markets to secure employment through economic growth. Instead of adjusting national prices to world market conditions by meddling with monetary conditions and depreciation of currency exchange rates, the achievement of greater labour productivity would become the unavoidable means of competitive adjustment. Like Hayek, Müller-Armack was opposed to economic *dirigisme* but not to a 'consciously steered market economy' (Müller-Armack 1947a, 95; 1960). The purpose of political 'steering' is the achievement and maintenance of conditions of complete competition.

By the late 1970s, in a context of economic turmoil, political crisis, labour militancy and Eurosclerosis, Hayek renounced his youthful views of the late 1930s.[31] Instead of supranational money, Hayek now advocated that money was to be issued by competing private banks (Hayek 1978). Hayek distinguishes between an entirely depoliticised monetary union as the gold standard of asserting freedom as a form of economic discipline and a democratic political union, in which the conduct of monetary policy is subject to political calculation and democratic demands.[32] The late Hayek seemed fearful that a single European currency would be prone to political interference by what Röpke had called 'European Saint-Simonism', that is economic planning by a controlling centre composed of technocrats, who given the opportunity would be intent on establishing an 'international welfare state', fully equipped with policies of full employment and redistribution of wealth associated with Keynesian demand management and deficit financing (Röpke 1998, 243). Instead of a federal Europe of independent nation states that govern their respective societies through a supranational framework of negative economic rights, competition law and sound money, political union brings to power an 'economocracy', that is, 'domination' by a centralised 'planning bureaucracy', which today's liberal-conservative detractors of European integration refer to as Eurocrats. Like Hayek, Röpke offers a stark choice: either political union or a federation of independent nation states (2002, 230), that is, either a 'bloc economy' or a community that facilitates decentralised decision making (231). 'Either it is right and desirable that money and credit policy should be operated like a switchboard by a government directly dependent upon a parliamentary majority or, worse still, upon some non-parliamentary group posing as the representative of public opinion. Or, conversely, it is right and desirable to counteract such dependency' (1998, 223) through a European *Stabilitätsgemeinschaft* committed to *Ordnungspolitik*.

CONCLUSION

The market liberal watchword for both Hayek's interstate federalism and Müller-Armacks's *Stabilitätsgemeinschaft* is subsidiarity. Subsidiarity entails a system of 'relative sovereignty' (Röpke 1954, 38), in which the fundamental freedoms of a social market economy, including monetary conditions and 'anti-trust rules and institutions for the supervision of state aid', are regulated by law-governed and rule-based supranational institutions that are not 'directly controlled by the electorate' (Engel 2003, 430). The 'disciplinary effect[s]' (Feld 2012, 410) of this arrangement depend on the capacity of the member states to translate and implement European Union rules and commitments into effective national politics, from fiscal retrenchment to removal of protectionist measures and from the abandonment of state aid to the achievement of competitive labour relations and markets. For Engel (2003, 430), the functioning system of supranational rule making and national implementation of the rules agreed upon would make 'Europe . . . the stronghold of the fight to save the Member States' civil society'. Subsidiarity fetters democratic government to transcendent structures of law and money. It thus limits mass democracy through 'denationalised' systems of economic governance at the Union level. The Union would have 'the negative power' which Hayek expected from his system of interstate federalism. In Hayek's view, its 'negative power' would prevent 'individual states from interfering with economic activity in certain ways, although it may not have the positive power of acting in their stead' (Hayek 1939, 267).

John Pinder (1968) recognised this negative power in his analysis of the implementation the provisions of the Treaty of Rome during the 1960s. It led him to characterise European integration as 'negative integration'. He reasoned that the European Economic Community created a common market that undercut domestic schemes of economic regulation.[33] Hallstein (1972, 111) argues similarly about the liberalising effect of the Treaty of Rome: 'What is irreversible is the opening-up of the internal markets' with the effect that 'enterprises are . . . no longer faced with conditions which distort free competition'. There is however no automaticity. Rather, and as I have argued throughout, the free economy amounts to a practice of government.

The following chapter explores the character of subsidiarity in the governance of the European monetary union. Hayek's programme of an interstate federalism provides useful insights into its structure of subsidiarity. He makes a robust distinction between the institutions responsible for monetary policy and fiscal policy, with fiscal policy a national responsibility and monetary policy a supranational matter (Hayek 1939, 267–268). He recognises clearly that economic planning by the free price mechanism amounts fundamentally to a political practice of enforcing the rules agreed upon.

NOTES

1. For an assessment of the influence of German ordoliberalism on European competition law, see Gerber (1998) and Wigger (2008).

2. Walter Hallstein was one of the founders of the European communities and the first president of the Commission of the European Economic Community, serving from 1958 to 1967. During the 1940s, Hallstein became a close associate of German ordoliberalism.

3. Christoph Engel is currently director of the Max Planck Institute for Research on Collective Goods.

4. This critique of the euro as being at the mercy of indebted member states found political expression in the creation of the *Alternative für Deutschland* (AfD). Originally, the AfD was formed as an anti-euro party in reaction to the euro crisis. It demanded that Germany leave the euro and return to the Deutschmark. The AfD has since trans-morphed into an electorally viable nationalist party. Its appeal is fuelled by anti-immigration. On the AfD, see Grimm (2015) and Schmitt-Beck (2016).

5. One of the first countries to be found out was however Germany in the early 2000s. It escaped censure by the European institutions. Nevertheless, the then Red-Green coalition government between the Social Democratic Party (SPD) and the Greens responded with a series of decisive labour market reforms under its Agenda 2010 programme. The reform programme has been an unpopular success. It helped the unemployed to price themselves into work and sustained Germany's economic

performance. It also has been met with sustained critique by the German public. The Social Democrats who initiated the reforms in 2003–2005 have yet to recover electorally (Jacobi and Kluve 2006; Schwander and Manow 2016).

6. Lars Peter Feld is director of the Walter Eucken Institute and professor for economic policy at the University of Freiburg. He has been a member of the German Council of Economic Experts since March 2011. In 2013 he joined the advisory board of the Stability Council, a body that was devised as part of Germany's implementation of the European Fiscal Compact. On the European Fiscal Compact, see chapter 7.

7. Similar commentary can be found in, for example, Brunkhorst (2014), Dardot and Laval (2013) and Bulmer and Paterson (2013).

8. For an exploration of this point, see MaCartney (2013).

9. In the 1950s Müller-Armack worked for the German Economic Ministry under Erhardt and was a leading member of the German Delegation to the Intergovernmental Conference on the Common Market and Euratom (Treaty of Rome). See Müller-Armack (1971) for an account.

10. Riker was an American political scientist. He argued that constitutional restriction and direction is about the structuring of the world so that you can win. See also Riker (1993). He had started out as a supporter of Roosevelt's New Deal, and in this context he saw federalism as an obstacle to the New Deal. Later in his career he turned against what he decried as 'big government', which he identified with Johnson's Great Society. Riker's libertarian turn led him to re-evaluate of the system of federalism, which he now endorsed as a protection against big government. Riker's account overlaps with Röpke's (1998, 226) argument about federalism as a means of thwarting the 'eternal Jacobins', from the Keynesian New Dealers to welfare state reformers like Beveridge in the UK.

11. The German original reads: Europe has to be an 'Einheit in der Vielfalt . . . , weshalb dann alles Zentristische Verrat und Vergewaltigung Europas ist, auch im wirtschaftlichen Bereich' (Röpke 2000, 12).

12. Böhm's idea of private law society is relevant here. It assumes a European dimension. In Böhmean phraseology, Europe constitutes an association based on abstract economic rights that protect the freedom to compete in decentralised market settings from coercion, public and private. On private law society, see chapter 4.

13. Röpke (2002, 230) makes this point in support of what he calls a 'genuine federation' which he defines as an arrangement against collectivism.

14. On democratic excess and the so-called independent will of the state, see chapter 3. See also chapter 8.

15. This insight derives from Walter Hallstein (1972, 28).

16. The term *Stabilitätsgemeinschaft* is Müller-Armack's (1971).

17. For a detailed exposition of the constitutive principles of free economy, see chapter 2.

18. On ordoliberalism as planning by the free price mechanism, see Balogh (1950).

19. As Eucken saw it, Lenin recognised what is at stake: 'In order to destroy bourgeois society, one has to devastate its finance' (quoted in Eucken 2004, 255).

20. The phrasing of this last sentence derives from Marx's insight that 'money is itself the real community and cannot tolerate none other standing above it' (Marx 1973, 223).

21. As MacCormick (1999, 146) put it when describing Brussels bureaucracy as a 'benign oligarchy': 'Given that wisdom in practical affairs, *prudentia*, seems to be very differently distributed among us, and possessed in exalted degree only by a few, there is something of an argument for aristocracy. Identifying the common good and the means of its pursuit is not an easy task, and only wise and experienced persons are likely to be good guides.' For a similar argument, see Böhm, Eucken and Grossmann-Doerth (1989). On the agents of the common good, see chapter 2.

22. For the wider significance of this point in contemporary political economy and public policy, see Burnham (2001, 2014).

23. See also Popper's verdict: 'Institutions must be like fortresses. They must be well planned and properly manned' (2002, 60).

24. In this context Röpke refers to the Nazi idea of a *Grossraumwirtschaft* and the Japanese idea of a 'co-prosperity sphere' as violations of federalism (2002, 231). In a later work, he also refers to the European Coal and Steel Community, which was formally established in 1951 by the Treaty of Paris, and to the European Common Market, which was created by the Treaty of Rome of 1957. In his view these treaties point towards the establishment of an 'international welfare state' (Röpke 1998, 243).

25. Röpke's reference to aristocratism is suggestive of Weber's (1994b) argument that in modernity aristocracy has been replaced by meritocracy. He conceives of this change as a process of expropriation. The means of administration had been the property of the aristocracy. They held office as members of the ancient regime, courtiers of king or queen. In distinction, meritocracy belongs to a rationalised mass society in which loyalty to king, queen and country, social position and Right have been replaced by employment contracts. Röpke's proclamation for aristocratism is part of his call for imbuing democracy with the values of an elite that has always '[carried] civilisation on' (Röpke 1942, 248). For further discussion, see chapters 3 and 8.

26. See also Haselbach (1991, 180).

27. On this, see also Wilkinson (2014).

28. MacCormick's argument is the most decisive. Bellamy (2007) is quietly in favour.

29. In this context, Habermas (2012, viii) refers to European agreements that intervene into 'the core domains of the national parliaments, from fiscal to economic policy, through social policy, to education and employment policy'.

30. For an account of the liberalising benefits of federalism in the context of the political economy of the US, see Riker (1987). In distinction to Riker, Hayek did not advocate the creation of a federal state system. He advocated an interstate system of law and money. On Riker see note 10.

31. Hayek thus disapproved of monetary union at the end of a decade that the neo-liberals characterise as one of lamentable political weakness (see chapter 3). The states of Western Europe, they argued, had become ungovernable as a consequence of unlimited mass democracy and socio-economic politicisation (see Crozier et al. 1975). European leaders first considered monetary union in the early 1970s against the background of the soon-to-be-terminal crisis of the Bretton Woods system. The plans were put forward in the Werner Report of 1971. On this effort, see Molle (1990, 391–394). See Clarke (1988) and Radice (2015) for accounts about the then

crisis of political economy and its aftershocks in the 1980s. The term Eurosclerosis was used to characterise the weakness and lack of direction of European integration during the 1970s (see McAllister 2009; Middlemas 1995). On the failure of European monetary intensions and turmoil of European currency relations in the 1970s, see Parboni (1981).

32. For a more recent endorsement of Hayek's 1930s view in relation to the EU, see Bernholz (1992). For an argument that the handling of the euro crisis politicised monetary policy, undermining European *Ordnungspolitik*, see Bernholz (2013) and also Sinn (2014).

33. De Gaulle understood this well when he outlined the reason behind his support for the Treaty of Rome, which was to assert useful competitive pressure on French industry. As he put it (1971, 143), 'International competition . . . offered a lever to stimulate our business sector, to force it to increase productivity . . . hence my decision to promote the Common Market which was still just a collection of paper'.

Chapter 7

European Monetary Union: Economic Constitution and *Ordnungspolitik*

INTRODUCTION

The euro is a stateless currency, and the European Central Bank (ECB) is a stateless central bank. Their stateless characters express a political decision and entail a sustained political practice of government in the euro member states. The *Ordnungspolitik* of monetary union posits the member states of the euro club as federated powers of supranational money. The euro requires enforcement of monetary discipline by the member states. It demands fiscal prudence. It focuses the economic adjustment of its federated economies to world market conditions on the achievement of competitive labour relations in territorialised markets. The stability of the euro, and indeed its very existence, is entirely dependent upon the capacity of the member states to act in concert to sustain it. Monetary union establishes the framework within which the economies of the Eurozone unfold. The member states govern within and through this framework. Failure on the part of a member state to secure the domestic requirements of euro membership affects monetary conditions in the Eurozone as a whole. It thereby becomes a collective problem of political authority in an intergovernmental setting.

The former president of the German Bundesbank, Hans Tietmeyer, saw clearly that the stability of monetary union depended on the solidarity of the member state to meet the purposes of monetary union in their own conduct, committing to fiscal discipline and achieving competitive labour markets. As Tietmeyer put it, 'Sustaining the monetary union might need perhaps more solidarity than beginning it' (cited in Eltis 2000, 146). The chapter argues that monetary union is dependent on the capacity of the member states to secure the economic constitution of Europe domestically and govern for the euro especially in times of economic downturn, populist backlash, mass

democratic challenges and, as especially the case of Greece showed, sustained and widespread social militancy and riotous opposition to the exacted
socio-economic costs of monetary union.[1]

The resolution to the euro crisis both reinforced the existing structure of
subsidiarity of monetary union and violated key rules of monetary union.
Whether its resolution was based entirely on ordoliberal 'economic' policy
descriptions or not (Blyth 2013; Young 2014; Feld, Köhler and Nientiedt
2015) is ultimately an idle question. By reducing ordoliberalism to a set of
economic instruments and policy objectives, such argument fails to account
for *Ordnungspolitik* as a *Gesamtentscheidung* – a complete and comprehensive decision about the character of political economy as a whole. The chapter
argues that the resolution to the euro crisis uncovered the decisive role of
the member state in sustaining the monetary framework within which social
reproduction in the Eurozone takes place. Indeed, the member states asserted
themselves as executive states (*Regierungsstaaten*) of sound money. This
notion, which belongs to Schmitt's political theology, is key to understanding the ordoliberal demand for state independence from democratic fetters
(Eucken 1932) and its characterisation as an authoritarian liberalism, which
identifies liberty as a political practice of government, acting as market police
(Rüstow 1942; Röpke 2009) or planner for competition (Hayek 1944). The
chapter concludes that monetary union entails the democratically constituted
member states as executive states of the supranational institutions of money,
law and market competition.

The chapter first establishes the governance structure of monetary union.
It then discusses the character of euro crisis management. The conclusion
explores the political character of the euro. With this, it establishes the
context for the concluding chapter, chapter 8, which analyses the emergent
character of the European executive state as a contemporary manifestation of
authoritarian liberalism in mass democracy.

SUBSIDIARITY, SOUND MONEY
AND ECONOMIC ADJUSTMENT

Padoa-Schioppa's (1994, 191) characterisation of EMU is succinct: 'Subsidiarity, not the Leviathan, is the catchword for European political union'.[2]
He explains that EMU is based on a collective decision-making process
that both undercuts national plurality of decision making and encourages
competition between territorially segmented labour markets. The institutional structure of EMU combines supranational conduct of monetary policy
with national state responsibility for the achievement of competitive labour

markets. Padoa-Schioppa's neo-Machiavellian view of EMU as a depersonalised 'collective prince' (1994, 151) is therefore apt.[3] EMU appears indeed to reduce government to governance, to the sphere of technical control and implementation, which flows from a set of rules that, despite proclamations of the sovereignty of a – territorialised – people, are founded on supranational law and money.

Padoa-Schioppa's depersonalised 'collective prince' appears to govern without government. Seemingly, it is a prince of economic governance. According to the rules of monetary union, the ECB cannot be given instruction by any conventionally conceived political body. It appears as if it were a court of law rather than an instrument of public policy. Its objective is to enhance and guarantee the credibility of monetary policy. 'One way to bolster credibility . . . is to assign the responsibility for monetary policy to an institution that is not subject to political influence' (Padoa-Schioppa 1994, 188). For monetary policy to be credible, its conduct has to be a rule-based and expert-led. A democratised central bank is deemed incredible; at least there is the risk of meddling and manipulation, and thus discretion towards, and potential comprise with, the so-called special interests, from a multitude of powerful economic lobbies to the labour movement and its demands for wage-led economic growth, employment and material security. In monetary union, 'false incomes and labour market policy' cease as government is no longer able to devalue its currency or manipulate the supply of money to protect labour markets from competitive pressures (Feld 2012, 412).[4] Monetary union established a currency that no individual government can create or print, inflate or deflate. For Feld, the depoliticised and stateless character of the euro is the embodiment of *Ordnungspolitik*. It 'guarantees Hayek's demands for the denationalisation of money' by other means (411).

Monetary union removes the conduct of monetary policy from the direct pressures of national labour markets. Its rule-based conduct appears entirely impartial towards a variety of national labour markets. It grants no privileges and extends no favours to the economic interests, social forces and the member states. Monetary policy is not made for Germany or for Greece. It is made to meet the statutory requirements of the euro as stateless currency of global importance and standing. Nevertheless, by treating differential conditions of labour competitiveness as equal before money, monetary union reinforces existing differentials with potentially devastating effect. Competitive national economies are usually reluctant to revalue 'while the weaker are often forced into devaluation' (Williams, Williams and Haslam 1992, 227).[5] Monetary union eliminates devaluation as an option for the weaker economies. Instead, it demands the achievement of greater labour productivity as the principal means of economic adjustment and catch-up.[6]

Expanding on Padoa-Schioppa's metaphor about EMU as a depersonalised prince, fiscal policy is its court, and the territorialised European working classes its Fourth Estate. Fiscal policy is the forte of neither the national state nor the Union – it is located in the twilight zone between member states and Union. EMU excludes transfer of fiscal responsibility to the Union, and the member states retain full fiscal sovereignty. The Union has no positive fiscal powers. Monetary union is not a fiscal union. However, the Union sets the framework for fiscal policy and polices observance of agreed fiscal conditions in member states. Monetary union requires that fiscal policy is in effect pro-cyclical. It rejects deficit financing and requires fiscal discipline instead, which is most difficult to come by at times of economic recession as tax income declines and demands on expenditure increase. Especially for states that face difficulties, euro fiscal rules reduce their fiscal sovereignty to a mere formality. The Union is responsible for the surveillance of fiscal conduct. The catchphrases are vigilance and coordination of national budgetary policies. Since fiscal policy is thus to support sound monetary conditions, it ceases as a means of economic adjustment through, for example, Keynesian fiscal expansionism and anti-cyclical demand management. In monetary union economic adjustment is to be achieved by 'labour movement from states in recession to states in high growth, or through labour market flexibility, with a reduction of wage and labour costs in states in recession to attract capital investment' (Hix 1999, 299–300).

The architecture of monetary union vindicates Padoa-Schioppa's view of EMU as resembling a modern version of Machiavelli's prince. This prince is, however, not a Leviathan. The Union does not possess political sovereignty. There is no European government. The Union is not a political union. It is a monetary union. Padoa-Schioppa's prince is a prince of money – this, as liberal economics has it, cunningly conceived technical instrument of economic calculation and medium of exchange that emerges from the pursuit of individual self-interest and comes to express the collective wisdom of society (see Menger 1963). Courted by fiscal policy it governs its subjects through the member states in the name of competitive labour markets. Its subjects are the territorially regimented European working classes. Their allocated position is that of the democratically accepted plebes, democratically accepted that is, in the republic of the market that is governed by the price competitiveness of differential rates of labour productivity. Within monetary union the sellers of labour power and their employers have thus to act with greater responsiveness to market pressure, and workers have to show greater entrepreneurial discipline and cunningness to sustain employment, particularly at times of glutted labour markets. Monetary union institutionalises the liberal objective of 'competitive order'. It is a regime for the achievement of complete competition based on economic performance in territorialised labour markets. It nudges the conduct of social policy in member states towards the enterprise society.[7] European *Ordnungspolitik* separates monetary policy and fiscal policy into supranational and national spheres of responsibility. It also creates a system of federated political responsibility, which undercuts traditional forms of democratic government and parliamentary democracy. It also creates a system of decentralised decision making in territorialised labour markets that are regulated by supranational rules and requirements (Sievert 1993). EMU emphasises market rule as the formative power of European society and recognises the role of the national state in securing market order. The following parts explore the federated principles of economic governance and market liberalisation in greater detail.

MONETARY POLICY AND THE EUROPEAN CENTRAL BANK

The sole task of the ECB is to guarantee price stability and achieve sound monetary conditions in the Eurozone. For the proponents of EMU, 'Expectations are at the heart of the inflation process' (Padoa-Schioppa 1994, 21). Monetary union therefore had to be well armed so that it can defend itself from the pressures of inflation inducing expectations. The ECB was thus built as a fortress.[8] It cannot be given instructions by *any* democratic body. . . as if it were a court of law rather than an instrument of public policy (Grahl 1997, 138). Furthermore, the ECB is 'specifically excluded from lending directly to government at EU and national level', and it is 'obliged to avoid the monetary finance of public sector deficits' (121, 131). In fact, the ECB is not meant to be 'involved in any way in the financial position of member states' because 'financial markets must be convinced that neither the central bank nor any other Community organisation implicitly guarantees the obligations of national governments' (Padoa-Schioppa 1994, 183). The ECB was not to act as lender of last resort to indebted states and insolvent banks. It was not meant to be liable for the failure of member states to conduct their affairs according to common rules. Nor was the ECB to refinance indebted member state or create money to boost demand. That is, the euro is not Keynesian money. Rather it was conceived as 'Austrian, ordoliberal and neoliberal money' (Streek 2015, 369).

From an *ordnungspolitical* point of view, it is therefore 'a major progress that the ECB is state independent . . . and primarily committed to the aim of stability' (Koch 2003, 238). By removing the conduct of monetary policy as far as possible from the influence of social struggles and conflicts, economic lobbies and meddling parliamentary majorities in member states, any 'economic failure' under EMU expresses a failure of government to secure the demands of supranational money internally through the achievement of competitive labour relations on a world market scale.[9] It would thus express a weak state response to the lack of entrepreneurial adjustment to the limits of the market and unresponsiveness and indeed 'unreasonableness of the actors who get a wage' (Williams, Williams and Haslam 1992, 221). Monetary union sets the standard of monetary conditions in the union as a whole, and the member states have a responsibility to sustain the euro by achieving greater labour productivity 'at home'. They also have an obligation towards each other to sustain the union by refraining from 'beggar my neighbour' fiscal policies.

FISCAL POLICY

Fiscal policy remains a national responsibility, which is shared with the Union. Fiscal policy is to be conducted within limits of the Stability and Growth Pact (1996) and the Fiscal Compact (2013) that strengthened the pact's resolve in response to the euro crisis.[10] The Compact did not in any way change the structure of subsidiarity, nor did it change the position of fiscal policy within the governance structure of EMU. It hardened its structure and reinforced its resolve.

For its proponents, EMU establishes a 'framework of incentives and constraints' that will 'condition national budgetary policies, for which the key-words will be autonomy (to respond to country specific problems), discipline (to avoid excessive deficits), and coordination (to assure an appropriate overall policy-mix in the Community)' (Emerson 1992, 11).[11] The positioning of fiscal policy, which combines national fiscal sovereignty with supranational fiscal rules, is a response to the 'risk' of fiscal profligacy in member states and a rejection of a centralised responsibility for fiscal policy. The latter would have reasserted the prospects of Keynesian deficit spending and interventionism at the supranational level. The former was seen to pose 'a major threat to the overall monetary stability' of the Union (Emerson 1992, 100). As Padoa-Schioppa (1994, 127) put it, the question was 'whether monetary union runs a serious risk of being undermined by independent and possibly uncoordinated budgetary policies by member states'. The transition arrangement to EMU, that is the convergence criteria, and the Stability Pact are geared against what is called 'unsustainable budgetary policies in a member state'.[12] Emerson (1992, 107) defined 'fiscal discipline . . . as the avoidance of an unsustainable build-up of public debt'. Further, the transition to EMU 'amplifies the domestic effectiveness of national fiscal policy for stabilization purposes' (115), requiring a tight control of member states 'if fiscal expansion were systematically beggar-thy-neighbour in character' (119). In short, 'surveillance will have to correct possible tendencies for budget deficits to become too large' and EMU relies on 'fiscal policy to reduce budget deficits' (100). During the euro crisis, Eurozone government reasserted these basic arrangements and confirmed their commitments towards fiscal discipline by strengthening the rules of fiscal governance. The Union has the power of coordination and surveillance, and the ability to recommend modifications of fiscal policy and apply sanctions against member states that breach agreed-upon rules. The Union requires member states to achieve balanced budgets.[13] For member states in difficulties this requirement is punishing.

Nevertheless, the Union has no positive fiscal competence. It has negative power. Its ultimate means of enforcement is the threat of insolvency, as exercised during the Greek crisis in the first half of 2015. During the euro crisis, the enforcement of fiscal rules in the Southern European member states entailed redistribution of wealth from labour to capital, privatisation of national assets, liberalisation of the economy, welfare state cuts and robust labour market reforms (Flassbeck and Lapavitsas 2015). The IMF was clear about the kind of economic adjustment that was needed. It argued that the strengthening of fiscal governance, including mechanisms for enforcing compliance with rules and surveillance to secure fiscal sustainability, required for its success key labour market reforms, 'making the labour market more effective, removing disincentives to work embedded in various public policies, enhancing wage bargaining flexibility, and further liberalizing services sectors' and privatising infrastructure and public enterprises (IMF 2010, 7).

In sum European monetary union has neither fiscal nor monetary flexibility. Fiscal policy is to support sound monetary conditions. It is not to weaken the euro through the so-called fiscal expansionism that is associated with Keynesianism or simply beggar-my-neighbour fiscal profligacy associated with free-riding. In either case, fiscal expansionism and free-riding involve the risk of moral hazard that might well endanger the *Ordnungspolitik* of the union as a whole. 'Especially the German designers of EMU had wanted to prevent [moral hazard] by excluding responsibility for financial stability from the ECB's narrowly defined objectives and tasks' (Tuori and Tuori 2014, 165). Sovereign debt was not to be discharged by the Union. It may only be discharged by the respective member states (see Varoufakis 2013).

MARKET ADJUSTMENT AND LABOUR

EMU places the responsibility of economic adjustment squarely on competitive labour markets and the achievement of competitive labour unit costs. With national currency devaluations eliminated, with monetary policy removed from the purview of the national state and with fiscal policy disciplined by monetary union, the 'wage-price flexibility remains the basic adjustment channel as a substitute for the nominal exchange rate' (Emerson 1992, 102). Indeed, EMU comprises two principal means of economic adjustment: 'a) workers can move; b) wages can change' (Currie 2000, 124).

EMU does not include any form of compensation between member countries that have highly divergent levels of competitiveness. Any form of transfer payment in aid of less competitive labour markets is ruled out. In the case of sovereign debt exposure, it is to be discharged by the respective member states through savings and productivity inducing labour market reforms. The responsibility of labour market adjustment is the preserve of member states. The common market comprises territorialised labour markets and stimulates competition between them. Each labour market is governed by supranational law, money, market pressures and binding commitments to fiscal discipline. It encourages competition through labour market deregulation, increased labour flexibility, wage discipline, labour mobility, lower indirect labour costs and so on. Increased competition within the EU is expected to 'result in an increased responsiveness of wages to unemployment', with 'labour market flexibility, and most importantly wage flexibility . . . the most important adjustment instrument' (Emerson 1992, 149). Lower unit labour costs are 'a condition to the relative price decrease needed to restore the competitive position of [member states] and to bring output and employment back into equilibrium, and 'factor mobility, in particular labour mobility', may solve the problem through migration' (147). That is, 'wage bargainers will be affected by a credible monetary union' as they will realise that excessive wage rises will not be underwritten by devaluations (24). In other words, the cost in terms of output and employment might not be high for as long as workers respond flexibly to market pressures and requirements, pricing themselves into employment. In the absence of competitive labour market adjustments, unemployment might result and the 'need' to migrate arise. That is, an unemployed worker is in fact a worker in transit, up and down the wage scale, from this activity to that activity, from this labour market to that labour market. Employment and unemployment converge in the form of the employable worker as embodiment of, and investor in, human capital.[14]

The architecture of monetary union vindicates Padoa-Schioppa's view of EMU as resembling a modern version of Machiavelli's prince. This prince is, however, not a Leviathan – it has no Republic to call upon and its rule is depersonalised, depoliticised and denationalised. The prince governs through the formalism of law and statuary requirements, which are administered by technical experts that conduct policy as modern-day aristocrats of the common good. It is a prince of sound money and rule-based conduct. Courted by fiscal policy, it governs its subjects through the democratic member states that, operating within a framework of supranational rules and surveillance, retain formal responsibility for fiscal policy and enforcement of austerity. Its subjects are the territorially regimented European working classes who comprise the mass democratic subjects of the member states, which are responsible for the achievement of competitive labour markets. Monetary union establishes a binding framework for the conduct of economic and social policy in the federated member states. It integrates the role of the state in securing sound monetary conditions through the achievement of competitive labour relations. However, although the Union does not possess political sovereignty, it would be wrong to conclude from this that it does not have the capacity for authoritative political decision making. The euro crisis exposed the European Council as the political executive committee for managing the common concerns of the Eurozone. The automaticity of economic governance in monetary union amounts, I argue, to a political practice of a union of liberalising executive states.

EURO CRISIS MANAGEMENT: ON THE QUESTION OF ORDER

I have argued that monetary union removes economic governance from conventional forms of democratic contestation and accountability. As an institution of *Ordnungspolitik*, monetary union is not about risk sharing, fiscal transfers and joint-liability. It was envisaged as neither a fiscal union nor a 'transfer union', in which the economically stronger member states support the weaker member states through fiscal transfers. In monetary union, each member is responsible for sustaining monetary union and discharges its responsibilities through the achievement of sound fiscal conditions and competitive labour relations. Padoa-Schioppa's notion of EMU as a depersonalised prince is therefore apt. It places the European economies under a supranational regime of law and money, which are administered by apolitical experts of administration, including a cabal of central bankers ostensibly fine-tuning monetary aggregates but in reality conducting monetary policy for the member states that have agreed to come under an obligation of governing within the framework of monetary union rules. The structure of EMU suggests the elimination of politics in favour of rule-based, technical decision making by unaccountable experts and subsequent action by the member states as agents of implementation. Indeed, the economic constitution of Europe seemed as infallible as an 'automatic' mechanism of market adjustment (Sievert 1993). It narrows the policy options available to the democratically constituted member states to the planning of competition. Its institutional structure establishes a clear boundary between market and state. That is, the European economic constitution is premised on a state that 'knows exactly where to draw the line' (Röpke 2009, 102). It recognises the role of the democratically constituted member states as federated executive states of supranational requirements. The structure of monetary union appears strong. Yet, and as the Eurozone crisis has shown, its seam is weak. The seam is all important. The European Union of stateless money depends in its entirety on the capacity of its federated member states to 'impose liberty' (Engel 2003). The strength of its structure depends thus on the *ordnungspolitical* capacity of the member states to enforce the conditions of monetary union internally. In EMU, the member states not only compete with each other for competitive advantage. They also depend on each other for securing and maintaining the European *Stabilitätsgemeinschaft*.

During the Eurozone crisis the solidarity shown by member states to prevent the collapse of monetary union has been immense. In the case of Greece, the commitment to Europe that was finally extracted under threat of expulsion in July 2015 put a whole political economy on the brink and led to the restructuring of its entire social contract. In the case of Italy (2011–2013) it led to the appointment of a technocratic government and *de facto* or formal governments of national unity in Spain and Portugal (2011–2014).[15] The euro crisis established the European Council comprising the euro club as the political decision maker. It has overseen the strengthening of fiscal rules and hardening of the entire system of fiscal governance, which now requires the achievement of balanced budgets and includes the requirement that member states submit their budgets to European assessors before they are presented to the national parliaments.

The Union adopted a number of *ad hoc* measures to counter the deepening crisis of the Eurozone, contain the sovereign debt crisis and prevent contagion.[16] In May 2010, the European Financial Stabilisation Mechanism (EFSM) was introduced. It was to provide funding on request to member states in financial difficulties and had an initial financial capacity of 60 billion euros. It was administered by Council and Commission, with the ECB in a consulting role. The Council decides whether to grant assistance to member states in acute financial distress to restore their capacity for borrowing from financial markets. In the autumn of 2010, the Commission introduced a legislative package which entered into force in December 2011. The package comprised five regulations and one directive, which led to the nickname 'six-pack'. The primary objective was to reinforce the efficacy, preventative capacity and surveillance procedure of the Stability and Growth Pact. The six-pack sought to ensure consistency of national fiscal planning within the fiscal rules of the Union. It established fiscal retrenchment and market liberalising economic restructuring as the preferred means of debt reduction and conditionality of financial support to tie distressed member states over.

The European Financial Stability Facility (EFSF) followed in January 2011. It has a 'capacity of 440 billion euro and is backed by member state guarantee commitments of 780 billion euro, allotted in accordance with the states' share in paid-up capital to the ECB. The upper limit of guarantee liabilities for each euro state was defined by its guarantee commitment'. The EFSF operates as a 'limited liability company under Luxembourg law' (Tuori and Tuori 2014, 92). The EFSF and the EFSM were intergovernmental in character and thus remained outside the legal structure of monetary union. In September 2012 both programmes were replaced by a permanent European Stability Mechanism (EMS), which is a special Eurozone-only treaty. It has the power to advance bailout loans to member states in financial distress and to governments that need to borrow to recapitalise distressed banks. The EMS has taken over functions of both EFSF and EFSM. It grants financial assistance, subject to strict conditionality. Its modus operandi led to the characterisation of the EMS as the IMF of the Eurozone. The mechanism has a maximum lending capacity of five hundred billion euros. Its capital is contributed by the member states and financed in the market. The EMS reflects the financial strength of the member states. Its voting rights are weighted according to capital contributions. It is governed by the Council of the European Finance Ministers of the Eurozone, which assumes the role of Board of Governors. 'Major decisions granting and financing assistance require mutual agreement, i.e., unanimity, in the Board of Governors. However, an emergency voting procedure allows decision-making by mutual agreement with a qualified majority of 85 per cent of the votes cast' (Tuori and Tuori 2014, 95). Its decision making is thus neither depoliticised, nor is it undertaken by technical experts. Decisions are made by political managers who also set out the conditionality of financial assistance. Loan agreements require parliamentary ratification by the recipient state, which translates the agreement into domestic law.

Then there is the Treaty on Stability, Coordination and Governance in the EMU (or Fiscal Compact). It introduced a stricter version of the Stability and Growth Pact. It was signed by 25 out of 27 member states in March 2012 and came into force on 1 January 2014.[17] The Fiscal Compact sets a binding limit of 0.05 per cent of GDP on the structural deficits in the annual budgets of individual member states.[18] The Compact subjects national parliamentary budgeting to Union oversight and empowers the Union to give its opinion on budgetary plans. Non-compliance with fiscal rules and obligations might lead to sanctions. Nevertheless, although the reforms of fiscal policy meant that the Union is much more directly involved in national budgets, it does not exercise fiscal powers. The Union has negative fiscal powers. The Fiscal Compact establishes compliance procedures for balanced national budgets and, in cohorts with the conditionality clauses and requirements of Union bailout agreements, it establishes fiscal retrenchment and market liberalisation as binding.

In sum, the tightening of fiscal governance integrates fiscal policy much more firmly into the economic constitution of monetary union while leaving the sovereignty of member parliaments over budgetary policy formally intact. However, the framework within which they express their sovereignty has become much narrower. Indeed, the Union determines the rules of the game, keeps parliamentary compliance under surveillance and offers hard-to-ignore opinions on submitted draft budgets before they are presented formally to the member parliaments for discussion and approval. The Union does not vote on national budgets. The procedure recognises parliamentary assembly as a sovereign source of legitimation.

In addition to the European Council, the ECB asserted itself as a forceful crisis manager. From May 2010 it started to purchase government bonds, softened conditions for credits, pumped money into banking system and acted as lender of last resort, particularly to the Greek government. It thus crossed the line between monetary policy and fiscal policy. Indeed, the ECB is 'prohibited. . . from financing governments'. In recognition of the situation it decided on what was necessary and acted outside the law. In this manner, argues Borrell (2015, 239) with reference to Schmitt, it asserted itself by 'extra-sovereign acts' (see also Tuori and Tuori 2014, 164–166; Jörges 2016a). For some commentators, the actions of the ECB opened the door to moral hazard. 'As the ECB has become a large lender to Member States' financial sector, and as it accepts government bonds as collateral, one can argue that the ECB cannot afford a state to default' (Tuori and Tuori 2014, 167). It is pure conjecture to suppose that the Syriza government in Greece, which had come to power in January 2015 with a clear anti-austerity mandate, negotiated for debt relief, further bailouts with no additional conditionality on the assumption that the ECB could not afford a sovereign default. What forced the hand of the Syriza government to accept a loan agreement with much stricter conditionality in July 2015 than was on offer in February 2015 was the action of the ECB to withhold liquidity from the Greek banking system, forcing Greece on to the precipice. In this manner, and following Wolfgang Streek (2015, 370), amid the hurly-burly of summit meetings, the ECB established itself as 'the only agent capable of taking decisive action'. During the financial crisis it 'acquired wide-ranging capacities to discipline the sovereign states and society in and under its jurisdiction, to make them pay proper respect to the rule of a neo-liberal money-*cum*-market regime. . . . [S]tates that refuse to follow its precepts as to their public finances, the size and composition of their public sector, and even the structure of their wage setting systems' might find that their political economies are at the 'discretion' of the ECB.

Sinn (2014) and Bernholz (2013) identify the actions of the ECB as clear violations of *Ordnungspolitik*. In their view, the 'Southern nations in the euro zone were only saved from government bankruptcy by billions of euros in help from the other member states (although this had been forbidden by the Maastricht Treaty) and the International Monetary Fund (IMF). Besides, the ECB granted help by softening conditions for credits, buying government bonds and allowing huge transfer obligations . . . to pile up of Southern Central Bank members of the European Monetary System' (Bernholz 2013).[19] When Greece faced bankruptcy, 'instead of allowing open bankruptcy . . . it received dramatic and escalating financial help' (Bernholz 2013), which in his view opened the door to the development of monetary union towards a fiscal union. For Sinn, too, bailouts and the actions by the ECB are indefensible. In his view they put the Union on a path towards a system of 'joint liability' and mutualisation, which leads 'to a unitary state' (Sinn 2014, 356) in which the dynamic of adjustment is reversed. That is the more competitive economies would be obliged to support the weaker economies by a system of fiscal transfers and the adoption of Keynesian demand-side interventions guaranteed by especially German economic prowess, which establishes deficit spending in support of consumption and employment-led growth in indebted member states. For Bernholz and Sinn the Eurozone crisis changed the character of monetary union from a 'regime of liberty' to a 'regime of cheap money', money for nothing.[20]

Lars Feld (2012, 412–444) is more cautious in his assessment. He warns against the introduction of fiscal union and political union by stealth. Monetary union has to guarantee national autonomy for fiscal, labour market and social policy. It has to exclude risk sharing. Instead it has to be a union of decentralised economic responsibility. In the name of individual autonomy the Union is to guarantee individual economic rights and provide the legal and monetary frameworks for economic activities in a single market, but it is not to be liable for outcomes. He thus rejects political union as a danger to *Ordnungspolitik* and opposes fiscal union as a means towards political union. He also rejects the role played by the ECB during the euro crisis as a violation of the rules of the game. By acting as lender of last resort the ECB endangered the Union as a *Stabilitätsgemeinschaft*. *Ordnungspolitik* relies on and ensures through the disciplinary effect of sound money. Any weakening in this resolve would lead to irreparable damage.[21] He advises that Germany would have to leave the monetary union should the identified risks to *Stabilitätsgemeinschaft* become systemic.

Ordoliberal disquietude about the real or potential dangers to *Ordnungspolitik* in monetary union discloses ordoliberal red-lines. For the ordoliberals, monetary union cannot be a Keynesian union. It is a union of sound money and competitive adjustment in decentralised markets. It is also a depoliticised union of law-governed and rule-based conduct by technocratic organisations that, removed from traditional forms of democratic account-ability and oversight, wield real political power. It also establishes a federated system of political states that both determine the rules of the game through the European Council and execute the rules agreed upon by means of gov-ernment. The structure of monetary union incorporates the member states as executive states committed to economic liberty, emasculating the democratic idea of the state as a legislative state of mass demands. That is, the European *Stabilitätsgemeinschaft* recognises the role of the state as a market liberalis-ing interventionist state. The euro member states established a monetary framework for the operation of a market liberal economic system that com-pels each one of them to take on the role as 'market police' (cf. Rüstow 1942; Röpke 2009). Each member state comes under the compulsion to govern as 'planners for competition' (cf. Hayek 1944). Monetary union 'anchors' the liberal utility of the state as political power of a competitive order.

Ordoliberalism is not unique in requiring sound money, fiscal discipline, predictability in the conduct of public policy, security of private property, freedom of contract, market competition, acceptance of at least limited liabil-ity and so on. Its distinctiveness has to do with the recognition that the inde-pendent power of the state is a necessity of economic liberty. The ordoliberal unease about the future direction of European monetary union brings this out. It identifies especially the Southern European states as weak states that, instead of governing for free economy, let things slip to the point of insol-vency. An ordoliberal *Stabilitätsgemeinschaft* cannot be built on weak states that protect workers from competitive pressures, guarantee employment in an ostensibly overblown public sector and support consumption-led growth by means of deficit financing, and that in this argument neither have the capacity nor the will to enhance economic competitiveness and confront vested inter-ests. Nor can it be constructed as a 'transfer union' that rewards irresponsible member states by punishing the more competitive 'enterprise states' (*Wettbe-werbsstaaten*). Indeed, any such acceptance of 'joint liability' is fatal to the ordoliberal notion of European civilisation, which stands for a civil society of liberty, one that is 'reigned by sovereign consumers' (Engel 2003, 430). Indeed a risk-sharing union amounts to a redistributive union that is charac-teristic of the sort of 'quantitative civilisation' that the founding ordoliberal thinkers rejected as 'proletarian'. Any such union would replace the system of subsidiarity, that is, a system of decentralised responsibility, with a system of central responsibility for socio-economic conditions, inserting the despised Keynesian principles of economic regulation and associated ideas about social justice into monetary union. For the ordoliberal critics, the idea of an ever closer (political) union is thus anathema. In the meantime, a closer look at the resolution of the euro crisis reveals that the bailout arrangements did not transform monetary union into a Keynesian union of demand-led central economic planning and interventionism. Rather they transformed especially the Greek state into an executive state of European Council decisions for austerity, privatisation and market-led socio-economic restructuring.

CONCLUSION: EMERGENCY AND ORDER

Emergencies are not resolved by the application of law by a court of justice that by means of legal argument adjudicates the clashes of interest. Nor are they resolved by a deliberative parliamentary assembly. Emergencies call for decisive decision making and action by governing executives. Tradition-ally, the institution that is in a position to step in is the political state. In the European context, the ECB and the European Council of the Heads of State of the Eurozone countries stepped in and assumed the role of independent decision makers. They decided what needed to be done to resolve the crisis within the limits of European economic constitution. The 'self-authorisation' of particularly the European Council as executive power of monetary union (Habermas 2011) uncovered the political power at the heart of the Eurozone.

Crisis management led to an unprecedented rise and exercise of execu-tive power beyond the rights conferred by the treaties. It included the use of punitive measures, for example, withholding liquidity, to force governments into line (Bengoetxea 2015; Jörges 2014; Wilkinson 2015). During the crisis, authoritative decision making by both the Council and the ECB was unbound by the formalism of law.[22] In the words of the president of the ECB, Mario Draghi, executive decision makers should feel free, as indeed they did, to do 'whatever it takes' to preserve EMU.[23] In distinction to the ordoliberal gloom merchants who bemoan the suspension of the rules of monetary union, Vik-tor Vanberg (2014, 15) makes clear that 'prudence does indeed require us to acknowledge that there may be emergency situations in which we need to temporarily disband rules that in ordinary times we consider binding'.[24] Necessity knows no law. Rather necessity calls for a government of order. Such government cannot be bound by the rule of law. Indeed, it suspends the rule of law until the emergency is revolved so that it may not be permanently damaged. As laid out in chapter 2, order is the premise of the rule of law.

Traditionally, the European Council lays down policy guidelines but is authorised neither to pass legislation nor to direct the Commission or liaise with the ECB. Notwithstanding the attempts by the Lisbon Treaty to recog-nise the institution of the European Council, its power is extra-constitutional. In Council, executive decision making is akin to a medieval conclave of sovereign territorial rulers (Anderson 1997; Bonefeld 2005; Habermas 2012, 44). It is a body that governs not on the basis of the rule of law. It governs by executive agreement. The 'pact for Europe' is a pact between federated political entities, each enjoying the status of democratically constituted monopoly holders of the legitimate use of violence for the enforcement of the 'rules decided upon', as Friedman put it in his account of the liberal state. During the euro crisis, the heads of the euro club decided to implement 'a catalogue of economic, social and wage policy measures in their respective countries which are in actuality matters for the national parliaments' (Habermas 2012, 129). Furthermore, ever vigilant and distrustful about the willingness and capacity of its constituent members, they also decided to meet every year for the specific purpose to determine whether their colleagues in government have 'brought debt levels, the retirement age and labour market deregulation, the social benefits and health care system, public sector wages, the wage ratio, corporation tax, and much else besides into conformity with the guidelines of the European Council' (130). In this context, deliberation in member state parliaments of Council decisions amounts essentially to a legitimising exercise. A parliamentary vote against Council decisions not only denies legitimation. It also stalls the actions agreed upon in Council. However, it does not amount to a vote of no-confidence in the collective wisdom of a 'conclave' of European executives. Rather, it casts in doubt the capacity of the member state to act as a reliable European partner. In the case of Greece, the response to its robust opposition to Council decisions on the conditionality of financial bailout agreements was ruthless. The ECB ensured compliance by cutting off vital financial support to its already-crippled banking system.

In the context of the Eurozone, the ordoliberal notion that democracy works best when fettered by transcendent structures of law and money is premised on the capacity of the member states to deliver the goods. In a properly ordered 'commonwealth' popular sovereignty is exercised within a framework of extra-democratic forms of law, money and market forces. In Europe political sovereignty is divided. On the one hand, it is depersonalised and appears in the form of sound money as the denationalised prince of liberty and competitiveness. On the other, it appears in the form of a collegial body of governing national executives who make law by agreement, decide on the framework of national law making in their respective parliaments and deliberate on whether its policy guidelines and rules have been implemented and adhered to 'at home'. In this manner, the member states are limited by European agreements on what they are permitted to do. Monetary union goes hand-in-hand with the limited state. In the ordoliberal argument the limited state is the strong state. It governs for what is right and necessary. It does not let itself become the prey of mass emotions and mass demands. In the case of Greece the Syriza government that had been swept to power by a powerful anti-austerity movement learned quickly enough about the limits of popular democracy. The struggle against austerity is a struggle for money as a means of access to subsistence. When the ECB withheld liquidity, the demand for money was confronted by bank closures and potential default of an entire political economy. Under duress Greece accepted that it too will limit itself to the 'rules of the game'. Since summer 2015 its nominally anti-austerity government has established itself as a strong government – it limits itself not just to the enforcement of austerity but, also, to marketisation of public services, privatisation of national assets, market-based restructuring of labour relations and containment of the movement against austerity.

Wolfgang Streek's (2015, 370) characterisation of the ECB as 'the ideal dictator' is apt, up to a point. In distinction to the seemingly endless deliberations in Council over how best to respond to the euro crisis, member state recalcitrance and sustained political uncertainty, it took a 'decisive action'. It decided to violate statutory requirements for the greater good of European order, and it decided to end the political debate about the prospects of Greece by switching off the financial tap, bringing Greece to heel. However, and in distinction to Streek, the ECB is a technocratic organisation that wields real political power for as long as there is social order. Its capacity to confront social disorder and govern for a return to order is limited. It is not the holder of the legitimate use of violence. That is, the euro crisis made clear that monetary union is entirely dependent on the capacity of the member states to translate European monetary policy into market enabling domestic policy, from fiscal policy to economic policy, and from labour market policy to competition policy and so on. The stateless character of the euro amounts indeed to a political practice of the member states as the 'national monopolists over the legitimate use of force' (Habermas 2012, 25). In distinction to Padoa-Schioppa's (1994) projection of monetary union as having a quasi 'automatic' mechanism of economic adjustment, it does not replace the political state. Rather, monetary union depends on the capacity of its federated governments to commit to monetary union as the guiding principle of government policy and thereby bestow the mechanisms of European economic governance with a political will and a legitimation.

The European Union does not force the member states into retreat. Rather, it supports them as liberal states. Monetary union requires them to act as committed executive states of sound money. In this context it is not the national parliaments that hold member states to account. Rather, within the framework of monetary union, it is the European institutions, from the European Court of Justice to the ECB, and from the Commission to the European Council as the primary body of European decision making. In monetary union, formally independent but in effect federated states of the supranational media of market, money and law are judged on their commitments towards enhanced competiveness and fiscal discipline by the institutions of European governance and adjudication. Their judgments are overseen by a conclave of the executive managers of European order, principally the heads of government of the euro member states.

The euro crisis demystified the stateless character of the euro as mere appearance. Its depoliticised character amounts to a political decision and a political practice. Indeed, the stability of the euro depends on the capacity of the member states to enforce its requirements domestically and to act in concert with each other to maintain its stateless character, sustain market conditions and resolve difficulties. The organisation for joint thinking and binding decision making is the European Council of the euro club. It is the institution of institutions. As such it is the primary institution of 'post-democratic executive federalism' (Habermas 2011) or of 'managerial decisionism' (Everson and Jörges 2013; Jörges and Weimer 2014; Jörges 2016b, esp. 154), executive solidarity and mutual vigilance. In the European Union it is the institution of institutions. In Europe political sovereignty is both federated to democratically accountable executive governments and centralised in the form of a decision-making executive council as the political decision maker to the ECB as the technocratic 'government . . . of liberal market economy' (Streek 2015, 370). Tietmeyer's warning that sustaining monetary union requires greater European solidarity between the member states than beginning it expresses an obvious truism – yet it says more than it seemed at first. It entails the transformation of the liberal-democratic member states into capable and wholly committed national executive states of monetary union.

NOTES

1. In parts the chapter draws on my 'European economic constitution and the transformation of democracy', in *European Journal of International Relations* 21(4): 867–886, 2015.

2. Tommaso Padoa-Schioppa was an Italian economist and served as Italy's minister of economy and finance from May 2006 to May 2008. During the 1980s he had argued for the completion of the single market through monetary union based on a single currency and a single European central bank. The Delors Report of 1989 endorsed his view and recommended European Monetary Union (EMU). Padoa-Schioppa worked on designing and setting up the European Central Bank (ECB) and became one of its first executive board members from June 1998 to May 2005. He was the intellectual force behind EMU.

3. On monetary union as resembling a depersonalised and depoliticised 'prince' without a Republic to call upon, see also Müller (2014).

4. On the national state, money and world market trade, see Radice (2015). See also Bonefeld (2000).

5. On this point, see also Carchedi (2001).

6. In this context, the trajectory of the former German Democratic Republic (GDR) since German unification in 1990, de-industrialisation, impoverishment and depopulation, appears to hold the mirror image of the pressures on member countries that find it difficult to compete with German levels of productivity. However, in

distinction to German unification where the new East German Länder have been in receipt of ongoing fiscal transfers from the West-German Länder, EMU specifically excludes fiscal transfer to distressed member states. At the same time, the resources from the European Regional Fund have been and are expected to remain limited.

7. The achievement of complete competition relies on the establishment of an undivided common market by the Single European Act. The act was agreed in principle at the Luxembourg Summit in December 1985. It came into force in the summer of 1987. The Single European Act revitalised European integration after the economic malaise of the 1970s which was summed up by the term 'Eurosclerosis'. The act aimed to remove all remaining barriers to the free movement and free exchange of goods, services and resources among member countries, including non-tariff barriers such as technical specifications and prohibitive national standards. The act pursued integration 'exclusively through the reinforcement of competition and market relations' (Grahl and Teague 1990, 13). The then British government under Margret Thatcher was an ardent supporter of the single market. On monetary union as completing the single market, one market, one money, see the Emerson Report to the European Commission in 1990 (Emerson 1992).

8. On the need for 'strong' institutions, see Popper (2002). See also chapter 6, note 23.

9. Vanberg (2014, 15) thus argues that 'crises as the one we are currently faced with in Europe do not come upon us like natural disasters. They are typically the cumulative outcome of a continued violation of the rules that, if they would have been followed, would not have allowed the crisis to come about in the first place'. Crises express a failure of government to stick to the rules of competitive order. Instead of liberal interventionism, government lacked in commitment and yielded to social pressures, 'paving the way for the current sovereign-debt crisis'. Monetary union cannot be founded on weak states that allow themselves to become the instrument of the economic groups. It requires strong states that stick to rules and do not yield.

10. The Stability and Growth Pact was put in place on German insistence. It institutionalised a harder version of the convergence criteria that prospective member states had to meet to qualify for membership in monetary union. The act responded to the potential threat of fiscal profligacy by member states on the stability of monetary union. However, once inside monetary union, EMU lacked a mechanism for fiscal discipline (see Garrett 1994). The Stability and Growth Pact was to guarantee fiscal discipline once monetary union was in operation. Nevertheless, no credible institutional arrangements were put in place to enforce fiscal discipline, including arrangement for dealing with sovereign insolvency and default (Feld 2012; Jessop 2014).

11. The Emerson Report evaluated the potential costs and benefits of monetary union and set out its economic governance mechanisms. The report is the blueprint of monetary union.

12. During the Eurozone crisis, the requirement to avoid excessive deficits changed to the requirement to achieve balanced budgets.

13. During the Eurozone crisis, it was decided that a fiscal rule-breaking state can be fined up to 0.1 per cent of its GDP. Ultimately, the fine is a matter of legal judgment that is delivered by the Court of Justice in the EU. It will have to decide on the policy intensions of 'imbalanced' member states. On this, see MaCartney (2013).

14. For an account of ordoliberal social policy, see chapter 5.

15. See Lapavitsas (2012) and Charnock, Purcell and Ribera-Fumaz (2014).

16. For a detailed account, see Tuori and Tuori (2014). See also Varoufakis (2016) and Sinn (2014).

17. The UK and the Czech Republic opted out.

18. Economic theory does not tell us what a balanced budget is. Its determination is a political decision, which, for the sake of appearing credible, needs to eliminate any doubt in its veracity to forgo adverse market reactions. Financial markets feed on deficits and react with herd-like runs if confidence is dented. During the Eurozone crisis, the euro club decided that a balanced budget amounts to a budget deficit of less than 3 per cent of GDP, requiring Greece to restructure its entire political economy, for the sake of confidence in the euro. What counts as a deficit and what needs to be done about it is a political decision. On this see Radice (2014).

19. The IMF, ECB and European Commission were nicknamed by the Greek opposition to austerity as the troika or the institutions. They stood accused of straight-jacketing Greek democracy.

20. On the political repercussions of the bailout agreements in Germany, especially populist rejection of monetary union, see Grimm (2015) and Schmitt-Beck (2016).

21. Feld (2012, 414) rejects any change in the mandate of the ECB. He characterises any such change as a *Sündenfall*, which translates as fall from grace, which in Christian mythology led to Man's expulsion from paradise.

22. Wilkinson (2015) argues that European crisis-resolution led to a 'judicial deficit' and identifies Council executive decision making as the emergence of 'authoritarian constitutionalism'. See also Oberndorfer (2015).

23. See 'Speech by Mario Draghi, President of the European Central Bank at the Global Investment Conference in London, 26 July 2012', available at www.ecb.europa.eu/press/key/date/2012/html/sp120726.en.html. Accessed March 2016. The phraseology is reminiscent of Schmitt's definition of the state of emergency as the time of the executive.

24. For similar formulation, see Röpke (2009, 52) and Rossiter (1948, 12). Vanberg's argument expresses the difficulties of finding a resolution to the conundrum of liberty and democracy, and emergency government too, see chapter 3. On the one hand, he acknowledges the need to 'temporarily disband rules that in ordinary times we consider binding'. Yet, on the other, he requires that the abandonment of binding rules has itself to be rule based, that is, 'we need to adopt rules for *when* and *by whom* and according to *what procedures* an emergency can be declared as well as rules that constrain what the authority in charge is allowed to do in such emergency situations' (2014, 15). Like Draghi, Vanberg's argument accepts that a state of emergency is about the preservation of binding rules. The rules of exception do not however trigger themselves. They are activated by extralegal authority, which decides on whether to govern through the existing rules or their suspension, unbound by the formalism of law.

Chapter 8

Authoritarian Liberalism and the Euro: On the Political Theology of the Executive State

INTRODUCTION

Ordoliberalism identifies liberal political economy as a practice of government. As laid out in the introduction, interpretations of ordoliberalism as a socially just alternative to neoliberalism depend for their view on a conception of state and market as distinct forms of social organisation. From this perspective political economy amounts either to an assertion of the market against the state or of the state against the market. In this context, neoliberalism is identified with market rule and ordoliberalism with state rule (Sheppard and Leitner 2010). Ordoliberalism is held as an alternative to neoliberalism because it fetters markets to rules and better still it projects a socially responsible market economy that enables the individuals to cope with market pressures (see Glasman 1996).

The account assembled in this book makes clear that the free economy leads to 'disorder' (Smith 1976b), that a society based solely on egoism is impossible (Kant 1971) and that the system of liberty is founded on irreconcilable class relations (Hegel 1967; Smith 1976a). Without the civilising power of the state the free economy tends to 'degenerate into a vulgar brawl' that breaks society up (Röpke 1982, 188). The ordoliberal argument for restraint and policing of the market is not at all directed against the free economy. Rather it is an argument about the indispensability of the state as the concentrated power to establish and sustain the free economy. In Viktor Vanberg's succinct formulation, *Ordnungspolitik* is about the creation of 'conditions under which the "invisible hand" that Adam Smith had described can be expected to do its work' (Vanberg 2015, 29).

Foucault's reading of ordoliberalism also assumes that state and economy are different forms of social organisation. His account differentiates between the logic of the market and the logic of the state. In his view, the state operates for ordoliberal ends because ordoliberalism 'adopt[s] the free market as the organizing and regulating principle of the state' (2008, 116), just as, as it were, socialism adopts the planned economy as the organising and regulating principles of the state, classical political economy adopts commercial society as the organising principle of the state and so on. The use of the word 'adoption' suggests that the character of the state is essentially undefined and that it therefore might be an ordoliberal state or, say, a Keynesian state, depending on which economic ideology has achieved hegemony at a given conjuncture of social struggle. In distinction, the book argued that ordoliberalism is a theoretical expression of definite social relations. The idea that their character has to do with the adoption of this or that guiding principle of political construction confuses the reality of a free labour economy with its ideology, which suggests flight from reality towards ideality. In distinction to Blyth (2013), therefore, austerity is not an ordoliberal idea. Nor is ordoliberalism distinct because it favours sound money as opposed to the fictitious money that is associated with neoliberal financial globalisation. The notion that the pursuit of fiscal discipline, sound money and market competition in the European monetary union presents a German ideology and projects German hegemonic power (Bulmer and Joseph 2016) tends to nationalise the critique of political economy, substituting analyses of the conditions of a free labour economy for the illusionary idea that European monetary union could 'adopt' an entirely benevolent reality if replaced by some other ideality of political construction.

Ryner's (2015) conception of Europe as an 'ordoliberal iron cage' has much to commend it by. However, the notion of an iron cage is potentially misleading. It implies automaticity of administrative processes and regulative interventions by means of technocratic economic governance. That is, it suggests that the European monetary union entails the retreat of the state in favour of quasi-judicial processes of depoliticised economic governance and technocratic decision making, especially about monetary policy. Ordoliberalism is not an argument about administrative processes and economic technique. It is an argument about the indispensability of the state as the concentrated power of the free economy. The characterisation of contemporary European integration as ordoliberal in character requires therefore analyses of the political character of monetary union. As laid out in the previous chapters, the stateless character of the euro amounts to a political practice, that is, a practice of 'market police'. European integration incorporates the liberal-democratic member states as federated executive states (*Regierungsstaaten*) of European money.

This chapter integrates the exposition of ordoliberal thought in the earlier chapters with the analyses of the ordoliberal elements of European monetary union in the previous chapters. It recasts the theoretical argument to establish the meaning of the executive state in the contemporary European Union. The argument is in three steps. First, it presents Schmitt's original depiction of the executive state. Following Heller (2015) his authoritarian liberalism presents the liberal state in its pure form. It then turns to the ordoliberal argument that the free economy presupposes the 'independence of political will' from mass democratic entanglements and the economic pressure groups (Eucken 1932, 307–308). The final section analyses the executive state in the European monetary union and concludes on the populist backlash against the European Union.

AUTHORITARIAN LIBERALISM AND POLITICAL THEOLOGY

Schmitt's political theology identifies modernity as a desacralised and grace-less manifestation of rationalism, egalitarianism, legal positivism and mass democratic dissolution of the divine Rights (*Rechte*) of government and property. Political theology entails a political metaphysics. It holds that 'the central concepts of modern state theory are all secularised theological concepts' (1985, 36). In line with the conservative critics of the Enlightenment, from Juan Donoso Cortes and Joseph de Maistre to Benjamin Constant, he asserts that with the French Revolution political concepts started to lose their metaphysical quality. The old concept of legitimacy, which had to do with divine Rights based on social distinction, clear relations of rule, social propriety and respect for (private) property, had given way to rational-legal forms of legitimation that supplant loyalty to king and country by principles of equal social and political rights. Nothing sacred remained. The sacred was replaced by the profane. In modernity, politics has become mass politics. It diminishes the political to administration and technical regulation, to questions of economic technique and adherence to disenchanted rules and procedures. In mass democracy the 'theistic and the deistic idea of God is unintelligible' (Schmitt, quoted in Cristi 1998, 112).

In Schmitt's argument existential problems appear as 'organisational-technical and economic-sociological ones' (Schmitt 1985, 65). In this sense, the 'de-theologised' world is a 'de-politicised' world of social administration, and engineering too (Schmitt 2008b, 128). It is supposed to be a world without divine authority, certainty of moral values, ready acceptance of social position, clarity of political purpose, willingness to serve and so on. Right (*Recht*) thus steps aside for the sake of egalitarian notions of distributive justice and material security, from the cradle to the grave. In the words of Schmitt, '[t]he state as an outgrowth of society, and thus no longer objectively distinguishable from society, occupies everything societal, that is, anything that concerns the collective existence of human beings. There is no longer any sphere of society in relation to which the state must observe the principle of absolute neutrality in the sense of non-intervention' (Schmitt 1996b, 79). In mass democracy the state is at the mercy of competing social forces and serves, in Eucken's (1932, 307) formulation, 'the will of the interested parties'. Whereas Man used to accept his or her 'responsibility to the state', now 'the state is responsible to man', as Marcuse (1988, 36) put it in his account of liberalism's turn towards authoritarianism towards the end of the Weimar Republic.

Schmitt's call for the recovery of the elements of metaphysics in the government of mass society presupposes, as Marcuse (1988, 36) recognised, the 'existentialization and totalization of the political sphere'. It amounts thus to the politicisation of the state as the independent power of social integration. The politicised state reacts to the 'threatened freedom and security of private property' and acts with unbound authority (36). The decision to act not only reveals the political sovereign, that is, 'he who decides on the exception' (Schmitt 1985, 5). It also asserts the power of the state as a 'Right producing' state (13).[1] Law does not apply to disorder. Order is a political category of disorder in the mode of being denied. Schmitt thus insists that 'all law is situational' (13) and at unpredictable times 'the power of real life breaks through the crust of a mechanism that has become torpid by repetition' (15). The state of exception recognises the unpredictable power of real life in the reality of the political situation. It spills blood for the sake of a rightful social order, for peace and tranquillity. For the sake of Right, it casts aside the legal formalism of a mass democratic age and opposes the 'democratically equal populace' with the 'myth of a hierarchically ordered and unified people' (Strong 1985, xxvii). In a state of exception, the sovereign transforms the myth of the Rights of the nation into action for the rightful nation, and endows it with a political will and an authoritarian consciousness. It thus enforces the illusory autonomy of national being over the mass democratic quarrels and class interests and struggles, restoring not only tranquillity, order and stability but also certainty of values, respect for private property and acceptance of social hierarchy and distinction. Any doubt in the veracity of the new order is eliminated by pursuit of the doubter. As Forsthoff (1933b, 29) put it, 'Attempts to dispute the state's newly gained effective right signify sabotage. . . . Relentlessly to exterminate this sort of thought is the noblest duty of the state today'.[2] Political theology, which had become unthinkable in a democratic context, asserts itself in the form of a leadership democracy that comprises a unity between movement and leader. For the sake of unity, the identification of the stranger to the relations of national harmony is of greatest importance. The identified stranger functions like metaphysical glue. It cements the bond between the leader and his movement.[3]

In his *The Guardian of the Constitution* Schmitt argues that the old liberal state possessed elements of an 'executive state' (*Regierungsstaat*) that was 'strong enough to stand above and beyond all social forces' (Schmitt 1996b, 73).[4] In Schmitt's argument the liberal state of old comprised a dual structure that embodied two different forms of state: a parliamentary 'legislative state' (*Gesetzgebungsstaat*), which was the representative body of the propertied classes and the educated (*Besitz und Bildung*), and an 'executive state' (*Regierungsstaat*), which expressed the interests of the ancient regime and was administered by aristocratic officeholders.

The dual structure comprised thus a democracy of liberal friends and government by the ancient regime. Schmitt acknowledges that this structure was contradictory and tension-ridden with traditional economic and political elites battling a liberal bourgeoisie demanding reforms in support of their own economic interests. Nevertheless, this conflict was between different property owners. It excluded the property-less.[5] Schmitt argues that the dual structure of the liberal state fell apart with the German democratic revolution of 1918. With the emergence of mass democracy the legislative state supplanted the executive state, making government dependent on the governed. Following William Scheuerman (1999, 89) 'the democratisation of parliament in conjunction with the simultaneous parliamentarization of the state means that no element of the state now "stands above and beyond the social forces"' (quoting Schmitt 1996b). The old executive state vanished because democratisation and parliamentarisation meant that it had literally lost its constituency (of friends). Schmitt summarises the socio-economic consequences of the struggle for political equality as follows: 'If society organises itself into the state, if state and society are to be basically identical, then all social and economic problems become immediate objects of the state' (Schmitt 1996b, 78–79).[6] Paraphrasing Schmitt, the stranger, this figure of the enemy within, enters the liberal state and asserts his interests as an equal; that is, in mass democracy control is exercised by those who need to be controlled.[7] Schmitt's argument is to the effect that, put crudely, the emergent 'legislative state' of mass democracy had replaced rightful government by mass 'voting' and law making by mass opinion. The mass state does not distinguish between the friends of private property and their enemies, legitimate Rights and the formalism of procedural law, sacred values and coarse demands for material security. The distinction between political state and depoliticised social relations appears lost inasmuch as the mass state does not draw a line between society and state.

In the Schmittean argument majoritarian democratic law making de-theologises the rule of law as a normative statement of divine socio-political Rights. It reduces law to a mere procedural formalism of majoritarian democracy. Legality is the principle of mass democratic law making, which attributes the legitimacy of law to legal-rational processes and procedures. It is, says Schmitt (2008b, 119), 'nothing more than mob rule'. Schmitt identifies the time of egalitarian mass democracy with mob rule and recognises it as a time of exception. The declaration of a state of exception is a matter of sovereign judgment about conditions deemed to amount to ungovernability and social anarchy. Since the law does not apply to disorder, the judgement about the state of disorder, of exception and emergency, is an extralegal one. It is a political judgement that requires political decision to set things right. This decision is political at its most intense. It abandons the formalism law. Instead it is guided by what needs to be done – 'whatever it takes'. The decision to suspend the rule of law and govern unbound by (the formalism of) law is true inasmuch as any doubt in its veracity is eliminated; at least this is its sovereign requirement. Decisionism, in which an unregulated act of power is taken, suspends the 'legislative state' of mass democracy and casts aside the formalism of law as the basis of government. If need be, blood is spilled to restore order, peace and tranquillity. As Rüstow (1959, 100) made clear, the (unbound) executive state governs with 'authority and leadership'. It asserts itself as an executive state of non-negotiable socio-economic Rights.[8]

Decisionism has reached its limits once the decision has been taken. It is not an alternative to the suspended system of majoritarian parliamentary democracy and regulation of the social relations by the rule of law. Decisionism is bound to the identified exception to order and tranquillity. Once the Nazi dictatorship was established its time had passed. Now the focus shifts to the establishment of a concrete order as a robust 'alternative' to the dethronement of Right by mass democracy (Cristi 1998, 159). As Schwab (1985, l–li) explains concrete order thinking focuses on 'devising a constitutional order that would once and for all drain society of political forces that could challenge the state's monopoly on politics'. Schmitt's concrete order is hierarchically structured and based on the leadership principle. It stands for entirely depoliticised socio-economic relations, from which 'all orderlessness' has been eradicated.[9] That is, the 'segregation of the state from non-state spheres . . . is . . . a political procedure' and the 'disengagement from politics is a specifically political act' (Schmitt 1998, 221). The organisation of a depoliticised social order was for Schmitt an outcome of politics in the specific use of state authority. It includes the establishment of depoliticised social organisations and cultural institutions, for example professional bodies, including labour unions, occupational interest groups, youth clubs, and state-organised forms of amusements and relaxation such as holiday camps. These establishments are part of the state-organised societal order and operate according to a centrally devised set of purposes. The notion of a concrete order does not recognise extra-political forms of interaction. Rather, extra-political forms of social interaction are political institutions. Schmittean concrete order thinking is about the establishment of institutional complexes that discharge specific functions of social organisation and oversee the conduct of its members according to regulative principles that derive their authority and legitimacy from a legally unregulated sovereign, the leader.[10] This figure of will and charisma commands not through the rationality of law but, rather, the illusion of omnipotence.[11]

The Schmittean state of concrete order governs through intermediary organisations that institutionalise diverse social practices. They establish federated or decentralised networks of interaction between the leader and the led. Since anybody could be designated the role of enemy, doubt in the veracity of the new order evaporates for reasons of personal security. In this manner, the concrete order holds together because it succeeds in creating the people's adherence to the way things are. The concrete order is thus more than just a structure of government and network of socio-economic institutions. It reaches into the inner recesses of the governed. It instils a certain type of relationship to a certain type of authority. The designated enemy defines the political friend (see Schmitt 1985). That is, the friends have to be committed followers so that they may not be designated as enemies, too. As Forsthoff (1933a, 25) explains, 'Reality is not admit of knowledge, only of acknowledgment'. In the words of Müller-Armack (1933, 22), it determines 'the living space for individual life'. Schmitt's concrete order appeared thus as a 'concrete mode of existence', that is, as the 'unified and closed system of supreme and ultimate norms' (Schmitt 1934, 4, 7). In Schmitt's concrete order the political state is the 'concrete order of orders, the institution of institutions' (47). His leadership principle, therefore, is the secularised substitute for the monarchical principle. It unseats the democratic legal state and establishes a metaphysical executive state. The federated system of concrete institutions does therefore not fragment the unity of the state. Rather, it establishes channels for the decisions of sovereign power.[12]

POLITICAL AUTHORITY, MORALITY AND FREEDOM

In the ordoliberal argument the free economy is a 'universal form of life' (Eucken 2004, 321). That is 'man exchanges because he is the only living being that is capable of this form of transaction without being in any way aware about the ingenious character of his behaviour' (Böhm, cited in Eucken 2004, 321). Ordoliberalism does not endorse the free economy in narrow economic terms. Rather it identifies the free economy as a definite moral order. The freedom to compete is intrinsic to human nature (see Eucken 1989, 34). In this claim there is a deeper meaning. If competition defines what it is to be human then those who set out to diminish it diminish humanity. It is dangerous to speak in the name of universal forms of humanity since all those who oppose must perforce appear as speaking against humanity. As an outlaw of humanity, this other is not an adversary, opponent and competitor. Rather, this other is the enemy – the disturber of human economy, disrupter of order, peace and tranquillity, and destroyer of a culture of achievement and self-earned property.

The 'friend and enemy' (Müller-Armack 1933, 31; Röpke 1998, 66; Eucken 2004, 185) constellation is central to ordoliberal concrete order thinking, from the more economic leaning idea of an *Ordnungspolitik* that is about the constitutionalisation of free economy and the achievement of complete competition as a legal obligation and public duty, via the ideological formation of self-responsible entrepreneurship as a character trait and fabrication of society as an enterprise society to the creation of depoliticised regulatory institutions that, removed from democratic influence and accountability, oversee the conduct of liberal economy on a rule-based and law-governed basis, supervised and enforced by public authority. ORDO is a metaphysical concept, an *ordo mundi*. Although it is founded on some assumed eternal natural human condition of a freedom to exchange and compete, its conduct has to be 'firmly contained within an all-embracing order of society', encompassing 'ethics, the natural conditions of life and happiness, the state, politics and power' (Röpke 1998, 91). The purpose of *Ordungspolitik* is to 'subordinate' society to the 'ethical' effects of free economy (see Müller-Armack 1981a, 124). For the ordoliberals the task of government is to provide the institutions necessary for a civil society of competing property owners. ORDO combines nature with power, order with happiness, freedom with politics and competition with morality.

In the free economy, struggle is incessant. The ordoliberals recognise this. It is the dynamic behind the transformation of society into a graceless and disenchanted world of 'greedy self-seekers' (Rüstow 1963, 255) and proletarianised workers who struggle to make ends meet. Their struggle for material security 'reinforces the general tendency towards state slavery [*Staatsklaverei*]' and represents the 'decomposition of the human substance' (Eucken 2004, 193, citing Köstler) to the detriment of social harmony and morality. In the ordoliberal view, the freedom to compete is a fundamental means of human freedom. For the sake of humanity it is non-negotiable. It recognises 'constant surveillance of the total economic process' (Müller-Armack 1981a, 124) as a moral requirement and identifies it as a means of freedom.

In the ordoliberals' conception, capitalist economy is a moral economy because '"man is free if he needs to obey no person but solely the law"' (Kant, citied in Hayek 1944, 58). Freedom expresses a definite legal order. There is no freedom without it. The rule of law makes freedom possible as a law-governed expression of free will. The ordoliberals' endorsement of Kant's dictum entails a critique of unlimited mass democracy. '[E]ven if individuals are only obliged to follow the law, their freedom is always threatened if these laws can be changed arbitrarily by... duly elected parliamentary majorities (that is minorities) [that] are allowed to introduce new laws or change old ones relating to any sphere of human existence' (Bernholz 2013). The danger, then, of mass democracy is that law (*Gesetz*) and Right (*Recht*) collapse into a purely formal rule of law, which is decided upon by unpredictable parliamentary majorities according to set procedures. It is in this context that Rüstow (2005) charges laissez-faire liberalism with suffering from the delusion of freedom. In the words of Röpke (2009, 50) '[t]he enemies profit by it, too, and are in the name of freedom given every conceivable opportunity to put an end to liberal democracy'. He argues with Schmittean insights that the mass democratic demand for 'equality' transformed the liberal executive state into a legislative state (*Gesetztgebungsstaat*) of mass opinion and mass demands. Mass democracy is based on the 'principle of sovereignty of the people, ascertained by majority decision and intended to realise the identity of people and government'. There can be no freedom of competition, no morality, in a mass democracy that does not know how to limit itself to the pursuit of liberty. To govern for freedom means to govern with a clear conception of 'the enemies' of freedom (Röpke 1998, 66).

Fundamentally, freedom amounts to a political decision and political event (Böhm 1973; Miksch 1947). Its premise is the independent will of government (see Eucken 1932, 307–308). Indeed, the free economy 'cannot function without authority [*Obrigkeit*]' (Böhm 2010, 167). 'Independent' decision making by the state (Röpke 1998, 142) is the bedrock of the system of liberty. It underscores the rule-based and law-governed conduct in a free labour economy and bestows the liberal rule of law with a will and a consciousness.

Eucken (2004) offers a succinct account of economic freedom as political decision and constant practice of government. He identifies the freedom to compete as an intrinsic human property and argues that 'nobody is authorized to abandon his or her moral autonomy' and become a mere tool for somebody else. 'But no one must also force the others to waive his or her moral autonomy'. Freedom is an (authorised) moral obligation, which 'serves' (*dient*) Man as a 'self-responsible' being (178). Self-responsible freedom is a function of order. 'Freedom and order are not opposites. They depend upon one another. *Ordering means the ordering of freedom*' (179). For the sake of the order of freedom, therefore, 'man has to behave in a disciplined manner' (197, citing Miksch) and such behaviour is possible only in conditions in which 'the necessity of a willed order is affirmed in the mentality of a properly understood freedom'. Only on this basis can 'the coordination of the economic participants be achieved, which is the essence of a competitive order' (197). Eucken thus argues that the freedom to compete is a function of order. Freedom has therefore 'its limits, namely there where the order is threatened by it' (197). Whether freedom persists as an expression of order or not is a matter of political judgement. If a decision needs to be made between freedom and order, freedom has to give for the benefit of order.[13] Eucken grants that the pursuit of liberty might establish 'new forms of order. These are justified for as long as they are in conformity with the order of competition' (197). Here, too, a decision needs to be made as to whether socio-economic developments are in accordance with the principles of economic constitution. *Ordnungspolitik* amounts thus to a sustained political decision about the character of economic development and the conduct of the market participants. Government constitutes the competitive order, governs for the completeness of competition, secures the self-responsible conduct of the individuals in support of that order, curtails the excess of freedom, civilises its conduct on the basis of law and decides whether the development of freedom is bounded by the principles of social order. Government is thus a constant force of ordering, enabling, authoritative decision making and moralising. The ordoliberals recognise the liberal state as the political form of the relations of private property, and conceive of it as an executive state of a 'private law society'. The (ordo-)liberal state is a moral institution and a moralising force. For the ordoliberals, too, it is the institution of institutions.

During the 1930s, the ordoliberal denunciation of Weimar democracy as an 'economic state' and the call for a strong state to 'recover' free economy also changed into 'concrete order thinking'. As Müller-Armack had already put it in 1932 (1932, 42), we need to 'invent (*erfinden*) an objective order constellation (*Ordnungsgefüge*)' to safeguard the free economy. Freiburg school *Ordnungspolitik* and the sociological liberalism associated with Rüstow, Röpke and Müller-Armack developed different aspects of concrete order thinking from the mid-1930s onwards. These efforts included arguments for an *Ordnungspolitik* based on an economic constitution of complete competition, and depoliticised forms of market supervision and enforcement, for example, a cartel office with quasi-judicial status independent of the established democratic system of government and central bank independence, which for Röpke (2009, 196) appeared as the last line of defence of liberty economy. It further included commitments for a market facilitating conduct of social policy and ideological cohesion of the social relations on the basis of Christian values, and the establishment of a liberal-democratic state that does not tolerate the enemies of its basic constitutional value commitments – a 'militant democracy' (Agnoli 1990; Müller 2012). That is, 'trust in freedom must be accompanied by a distrust of forces that abolish freedom or interfere with it' (Lenel 1989, 21). Surveillance is the condition of trust. It is the premise of the freedom to exchange and compete on depoliticised labour markets. Safeguarding the free economy requires institutions that are well built to withstand mass demands for conditions. In the early 1930s, ordoliberal thinkers argued with Schmitt for the suppression of class struggle by commissarial dictatorship. In the post-war period they argued for the transformation of mass democracy into a liberal democracy, in which the democratic idea of one person one vote is tied to the liberal principle of government. As argued previously, the incorporation of parliamentary democracy into a European framework of law, money and market offered a supranational *Ordnungsgefüge* for the pursuit of liberty within mass democracy.

ON THE *ORDNUNGSGEFÜGE* OF THE EUROPEAN UNION

Mestmäcker (2003) characterises European Economic Community as a comprehensive decision (*Gesamtentscheidung*) about the economic constitution of Europe. Its principal elements are the free movement of goods, capital, services and labour and competition law. Competition between territorialised labour markets also includes the institutional systems, from taxation to social protection (see Dardot and Laval 2013, 208–212). The regulative institutions of the European Union are law, money and market. They are developed, administered and enforced by European institutions that operate removed from traditional democratic principles of parliamentary law making, oversight and accountability. Within the 'concrete order' (*Ordungsgefüge*) of Europe only the European Parliament is directly elected by a European citizenry which as such does not exist.[14] It is a forum for discussion, argument and deliberative formality. It represents the spectre of democratic pluralism at its most harmless. It has no executive to control, lacks the right of legislative initiative and cannot change the constitution of Europe because none exists, at least not in traditional form. European integration is based on international treaties between sovereign states. In the European Parliament the democratic groupings do not comprise governing majorities and opposition parties since there is no European government in the traditional sense. As a mass democratic body, it is without bite and consequence. The European Parliament is not an institution of a European legislative state. It is a deliberative institution of a union of executive states.

In this system, the European Commission, too, is a most curious institution. It is composed of the College of Commissioners, one from each member state. It is the executive body of the European Union. Its main roles are to propose legislation, enforce European law without power of state, implement EU policies, represent the EU outside Europe and set objectives for actions. It holds collective responsibility for the EU. The Commission operates akin to a technocratic cabinet government without democratic foundation and statehood. The European Court of Justice, now the Court of Justice of the European Union, emerged from being the authoritative interpreter of European competition law of the kind developed by German ordoliberalism (see Gerber 1994) as the legal guardian of the European market society. It adjudicates on stateless law that is superior to law made by national parliaments and in most cases directly applicable in member states.[15] The European Central Bank is the sovereign institution of European money. It is the most independent and depoliticised Central Bank. Indeed it is a stateless central bank and is not answerable to any government or any other European institutions. It regulates a stateless currency and determines the monetary framework for the conduct of public policy in the member states.

The political institution of the European Union is the European Council, which comprises the heads of member governments. It is supported by various ministerial councils. The Council is the membership organisation of national executives. It is the de facto European legislator and policy maker in one. In distinction to parliamentary law making, in the European Union law is made by councils composed of government executives. Executive law making is unique in contemporary historical perspective.

The Eurozone crisis uncovered the European Council as the Union's core decision maker. Its decisions entail the member states as federated executive states. Within the framework of 'executive federalism' (Habermas 2012, 129) national parliaments may oppose the ratification of policy decisions by European Councils but their powers remain purely negative. Member state parliaments do not make European policy or law. The Council operates akin to a medieval conclave of sovereign kings and queens who are united in their efforts to find resolutions to conflicts that in the past pitted them against each other. Their efforts are supported by a number of legal and technocratic institutions that act on the basis of the agreements that they have reached. The troublesome populace is kept out of the bargain.

The concrete order of the EU – its *Ordnungsgefüge* – forecloses, as Wilkinson (2015, 323) has argued, traditional 'route[s] of parliamentary, political contestation'. In its stead it establishes a fraternity of trade, commerce and exchange and institutes a market liberal framework for the pursuit of individual economic rights in competing territorialised labour markets.[16] Within this framework the member states act as executive states of a European economic constitution and they do so akin to the ordoliberal characterisation of the liberal state as the concentrated power of 'liberal interventionism' (Rüstow 1963, 252). The formative power of the European Union is market rule through the integration of the role of the state as market police.[17]

In 1933, Heller (2015) had argued that the authoritarian liberal scheme could not be maintained in democratic form. A state 'that is determined to secure "the free labour power of those people active in the economy" will . . . have to act in an authoritarian way' (Heller 2015, 301, citing Schmitt 1998). The concrete order of the European Union suggests that it is however possible to achieve the freedom of labour within a democratic form. Its *Ordnungsgefüge* respects in its entirety the traditional forms of parliamentary democracy in member states. Indeed it makes the establishment of parliamentary democracy a condition of membership. Nevertheless, by placing economic governance into a supranational structure, parliamentary democracy in the member states comes under a regime of liberty.[18] Within the European institutional structure, therefore, the member states achieve a degree of independence from traditional forms of democratic contestation. As argued by Hayek (1939) a federated system of containing mass democracy does not in any way curtail the liberal state as the independent power of society. Rather, it provides the means for its independence. In the European Union the member states govern the territorialised labour relations through European structures of money, law and market.

I have argued that the institutional structure of the European Union integrates the role of the member state not only in 'establishing the framework within which economic activity takes place' (Hallstein 1972, 28) but also as federated executive states of Union rules. Against this background the national parliaments have largely become assemblies for deliberation and legitimation. In contrast to the heterogeneous character of national parliaments, the Council assumes the role of an assembly of friends – each committed to the bargain in, at times, heated debate how best to sustain the European idea. However, in the first half of 2015 the election victory in Greece of a resolutely anti-austerity government led by Syriza challenged the fundamental homogeneity of Council interests. Instead of containing the mutinous character of the Greek opposition to austerity through the institutional *Ordnungsgefüge*, the anti-austerity movement gained entry not just into the Greek parliament. It also gained the seat of government in Greece and thus became a member of the Council, shattering its homogeneity. Concerted action between the ECB and Council majority in the euro club compelled the Greek government to recognise the limits of liberal democracy and accept its responsibilities as a member of the European executive council. Indeed, by accepting the conditionality of the bailout agreements in full, the Greek state has, to all intents and purposes, acknowledged its position as a federated executive manager of European Council decisions, without mitigation. 'Sovereignty ends when solvency ends' (Müller 2014, 262).

The European system of liberal democracy not only stimulates competition between territorialised labour markets. It also tends to nationalise the protest against the supranational regime of market liberty, federated executive states and deliberative democratic assemblies. The proliferation of the extreme right, including the neo-fascists, from the National Front in France to Golden Dawn in Greece, and the ADF in Germany, too, has seemingly become the 'new normal' in Euro-land. The curtailment of traditional forms of parliamentary democracy suffocated not only traditional forms of political legitimation. It also disarmed a whole tradition of left internationalism in Europe and reinforced entirely illusory ideas about the national state as an allegedly progressive alternative to the European Union.[19]

For its stability and future prospects the Europe an Union requires unbending solidarity between its member states – 'whatever it costs'. European government by Council executive decisions and technocratic regulation of the liberal market economy by the ECB depends on the capacity of the member states to act as committed executive states. For as long as the nationalist populist backlash is contained in national parliaments, the basic structure of the European order will not be under threat. Should Council solidarity however weaken and fragment, the question of who is the European sovereign will come to the fore again. In this case the 'managerial decisionism' (Jörges 2016b) or the 'executive federalism' (Habermas 2011) that the euro crisis uncovered might no longer do.[20] Only a state has the power to stop people running through the door. What is the state's name that has the courage and power of authoritative enforcement of the rules agreed upon?

Clearly, this state is not the UK. It never fully committed itself to Europe and lacking in courage it caved in at the first sign of serious trouble, first to populist flag-bearers and then to populist backlash, rejecting the free movement of labour. 'Brexit' articulates the idea of national self-determination as a perverted alternative to the European system of liberty by federated executive government. Rather than overcoming the tradition of authoritarian liberalism it posits it at its most dangerous, as a movement of national purposes.[21]

NOTES

1. Translation amended. In the German original, *Politische Theologie* (Berlin: Duncker & Humblot 1990, 20), Schmitt writes 'Recht zu schaffen', that is, to produce Right (*Recht*) or to make Right (*Recht*). In the English version this is translated as 'to produce law' (*Gesetz*). On the distinction between law and Right and the notion of the *Rechtsstaat*, see chapters 2 and 4.

2. Ernst Forsthoff was a student of Schmitt. He held various professorships during Nazism and was dismissed from his teaching post by order of the American military government. He resumed teaching at Heidelberg University in 1952. Forsthoff was the leading author of the *Constitution of Cyprus* and was president of the Supreme Constitutional Court of Cyprus from 1960 to 1963.

3. Traditionally the image of the Jew provided the metaphysical glue of national being. Schmitt's antisemitism is contested. Some say he inserted antisemitic formulations into his writings during Nazism in order to protect himself from Nazi persecution. On Schmitt's antisemitism, see Gross (2008).

4. On the Schmitt's notion of the *Regierungsstaat*, see also his *Legalität und Legitimität* (*Legality and Legitimacy*) (Schmitt 1988b). Eucken (1932, 307) refers to Schmitt's *Der Hüter der Verfassung – The Guardian of the Constitution* (Schmitt 1996b) as the authoritative account behind his argument. Hayek (1960, 485), too, refers to this text by Schmitt as the most learned and perspective analysis of the ills of Weimar democracy.

5. On the reconcilability of the competing social interests and irreconcilability of social antagonism, see chapter 2.

6. In this context Eucken writes about the 'economic state', which he defines with reference to Schmitt as a quantitatively total state (cf. Eucken 1932, 301 fn. 78, with Schmitt 1998). The economic state is a state of 'lamentable weakness'; it had lost its 'independence of will'.

7. Schmitt's account restates early arguments by Benjamin Constant. Constant conceived of the state as the political institution of private property and saw mass democracy as a danger to liberty. As he put it, '[i]f, to the freedom to use their talents and industry, which you owe them, you add political rights, which you do not owe them, these rights, in the hands of the greatest number, will inevitably serve to encroach upon property. . . . In all those countries which have representative assemblies it is essential that those assemblies, whatever their further organization, should be formed by property holders' (1988, 215).

8. This part draws on Marcuse (1988, 37).

9. This formulation derives from Böhm (1937, 150).

10. See also Müller-Armack (1933, 20–21, 31) argument for the total politicisation of society in the form of a unity between movement and leader who is himself not constrained by law. See also chapter 2.

11. Following Scheuerman (1999, 123), Schmitt endorsed 'the Nazi labor reforms of 1934' enthusiastically as 'the clearest expression of concrete order thinking'. The reforms stripped workers of 'basic workplace protection', reclassified them as 'disciples' (*Gefolgsschaft*) and introduced 'Leader (*Führer*) as concept of the legally unregulated leader'.

12. The final part draws on Cristi (1998, 162–165).

13. 'In a conflict between freedom and order, order is the unconditional priority' (Böhm 1937, 101).

14. This part draws on Streek's (2015) insightful account.

15. Primary legislation is directly applicable. Secondary legislation that has to do with regulative mechanisms of implementation might not be. The European Court of Justice established these principles by itself. In two landmark cases in 1963 and 1964 it ruled that the community constitutes a new legal order and that its laws therefore supersede national law. The ECJ is a stateless judicial institution that developed its own powers by activist interpretation of a stateless canon of law that cannot be overridden by parliamentary law in member states. It recognises as its subjects not only the member states but also their nationals. See, Craig and De Burca (2015).

16. For a systematic argument setting this out, see Hayek (1939) as discussed in chapter 6.

17. In the words of the former EU Competition Commissioner and former Italian prime minister Mario Monti, market is 'strikingly modern' term 'to which many policy choices can be traced back' (quoted in Dale and El-Enany 2013, 615, 616).

18. As Streek (2015, 366) put it, '[w]here there are still democratic institutions in Europe, there is no economic governance any more. . . . And where there *is* economic governance, democracy is elsewhere'.

19. Since the early 1990s state-centric critiques of globalisation, which advocated for a national Keynesianism, helped to revive nationalist perspectives as allegedly progressive in character. See Bonefeld (2006c) and Radice (2000).

20. The spectre of a Le Pen Presidency in France is most disconcerting.

21. 'Brexit' is a misnomer. It is an English projection of British peculiarity. Brexit was fed by impotent rage and pitiful delusions about 'land and sea' (Schmitt 2015). The one rejects the continent as a land-based power of rule-based and law-governed conduct; the other summons the buccaneering Palmerstonian spirit of old as a manifest destiny. For the English nationalist elite, the delusion of a long-lost empire as a sea-based commonwealth for private enrichment lingers on and informs its demagogy for British freedom. Impotent rage characterises the anti-EU revolt by the impoverished. After years of utter neglect and of being subjected to abject austerity, they had nothing to lose and gained the promise of further hardship.

Bibliography

Abelshausen, Werner. 1983. *Wirtschaftsgeschichte der Bundesrepublik Deutschland (1945–1980)*. Frankfurt: Suhrkamp.

Agnoli, Johannes. 1990. *Die Transformation der Demokratie und andere Schriften zur Kritik der Politik*. Freiburg: Ca Ira Verlag.

Agnoli, Johannes. 2003. 'Destruction as the Determination of the Scholar in Miserable Times'. In *Revolutionary Writing*, edited by Werner Bonefeld, 25–37. New York: Autonomedia.

Altmann, Rüdiger. 1960. *Das Erbe Adenauers*. Stuttgart: Seewald.

Ancil, Ralph E. 2012. 'Röpke and the Restauration of Property: The Proletarianized Market'. *The Imaginative Conservative*. Accessed 24 October 2016. www.theimaginativeconservative.org/2012/10/roepke-proletarianized-market.html.

Anderson, Perry. 1997. 'The Europe to Come'. In *The Question of Europe*, edited by Peter Gowan and Perry Anderson, 126–45. London: Verso.

Balogh, Thomas. 1950. *An Experiment in 'Planning' by the 'Free' Price Mechanism*. Oxford: Basil Blackwell.

Barry, Norman P. 1989. 'Political and Economic Thought of German Neoliberalism'. In *Germany Neoliberals and the Social Market Economy*, edited by Alan Peacock and Hans Willgerodt (with the assistance of Daniel Johnson), 105–24. London: Palgrave.

Beck, Ulrich. 2013. *German Europe*. Cambridge: Polity.

Becker, Gary. [1964] 1993. *Human Capital: A Theoretical and Empirical Analysis, with Special Reference to Education*. Chicago, IL: University of Chicago Press.

Bellamy, Richard. 2007. *Political Constitutionalism: A Republican Defence of the Constitutionality of Democracy*. Cambridge: Cambridge University Press.

Bengoetxea, Joxerramon. 2015. 'The Current European Crises: The End of Pluralism'? In *The Future of Europe. Democracy, Legitimacy and Justice after the Euro Crisis*, edited by Serge Champeau, Carlos Closa, Daniel Innerarity and Miguel Poaires Maduro, 57–73. London: Rowman & Littlefield.

171

Benjamin, Walter. [1921] 2007. 'Critique of Violence'. In *Reflections*, edited by Peter Demetz, 277–300. New York: Random House.

Bentin, Lutz Arwed. 1972. *Johannes Popitz und Carl Schmitt*. München: Beck.

Berghahn, Volker, and Brigitte Young. 2013. 'Reflections on Werner Bonefeld's "Freedom and the Strong State" and the Continuing Importance of the Ideas of Ordoliberalism to Understand Germany's (Contested) Role in Resolving the Euro-zone Crisis'. *New Political Economy* 187 (5): 768–78.

Bernholz, Peter. 1992. 'Constitutional Aspects of the European Integration'. In *The European Community after 1992*, edited by Silvio Borner and Herbert Grubel, 45–60. London: Palgrave.

Bernholz, Peter. 2013. 'The Slow and Hidden Road to Serfdom'. *Frankfurter Allgemeine Zeitung*. Accessed 21 March 2016. http://blogs.faz.net/fazit/2013/06/20/the-slow-and-hidden-road-to-serfdom-1933/.

Biebricher, Thomas. 2014. 'The Return of Ordoliberalism in Europe – Notes on a Research Agenda'. *i-lex* 9: 1–24.

Biebricher, Thomas. 2015. 'Neoliberalism and Democracy'. *Constellations* 22 (2): 255–66.

Blyth, Mark. 2013. *Austerity: The History of a Dangerous Idea*. Oxford: Oxford University Press.

Bofinger, Peter. 2016. 'German Macroeconomics: The Long Shadow of Walter Eucken'. *VOX Cerp's Policy Portal*. Accessed 9 June 2016. http://voxeu.org/article/german- macroeconomics-long-shadow-walter-eucken.

Böhm, Franz. 1933. *Wettbewerb und Monopolkampf*. Berlin: Heymann.

Böhm, Franz. 1936. 'Die Wirtschaftsordnung als Zentralbegriff des Wirtschafts-rechts'. *Mitteilungen des Jenaer Instituts für Wirtschaftsrecht* 31: 3–14.

Böhm, Franz. 1937. *Ordnung der Wirtschaft*. Berlin: Kohlhammer.

Böhm, Franz. 1950. 'Die Idee des ORDO im Denken Walter Euckens – Dem Freunde und Mitherausgeber zum Gedächnis'. *Ordo* 3: xc–lxiv.

Böhm, Franz. [1928] 1960. 'Das Problem der privaten Macht'. In *Reden und Schriften über die Ordnung einer freien Gesellschaft, einer freien Wirtschaft und über die Wiedergutmachung*, edited by Ernst Joachim Mestmäcker, 25–40. Karlsruhe: Müller.

Böhm, Franz. 1961. 'Demokratie und ökonomische Macht'. In *Kartelle und Mono-pole im modernen Recht*, edited by Institut für Ausländisches und Internationales Wirtschaftsrecht, 1–24. Karlsruhe: Müller.

Böhm, Franz. 1969. *Reden and Schriften*. Karlsruhe: Müller

Böhm, Franz. 1973. 'Die Kampfansage an Ordnungstheorie und Ordnungspolitik. Zu einem Aufstaz im Kyklos'. *Ordo* 24: 11–48.

Böhm, Franz. [1950] 1980a. 'Wirtschaftsordnung und Staatsverfassung'. In *Frei-heit und Ordnung in der Marktwirtschaft*, edited by Ernst Joachim Mestmäcker, 53–103. Baden-Baden: Nomos.

Böhm, Franz. [1958] 1980b. 'Wettbewerbsfreiheit und Kartellfreiheit'. In *Freiheit und Ordnung in der Marktwirtschaft*, edited by Ernst Joachim Mestämcker, 233–62. Baden-Baden: Nomos.

Böhm, Franz. [1966] 2010. 'Extracts from Franz Böhm: "Private Law Society and Market Economy"'. In *The Theory of Capitalism in the German Economic*

Tradition, edited by Peter Koslowski, 148–88. Berlin: Springer. [Truncated translation is also available in *Germany's Social Market Economy: Origins and Evolution*, edited by Alan Peacock and Hans Willgerodt, 46–67 (London: Palgrave, 1989).]

Böhm, Franz, Walter Eucken and Hans Grossmann-Doerth. [1936] 1989. 'The Ordo Manifesto of 1936'. In *Germany's Social Market Economy: Origins and Evolution*, edited by Alan Peacock and Hans Willgerodt, 15–26. London: Palgrave.

Bonefeld, Werner. 1993. *The Recomposition of the British State during the 1980s*. Aldershot: Dartmouth.

Bonefeld, Werner. 1995. 'The Politics of Debt'. *Common Sense* 17: 69–91.

Bonefeld, Werner. 2000. 'The Spectre of Globalization'. In *The Politics of Change. Globalization, Ideology and Critique*, edited by Werner Bonefeld and Kosmas Psychopedis, 31–68. London: Palgrave.

Bonefeld, Werner. 2005. 'Europe, the Market and the Transformation of Democracy'. *Journal of Contemporary European Studies* 13 (1): 93–106.

Bonefeld, Werner. 2006a. 'Democracy and Dictatorship'. *Critique* 34 (3): 237–52.

Bonefeld, Werner. 2006b. 'Human Progress and Capitalist Development'. In Andreas Bieler, Werner Bonefeld, Peter Burnham and Adam Morton, *Global Restructuring, State, Capital and Labour*, 133–52. London: Palgrave.

Bonefeld, Werner. 2006c. 'Anti-Globalisation and the Question of Socialism'. *Critique* 34 (1): 39–59.

Bonefeld, Werner. 2011. 'Primitive Accumulation and Capitalist Accumulation'. *Science & Society* 35 (3): 379–99.

Bonefeld, Werner. 2013. 'Human Economy and Social Policy'. *History of Human Sciences* 26 (2): 106–25.

Bonefeld, Werner. 2014. *Critical Theory and the Critique of Political Economy*. London: Bloomsbury.

Bonefeld, Werner. 2015. 'Big Society and Political State'. *British Politics* 10 (4): 413–28.

Bonefeld, Werner, and Peter Burnham. 1998. 'The Politics of Counter-Inflationary Credibility in Britain, 1990–1994'. *Review of Radical Political Economics* 30 (1): 30–52.

Borrell, Josep. 2015. 'About the Democratic Governance of the Euro: How the Crisis Is Changing Europe'. In *The Future of Europe. Democracy, Legitimacy and Justice after the Euro Crisis*, edited by Serge Champeau, Carlos Closa, Daniel Innerarity and Miguel Poaires Maduro, 235–45. London: Rowman & Littlefield.

Brennan, Geoffrey, and James M. Buchanan. 1980. *The Power to Tax*. Cambridge: Cambridge University Press.

Brennan, Geoffrey, and James M. Buchanan. 2000. *The Reason of Rules: Constitutional Economics*. Indianapolis: Liberty Fund.

Brittan, Samuel. 1976. 'The Economic Contradictions of Democracy'. In *Why Is Britain Harder to Govern?* edited by Anthony King, 96–137. London: BBC Books.

Brittan, Samuel. 1977. *The Economic Consequences of Democracy*. London: Temple Smith.

Brittan, Samuel. 1984. 'The Politics and Economics of Privatisation'. *Political Quarterly* 55 (2): 109–28.

Brittan, Samuel. 1986. 'Privatisation: A Comment on Kay and Thompson'. *Economic Journal* 96 (1): 33–38.

Brittan, Samuel. 2004. 'Hayek, Friedrich August (1899–1992)'. In *Oxford Dictionary of National Biography*, edited by Leslie Stephen, Sidney Lee and Christine Nicholls. Oxford: Oxford University Press. Accessed 24 October 2016. http://www. oxforddnb.com/index/51/101051095/.

Brunkhorst, Hauke. 2014. *Das Doppelte Gesicht Europas*. Berlin: Suhrkamp.

Buchanan, James M. 1990. 'The Domain of Constitutional Economics'. *Constitutional Political Economy* 1: 1–18.

Buchanan, James M., and Gordon Tullock. 1962. *The Calculus of Consent – Logical Foundations of Constitutional Democracy*. Ann Arbor, MI: University of Michigan Press.

Buchanan, James M., and Richard E. Wagner. 1977. *Democracy in Deficit – The Political Legacy of Lord Keynes*. New York: Academy Press.

Buchanan, James. M., and Richard E. Wagner, eds. 1978. *Fiscal Responsibility in Constitutional Democracy*. Boston: Martinus Nijhoff.

Bulmer, Simon. 2014. 'Germany and the Eurozone Crisis: Between Hegemony and Domestic Politics'. *West European Politics* 37 (6): 1244–63.

Bulmer, Simon, and Jonathan Joseph. 2016. 'European Integration in Crisis? Of Supranational Integration, Hegemonic Projects and Domestic Politics'. *European Journal of International Relations* 22 (4): 725–48.

Bulmer, Simon, and William Paterson. 2013. 'Germany as the EU's Reluctant Hegemon? Of Economic Strength and Political Constraints'. *Journal of European Public Policy* 20 (10): 1387–405.

Burgin, Angus. 2012. *The Great Persuasion: Reinventing Free Markets since the Great Depression*. Cambridge, MA: Harvard University Press.

Burnham, Peter. 1995. 'Capital, Crisis and the International State System'. In *Global Capital and National State*, edited by Werner Bonefeld and John Holloway, 92–115. London: Palgrave.

Burnham, Peter. 2001. 'New Labour and the Politics of Depoliticisation'. *British Journal of Politics and International Relations* 3 (2): 127–49.

Burnham, Peter. 2014. 'Depoliticisation: Economic Crisis and Political Management'. *Policy & Politics* 42 (2): 189–206.

Campbell, William F. 2002. 'Wilhelm Röpke and the City of Man'. Introduction to the Transaction Edition of Willelm Röpke, *The Moral Foundation of Civil Society*, ix–xxvi. New Brunswick, NJ: Transaction Publishers.

Carchedi, Guglielmo. 2001. 'The EMU, Monetary Crises, and the Single European Currency'. In *The Politics of Europe, Monetary Union and Class*, edited by Werner Bonefeld, 37–63. London: Palgrave.

Cassel, Dieter, and Siegfried Rauhut. 1999. 'Soziale Marktwirtschaft: Eine wirtschaftspolitische Konzeption auf dem Prüfstand'. In *50 Jahre Sozial Marktwirtschaft*, edited by Dieter Cassel, 3–31. Stuttgard: Lucius & Lucius.

Cerny, Phil. 1997. 'Paradoxes of the Competition State: The Dynamic of Political Globalization'. *Government and Opposition* 32 (2): 251–74.

Charnock, Greig. 2014. 'Lost in Space? Lefebvre, Harvey, and the Spatiality of Negation'. *South Atlantic Quarterly* 113 (2): 313–26.

Charnock, Greg, Thomas Purcell, and Ramon Ribera-Fumas. 2014. *The Limits to Capital in Spain*. London: Palgrave.

Clarke, Simon. 1988. *Keynesianism, Monetarism and the Crisis of the State*. Aldershot: Edward Elgar.

Clarke, Simon. 1992a. 'The Global Accumulation of Capital and the Periodisation of the Capitalist State'. In *Open Marxism*, volume I, edited by Werner Bonefeld, Richard Gunn and Kosmas Psychopedis, 133–50. London: Pluto.

Clarke, Simon. 1992b. *Marx, Marginalism and Modern Sociology*. London: Palgrave.

Constant, Benjamin. 1998. *Political Writings*. Cambridge: Cambridge University Press.

Craig, Paul, and Grainne De Burca. 2015. *EU Law. Text, Cases and Materials*. Oxford: Oxford University Press.

Cristi, Renato. 1998. *Carl Schmitt and Authoritarian Liberalism*. Cardiff: University of Wales Press.

Crozier, Michel, et al. 1975. *The Crisis of Democracy*. New York: New York University Press.

Currie, David. 2000. 'EMU: Threats and Opportunities for Companies and National Economies'. In *The Impact of the Euro*, edited by Mark Baimbridge, Brian Burkett and Philip Whyman, 113–38. London: Palgrave.

Dale, Garreth, and Nadine El-Enany. 2013. 'The Limits of Social Europe: EU Law and the Ordoliberal Agenda'. *German Law Journal* 40 (5): 613–49.

Dardot, Pierre, and Christian Laval. 2013. *The New Way of the World: On Neoliberal Society*. London: Verso.

Davies, William. 2015. 'The Return of Social Government: From "Socialist Calculation" to "Social Analytics"'. *European Journal of Social Theory* 18 (4): 431–50.

De Gaulle, Charles. 1971. *Memoirs of Hope: Renewal and Endeavour*. London: Simon and Schuster.

Dinerstein, Ana, and Mike Neary, eds. 2002. *The Labour Debate*. Aldershot: Ashgate.

Director, Aaron, and Edward Hirsch Levi. 1956. 'Trade Regulation'. *Northwestern University Law Review* 51: 281–96.

Eichengreen, Barry. 1995. *Golden Fetters: The Gold Standard and the Great Depression, 1919–1939*. Oxford: Oxford University Press.

Eltis, Walter. 2000. 'British EMU Membership Would Create Instability and Destroy Employment'. In *The Impact of the Euro*, edited by Mark Baimbridge, Brian Burkett and Philip Whyman, 139–59. London: Palgrave.

Emerson, Michael. 1992. *One Market, One Money*. Oxford: Oxford University Press.

Engel, Christoph. 2003. 'Imposed Liberty and Its Limits'. In *Spontaneous Order, Organization and the Law: Roads to a European Civil Society*, edited by Talia Einhorn, 429–37. The Hague: Asser Press.

Erhard, Ludwig. 1958. *Prosperity through Competition*. London: Thames & Hudson.

Eucken, Walter. 1932. 'Staatliche Strukturwandlungen und die Krise des Kapitalismus'. *Weltwirtschaftliches Archiv* 36: 297–321.

Eucken, Walter. 1952. *This Unsuccessful Age*. London: Hodge.

Eucken, Walter. [1937] 1959. *Die Grundlagen der Nationalökonomie*. Berlin: Springer.

Eucken, Walter. [1948] 1989. 'What Kind of Economic and Social System'? In *Germany's Social Market Economy: Origins and Evolution*, edited by Alan Peacock and Hans Willgerodt, 27–45. London: Palgrave.

Eucken, Walter. [1952] 2004. *Grundsätze der Wirtschaftspolitik*. Tübingen: Mohr Siebert.

Everson, Michelle. 1995. 'Economic Rights within the European Union'. In *Democracy and Constitutional Culture in the Union of Europe*, edited by Richard Bellamy, Vittorio Bufacchi and Dario Castiglione, 137–52. London: Lothian Foundation Press.

Everson, Michelle, and Christian Jörges. June 2013. 'Who Is the Guardian for Constitutionalism in Europe after the Financial Crisis'? *LSE Europe in Question Discussion Paper Series* 63.

Farrant, Andrew, Edward McPhail and Sebastian Berger. 2012. 'Preventing the "Abuses" of Democracy: Hayek, the "Military Usurper" and Transitional Dictatorship in Chile'? *The American Journal of Economics and Sociology* 71 (3): 513–38.

Feld, Lars. 2012. 'Europa in der Welt von heute: Wilhelm Röpke und die Zukunft der Europäischen Währungsunion'. *ORDO* 63: 429–48.

Feld, Lars, and Ekkehard Köhler. 2011. 'Zur Zukunft der Ordnungsökonomie'. Freiburg Discussion Papers on Constitutional Economics 11/2. Freiburg: Walter Eucken Institut.

Feld, Lars, Ekkehard Köhler, and Daniel Nientiedt. 2015. 'Ordoliberalism, Pragmatism and the Eurozone Crisis: How the German Tradition Shaped Economic Policy in Europe'. *European Review of International Studies* 2 (3): 48–61.

Ferrero, Guglielmo. 1963. *The Reconstruction of Europe: Talleyrand and the Congress of Vienna, 1814–1815*. New York: Norton.

Fine, Robert. 2002. *Democracy and the Rule of Law*. Caldwell, NJ: The Blackburn Press.

Flassbeck, Heiner, and Costas Lapavitsas. 2015. *Against the Troika: Crisis and Austerity in the Eurozone*. London: Verso.

Forststoff, Ernst. 1933a. *Das Ende der humanistischen Illusion*. Berlin: Furche-Verlag.

Forsthoff, Ernst. 1933b. *Der totale Staat*. Hamburg: Hanseatische Verlags-Anstalt.

Foucault, Michel. 1991. 'Governmentality'. In *The Foucault Effect: Studies in Governmentality*, edited by Graham Burchell, Colin Gordon and Peter Miller, 87–104. London: Harvester Wheatsheaf.

Foucault, Michel. 1997. *Ethics: Subjectivity and Truth*. London: Penguin.

Foucault, Michel. 2008. *The Birth of Biopolitics*. London: Palgrave.

Fried, Ferdinand. 1950. *Der Umsturz der Gesellschaft*. Stuttgart: Union Deutsche Verlagsgesellschaft.

Friedman, Milton. 1951. 'Neo-Liberalism and Its Prospects'. *Farmand* 17: 89–93.

Friedman, Milton. 1962. *Capitalism and Freedom*. Chicago, IL: University of Chicago Press.

Friedman, Milton. 1976. 'The Fragility of Freedom'. In *Milton Friedman in South Africa*, edited by Meyer Feldberg, Kate Jowell and Stephen Mulholland. Cape Town and Johannesburg: Graduate School of Business of the University of Cape Town and the Sunday Times. Electronic copy version accessed 21 September 2016. http://0055d26. netsolhost.com/friedman/pdfs/other_commentary/SundayTimes.1976. 4.pdf.

Friedrich, Carl. 1955. 'The Political Thought of Neo-Liberalism'. *The American Political Science Review* 49 (2): 509–25.

Friedrich, Carl. [1941] 1968. *Constitutional Government and Democracy; Theory and Practice in Europe and America*. London: Blaisdell Publishing.

Gamble, Andrew. 1979. 'The Free Economy and the Strong State'. In *Socialist Register 1979*, edited by Ralph Miliband and John Saville, 1–25. London: Merlin Press.

Gamble, Andrew. 1988. *The Free Economy and the Strong State*. London: Palgrave.

Garrett, Geoffrey. 1994. 'The Politics of Maastricht'. In *The Political Economy of European Monetary Unification*, edited by Barry Eichengreen and Jeffry Frieden, 111–29. Boulder, CO: Westview.

Gerber, David. 1994. 'Constitutionalising the Economy: German Neo-Liberalism, Competition Law and the "new" Europe'. *American Journal of Comparative Law* 42 (1): 25–74.

Gerber, David. 1998. *Law and Competition in the Twentieth Century Europe: Protecting Prometheus*. Oxford: Oxford University Press.

Giddens, Anthony. 1998. *The Third Way*. Cambridge: Polity.

Gill, Stephen. 2013. *Power and Resistance in the New World Order*. London: Palgrave.

Glasman, Maurice. 1996. *Unnecessary Suffering*. London: Verso.

Grahl, John. 1997. *After Maastricht*. London: Lawrence & Wishart.

Grahl, John, and Paul Teague. 1990. *1992 – The Big Market. The Future of the European Community*. London: Lawrence & Wishart.

Gregg, Samuel. 2014. 'An Economist of Our Time'. Introduction to the paperback edition of Wilhelm Röpke, *The Human Economy*, vii–xvi. Wilmington, DE: ISI Books.

Grimm, Robert. 2015. 'The Rise of the German Eurosceptic Party Alternative für Deutschland, between Ordoliberal Critique and Popular Anxiety'. *International Political Science Review* 36 (3): 264–78.

Gross, Raphael. 2008. *Carl Schmitt and the Jews*. Madison, WI: University of Wisconsin Press.

Habermas, Jürgen. 2011. 'A Pact for or against Europe'? In *What Does Germany Think about Europe?*, edited by Ulrike Guerot and Jacqueline Henard, 83–89. London: European Council on Foreign Relations.

Habermas, Jürgen. 2012. *The Crisis of European Union*. Cambridge: Polity.

Habermas, Jürgen. 2015. *The Lure of Technocracy*. Cambridge: Polity.

Hallstein, Walter. 1972. *Europe in the Making*. London: Georg Allen & Unwin.

Haselbach, Dieter. 1991. *Autoritärer Liberalismus und Soziale Marktwirtschaft*. Baden-Baden: Nomos.

Haselbach, Dieter. 1994. '"Soziale Marktwirtschaft" als Gründungsmythos. Zur Identitätsbildung im Nachkriegsdeutschland'. In *Zwischen Traum und Trauma*, edited by Claudia Mayer-Iswandy, 255–66. Tübingen: Stauffenburg.

Hayek, Friedrich. 1939. 'The Economic Conditions of Interstate Federalism'. *New Commonwealth Quarterly* 5 (2): 130–49. Reprinted in Friedrich Hayek. 1949. *Individualism and Economic Order*, 255–73. London: Routledge and Kegan Paul.

Hayek, Friedrich. 1944. *The Road to Serfdom*. London: Routledge.

Hayek, Friedrich. 1949. *Individualism and Economic Order*. London: Routledge and Kegan Paul.

Hayek, Friedrich. 1960. *The Constitution of Liberty*. London: Routledge.

Hayek, Friedrich. 1972. *A Tiger by the Tail*. London: London Institute of Economic Affairs.

Hayek, Friedrich. 1976. 'Socialism and Science'. *A Lecture Delivered to the Economic Society of Australia and New Zealand*. Accessed 25 October 2016. https://ipa. org.au/library/publication/1213763502_document_review30- 4_hayek_socialism_ science.pdf.

Hayek, Friedrich. 1978. *Denationalization of Money. The Argument Refined*. Hobart Paper 70. London: Institute of Economic Affairs.

Hayek, Friedrich. 1979. *Law, Legislation and Liberty*. London: Routledge.

Hayek, Friedrich. 2013. *The Fatal Conceit. The Errors of Socialism*. London: Routledge.

Hegel, Georg W.F. 1932. *Jenenser Realphilosophie*. Leipzig: Meiner.

Hegel, Georg W.F. 1967. *Philosophy of Right*. Oxford: Clarendon Press.

Heller, Hermann. [1933] 2015. 'Authoritarian Liberalism'. *European Law Journal* 21 (3): 295–301.

Hildebrand, Rainer. 2015. 'Germany and Its Eurozone Crisis Policy: The Impact of the Country's Ordoliberal Heritage'. *German Politics and Society* 33 (1–2): 6–24.

Hirsch, Joachim. 1991. *Der Sicherheitsstaat*. Frankfurt: Europäische Verlagsanstalt.

Hirsch, Joachim. 1995. *Der nationale Wettbewerbsstaat*. Berlin: Id-Verlag.

Hirschman, Albert. 1977. *The Passions and the Interests*. Princeton, NJ: Princeton University Press.

Hix, Simon. 1999. *The Political System of the European Union*. London: Palgrave.

Holloway, John. 1995a. 'Global Capital and the National State'. In *Global Capital, National Sate and the Politics of Money*, edited by Werner Bonefeld and John Holloway, 116–40. London: Palgrave.

Holloway, John. 1995b. 'The Abyss Opens: The Rise and Fall of Keynesianism'. In *Global Capital, National Sate and the Politics of Money*, edited by Werner Bonefeld and John Holloway, 7–34. London: Palgrave.

Hunt, Kay. 2003. *Property and Prophets. On the Evolution of Economic Institutions and Ideologies*. Armonck, NY: M.E. Sharp.

Hutchinson, Terrence. 1981. *The Politics and Philosophy of Economics*. Oxford: Basil Blackwell.

IMF (International Monetary Fund). 2010. 'Concluding Statement of the IMF Mission on Euro-Area Politics'. Accessed 15 May 2016. www.imf.org/external/np/ ms/2010/0600710a.htm.

Jackson, Ben. 2010. 'At the Origins of Neo-Liberalism: The Free Economy and the Strong State, 1930–1947'. *The Historical Journal* 53 (1): 129–51.

Jacobi, Lena, and Jochen Kluve. 2006. *Before and after the Hartz Reforms: The Performance of Active Labour Market Policy in Germany*. Discussion Paper No. 2100. Bonn: Forschungsinstitut zur Zukunft der Arbeit.

Jessop, Bob. 1993. 'Towards a Schumpeterian Workfare State'? *Studies in Political Economy* 40: 7–39.

Jessop, Bob. 2010. 'The "Return" of the National State in the Current Crisis of the World Market'. *Capital & Class* 34 (1): 38–43.

Jessop, Bob. 2014. 'Variegated Capitalism, das Modell Deutschland and the Euro-zone Crisis'. *Journal of Contemporary European Studies* 22 (3): 248–60.

Jevons, William Stanley. [1871] 1988. *The Theory of Political Economy*. Accessed 30 August 2016. http://www.econlib.org/library/YPDBooks/Jevons/jvnPE.html.

Jörges, Christian. 2005. 'What Is Left of the European Economic Constitution? A Melancholic Eulogy'. *European Law Review* 30 (4): 461–89.

Jörges, Christian. 2014. 'Europe's Economic Constitution in Crisis and the Emergence of a New Constitutional Constellation'. In *The European Union in Crises or the European Union as Crisis*, edited by John Eric Fossum and Agustin Jose Menendez, 279–334. Oslo: ARENA, Centre for European Studies.

Jörges, Christian. 2016a. 'Pereat Iustitia, Fiat Mundus: What Is Left of the European Economic Constitution after the Gauweiler Litigation'. *Maastricht Journal of European and Comparative Law* 23 (1): 99–118.

Jörges, Christian. 2016b. 'What is left of the European Economic Constitution II?: From Pyrrhic Victory to Cannae Defeat'. In *Critical Theories of Crisis in Europe: From Weimar to the Euro*, edited by Poul F. Kjaer and Niklas Olsen, 143–160. London: Rowman & Littlefield.

Jörges, Christian, and Maria Weimer. 2014. 'A Crisis of Executive Managerialism in the EU: No Alternative'. In *Critical Legal Perspectives on Global Governance. Liber Amicorum for David M Trubek*, edited by Grainne de Burca, Claire Kilpatrick and Joanne Scott, 295–322. Oxford: Hart.

Joseph, Keith. 1975. *Freedom and Order*. London: Centre for Policy Studies.

Joseph, Keith, and Jonathan Sumption. 1979. *Equality*. London: John Murray.

Kant, Immanuel. 1971. *Political Writings*. Cambridge: Cambridge University Press.

Karacimen, Elif. 2014. 'Interlinkages between Credit, Debt and the Labour Market: Evidence from Turkey'. *Cambridge Journal of Economics* 39 (3): 751–67.

Kelsen, Hans. [1934] 2009. *Pure Theory of Law*. Clark, NJ: The Lawbook Exchange.

Kerber, Wolfgang, and Viktor Vanberg. 2001. 'Constitutional Aspects of Party Autonomy and Its Limits – The Perspective of Constitutional Economics'. In *Party Autonomy and the Role of Information in the Internal Market*, edited by Stefan Grundmann, Wolfgang Kerber and Stephen Weatherill, 49–79. Berlin: Walter de Gruyter.

Kiely, Ray. 2016. 'From Authoritarian Liberalism to Economic Technocracy: Neoliberalism, Politics and "De-democratization"'. *Critical Sociology*, Onlinefirst. doi: 10.1177/0896920516668386.

King, Anthony. 1976. 'The Problem of Overload'. In *Why Is Britain Harder to Govern?* edited by Anthony King, 8–30. London: BBC Books.

Kirkpatrick, Jean. November 1979. 'Dictatorship & Double Standards'. *Commentary Magazine* 1. Accessed 10 October 2016. https://www.commentarymagazine.com/articles/dictatorships-double-standards/.

Klincewicz, Krzysztof. 2010. 'Discussion Summary – Christian Watrin: Alfred Müller-Armack – Economic Policy-Maker and Sociologist of Religion'. In *The Theory of Capitalism in the German Economic Tradition*, edited by Peter Koslowski, 221–23. Berlin: Springer.

Koch, Eckart. 2003. 'Money, Civil Law and European Integration'. In *Spontaneous Order, Organization and the Law*, edited by Talia Einhorn. 229–39. The Hague: Asser Press.

Koslowski, Peter, ed. 2010. *The Theory of Capitalism in the German Economic Tradition*. Berlin: Springer.

Lapavitsas, Costas. 2012. *Crisis in the Eurozone*. London: Verso.

Lazzarato, Maurizio. 2012. *The Making of Indebted Man*. Cambridge, MA: MIT Press.

Lemke, Thomas. 1997. *Eine Kritik der politischen Vernunft: Foucaults Analyse der modernen Gouvernementatlität*. Hamburg: Argument Verlag.

Lenel, Hans Otto. 1989. 'Evolution of the Social Market Economy'. In *German Neoliberals and the Social Market Economy*, edited by Alan Peacock and Hans Willgerodt (with the assistance of Daniel Johnson), 16–39. London: Palgrave.

MaCartney, Huw. 2013. *The Debt Crisis and European Democratic Legitimacy*. London: Palgrave.

MaCartney, Huw. 2014. 'The Paradox of Integration'. *Cambridge Review of International Affairs* 27 (2): 401–23.

MacCormick, Neil. 1995. 'Sovereignty, Democracy and Subsidiarity'. In *Democracy and Constitutional Culture in the Union of Europe*, edited by Richard Bellamy, Vittorio Bufacchi and Dario Castiglione, 95–104. London: Lothian Foundation Press.

MacCormick, Neil. 1999. *Questioning Sovereignty*. Oxford: Oxford University Press.

Manow, Phillip. 2001. 'Ordoliberalismus als ökonomische Ordungstheologie'. *Leviathan* 29: 179–98.

Manow, Phillip. 2008. *Religion und Sozialstaat. Die konfessionellen Grundlagen europäischer Wohlfahrtsregime*. Frankfurt: Campus.

Marbach, Fritz. 1965. 'Zur Frage wirtschaftlicher Macht'. In *Vom Sinn der Konzentration*, edited by Hermann Josef Abs and Volkmar Muthesius, 19–29. Frankfurt: Knapp.

Marcuse, Herbert. [1934] 1988. 'The Struggle against Liberalism in the Totalitarian View of the State'. In *Negations*, 3–42. London: Free Association Books.

Marx, Karl. [1858] 1973. *Grundrisse*. London: Penguin.

Marx, Karl. [1845] 1975. *The Holy Family*. Moscow: Progress Publishers.

Marx, Karl. [1857–1858] 1987. *From the Preparatory Materials*. In Marx Engels Collected Works 29. London: Lawrence & Wishart.

Marx, Karl. [1867] 1990. *Capital*, volume I. London: Penguin.

Marx, Karl, and Friedrich Engels. [1846] 1976. *The German Ideology*. In Marx Engels Collected Works 5. London: Lawrence & Wishart.

Marx, Karl, and Friedrich Engels. [1848] 1996. *The Communist Manifesto*. London: Pluto.

Maus, Ingeborg. 1976. *Bürgerliche Rechtstheorie und Faschismus. Zur sozialen Funktion und aktuellen Wirkung der Theorie Carl Schmitts*. München: Wihlhelm Fink Verlag.

May, Christopher. 2014. *The Rule of Law: The Common Sense of Global Politics*. Aldershot: Edward Elgar.

McAllister, Richard. 2009. *From EC to EU*. London: Routledge.

Menger, Carl. [1883] 1963. *Problems of Economics and Sociology*. Urbana, IL: University of Illinois Press.

Mestmäcker, Ernst-Joachim. 1993. *Recht in der offenen Gesellschaft*. Baden-Baden: Nomos.

Mestmäcker, Ernst-Joachim. 2003. *Wirtschaft und Verfassung in der Europäischen Union: Beiträge zur Rechtstheorie und Politik der Europäischen Integration*. Baden-Baden: Nomos.

Mestmäcker, Ernst-Joachim. 2007a. *A Legal Theory without Law*. In *Beiträge zur Rechtstheorie und Politik der Europäischen Integration* 174, edited by Walter Eucken Institut. Tübingen: Mohr Siebeck.

Mestmäcker, Ernst-Joachim. 2007b. 'European Touchstones of Dominion and Law'. *ORDO* 58: 3–16.

Middlemas, Keith. 1995. *Orchestrating Europe*. London: Fontana.

Miksch, Leonard. 1947. *Wettbewerb als Aufgabe. Grundsätze einer Wettbewerbsordnung*. Bad Godesberg: Kuepper.

Mirowski, Philip. 2013. *Never Let a Serious Crisis Go to Waste*. London: Verso.

Mirowski, Philip, and Dieter Plehwe. eds. 2009. *The Road from Mont Pélerin*. Cambridge, MA: Harvard University Press.

Molle, Willem. 1990. *The Economics of European Integration*. Aldershot: Dartmouth.

Möschel, Wernhard. 1989. 'Competition Policy from an Ordo Point of View'. In *German Neo-Liberals and the Social Market Economy*, edited by Alan Peacock and Hans Willgerodt (with the assistance of Daniel Johnson), 142–59. London: Palgrave.

Möschel, Wernhard. 2003. 'Competition as a Basic Element of the Social Market Economy'. In *Spontaneous Order, Organization and the Law: Roads to a European Civil Society*, edited by Talia Einhorn, 285–93. The Hague: Asser Press.

Moss, Bernie. 2000. 'The European Community as Monetarist Construction'. *Journal of European Area Studies* 8 (2): 247–65.

Mouffe, Chantal. 1999. *The Challenge of Carl Schmitt*. London: Verso.

Müller, Jan-Werner. 2011. *Contesting Democracy: Political Ideas in the Twentieth Century*. New Haven, CT: Yale University Press.

Müller, Jan-Werner. 2012. 'Militant Democracy'. In *Oxford Handbook of Comparative Constitutional Law*, edited by Michel Rosenfeld and Andras Sajo, 253–69. Oxford: Oxford University Press.

Müller, Jan-Werner. 2014. 'Who Is the European Prince?'. *Social Research: An International Quarterly* 81 (1): 243–67.

Müller-Armack, Alfred. 1932. *Entwicklungsgesetze des Kapitalismus*. Berlin: Junker & Dünnhaupt.

Müller-Armack, Alfred. 1933. *Staatsidea und Wirtschaftsordnung im neuen Reich*. Berlin: Junker & Dünnhaupt.

Müller-Armack, Alfred. 1947a. *Wirtschaftslenkung und Marktwirtschaft*. Hamburg: Verlag für Wirtschaft und Sozialpolitik.

Müller-Armack, Alfred. 1947b. 'Die Wirtschaftsordnungen sozial gesehen'. *ORDO* 1: 125–55.

Müller-Armack, Alfred. 1947c. 'Soziale Markwirtschaft'. *Wirtschaftsspiegel* 2: 480–84.

Müller-Armack, Alfred. 1955. 'Wirtschaftspolitik in der sozialen Marktwirtschaft'. In *Der Christ und die Soziale Marktwirtschaft*, edited by Patrick M. Boarman, 75–99. Stuttgart: Kohlhammer.

Müller-Armack, Alfred. 1956. 'Soziale Marktwirtschaft'. In *Handbuch der Sozial-wissenschaften*, volume 9, edited by Erwin von Beckerath and Carl Brinkman, 390–92. Stuttgart: Fischer.

Müller-Armack, Alfred. 1960. *Studien zur sozialen Marktwirtschaft*. Köln: Institut für Wirtschaftspolitik.

Müller-Armack, Alfred. 1971. *Auf dem Weg nach Europa. Erinnerungen und Aus-blicke*. Tübingen: Wunderlich.

Müller-Armack, Alfred. 1976. *Wirtschaftsordnung und Wirtschaftspolitik*. Stuttgart: Paul Haupt.

Müller-Armack, Alfred. 1978. 'The Social Market Economy as an Economic and Social Order'. *Review of Social Economy* 36 (3): 325–31.

Müller-Armack, Alfred. 1979. 'Thirty Years of Social Market Economy'. In *Economy and Development*, edited by Josef Thesing, 146–62. Mainz: Hase und Köhler.

Müller-Armack, Alfred. 1981a. *Diagnose unserer Gegenwart*. Stuttgart: Paul Haupt.

Müller-Armack, Alfred. 1981b. *Genealogie der Sozialen Marktwirtschaft*. Stuttgart: Paul Haupt.

Müller-Armack, Alfred. 1981c. *Religion und Marktwirtschaft*. Stuttgart: Paul Haupt.

Müller-Armack, Alfred. 1989. 'The Meaning of the Social Market Economy'. In *Germany's Social Market Economy: Origins and Evolution*, edited by Alan Peacock and Hans Willgerodt (with the assistance of Daniel Johnson), 82–86. London: Palgrave.

Nedergaard, Peter, and Holly Snaith. 2015. 'As I Drifted on a River I Could Not Control: The Unintended Ordoliberal Consequences of the Eurozone Crisis'. *Journal of Common Market Studies* 53 (5): 1094–109.

Nicholls, Anthony. 1994. *Freedom with Responsibility*. Oxford: Oxford University Press.

Norman, Jesse. 2010. *The Big Society*. London: University of Buckingham Press.

Nörr, Knut Wolfgang. 2003. 'Economic Power: A Productive Concept for the Law'? In *Spontaneous Order, Organization and the Law*, edited by Tania Einhorn. 295–310. The Hague: Asser Press.

Nörr, Knut Wolfgang. 2010. 'Franz Böhm and the Theory of the Private Law Society'. In *The Theory of Capitalism in the German Economic Tradition*, edited by Peter Koslowski, 148–60. Berlin: Springer.

Oberndorfer, Lukas. 2012. 'Die Renaissance des autoritären Liberalismus? – Carl Schmitt und der deutsche Neoliberalismus'. *PROKLA* 168: 413–31.

Oberndorfer, Lukas. 2015. 'From New Constitutionalism to Authoritarian Constitutionalism: New Economic Governance and the State of European democracy'. In *Asymmetric Crisis in Europe and Possible Futures*, edited by Johannes Jäger and Elisabeth Springler, 186–207. London: Routledge.

Ojala, Markus, and Timo Harjuniemi. 2016. 'Mediating the German Ideology: Ordoliberal Framing in European Press Coverage of the Eurozone Crisis'. *Journal of Contemporary European Studies* 24 (3): 414–30.

Opitz, Reinhard. 1965. 'Der grosse Plan der CDU: die "Formierte Gesellschaft"'. *Blätter für internationale und deutsche Politik* 10: 750–77.

Ortega y Gasset, Jose. [1930] 1994. *The Revolt of the Masses*. New York: Norton.

Oswalt, Walter. 2012. 'Die falschen Freunde der offenen Gesellschaft'. In Walter Eucken, *Wirtschaftsmacht und Wirschaftsordnung*, 87–152. Münster: LIT Verlag.

Padoa-Schioppa, Tomasso. 1994. *The Road to Monetary Union*. Oxford: Clarendon Press.

Parboni, Ricardo. 1981. *The Dollar and Its Rivals*. London: Verso.

Pashukanis, Evgeny. [1924] 1987. *The General Theory of Law and Marxism*. London: Pluto.

Peacock, Alan, and Hans Willgerodt. 1989. 'Preface'. In *German Neo-Liberals and the Social Market Economy*, edited by Alan Peacock and Hans Willgerodt (with the assistance of Daniel Johnson), xvii–xviii. London: Palgrave.

Peacock, Alan, and Hans Willgerodt, eds. 1989. *German Neo-Liberals and the Social Market Economy*. London: Palgrave.

Peck, Jamie. 2010. *Constructions of Neoliberal Reason*. Oxford: Oxford University Press.

Peukert, Helge. 2009. 'Wilhelm Röpke als Pionier einer ökologischen Ökonomik'. In *Wort und Wirkung: Wilhelm Röpkes Bedeutung für die Gegenwart*, edited by Heinz Rieter and Joachim Zweynert, 123–62. Marburg: Metropolis.

Peukert, Helge. 2010. 'Walter Eucken (1891–1950) and the Historical School'. In *The Theory of Capitalism in the German Economic Tradition*, edited by Peter Koslowski, 93–145. Berlin: Springer.

Pinder, John. 1968. 'Positive and Negative Integration: Some Problems of Economic Union in the EEC'. *The World Today* 24 (3): 88–110.

Popper, Karl. [1957] 2002. *The Poverty of Historicism*. London: Routledge.

Posner, Richard. 2003. *Law, Pragmatism, and Democracy*. Cambridge, MA: Harvard University Press.

Postone, Moishe. 1993. *Time, Labor, and Social Domination*. Cambridge: Cambridge University Press.

Ptak, Ralf. 2004. *Vom Ordoliberalismus zur Sozialen Marktwirtschaft*. Opladen: Leske & Buderich.

Ptak, Ralf. 2007. 'Grundlagen des Neoliberalismus'. In *Kritik des Neoliberalismus*, edited by Christoph Butterwegge, Bettina Lösch and Ralf Ptak, 12–86. Wiesbaden: VS.

Ptak, Ralf. 2009. 'Neoliberalism in Germany: Revisiting the Oroliberal Foundations of the Social Market Economy'. In *The Road from Mont Pélerin. The Making of the Neoliberal Thought Collective*, edited by Philip Mirowski and Dieter Plehwe, 98–138. Cambridge, MA: Harvard University Press.

Quinn, Dermont. 1998. 'Introduction'. In Wilhelm Röpke, *A Human Economy*, iii–xx. Wilmington, DE: ISI Books.

Radice, Hugo. 2000. 'Responses to Globalisation: A Critique of Progressive Nationalism'. *New Political Economy* 5 (1): 5–19.

Radice, Hugo. 2014. 'Enforcing Austerity in Europe: The Structural Deficit as a Policy Target'. *Journal of Contemporary European Studies* 22 (2): 318–28.

Radice, Hugo. 2015. *Global Capitalism*. London: Routledge.

Ranciere, Jacques. 2001. 'Ten Theses on Politics'. *Theory & Event* 5 (3): 1–16. Electronically available at www.after1968.org/app/webroot/uploads/Ranciere THESESONPOLITICS.pdf.

Rath, Corinna. 1998. *Staat, Gesellschaft und Wirtschaft bei Max Weber und Walter Eucken*. Hohenhausen: Hönzel.

Riese, Hajo. 1972. 'Ordnungsidee und Ordnungspolitik: Kritik einer wirtschaftspolitischen Konzeption'. *Kyklos* 25 (1): 24–48.

Rieter, Heinz, and Matthias Schmolz. 1993. 'The Ideas of German Ordoliberalism 1938–45: Pointing the Way to a New Economic Order'. *The European Journal of the History of Economic Thought* 1 (1): 87–112.

Riker, William H. 1982. *Liberalism against Populism: A Confrontation between the Theory of Democracy and the Theory of Social Choice*. San Francisco, CA: Freeman.

Riker, William H. 1987. *The Development of American Federalism*. Boston, MA: Kluwer Academic.

Riker, William H. 1993. *Agenda Formation*. Ann Arbor, MI: Michigan University Press.

Ronge, Bastian. 2015. *Das Adam-Smith-Projekt*. Wiesbaden: Springer.

Röpke, Wilhelm. 1936. *Crisis and Cycles*. London: Hodge.

Röpke, Wilhelm. 1942. *International Economic Disintegration*. London: Hodge.

Röpke, Wilhelm. 1950a. *Mass und Mitte*. Zürich: Rentsch.

Röpke, Wilhelm. 1950b. *Ist die Deutsche Wirtschaftspolitik richtig?* Stuttgart: Kohlhammer.

Röpke, Wilhelm. 1954. *Internationale Ordnung – heute*. Erlenbach-Zuerich: Eugen Rentsch.

Röpke, Wilhelm. 1955. *Economic Order and International Law*. Leiden: Sijthoff.

Röpke, Wilhelm. 1957. *Welfare, Freedom and Inflation*. London: Pall Mall Press.

Röpke, Wilhelm. 1959a. *International Order and Economic Integration*. Dodrecht: Reidel.

Röpke, Wilhelm. [1923] 1959b. 'Wirtschaftlicher Liberalismus und Staatsgedanke'. In Wilhelm Röpke, *Gegen die Brandung*, 42–46. Zürich: Rentsch.

Röpke, Wilhelm. 1964. *Wort und Wirkung*. Ludwigsburg: Hoch.

Röpke, Wilhelm. 1969. *Against the Tide*. Vienna: Ludwig von Mises Institute.

Röpke, Wilhelm. [1944] 1982a. 'The Guiding Principles of the Liberal Programme'. In *Standard Texts on the Social Market Economy – Two Centuries of Discussion*, edited by Wolfgang Stützel, Christian Watrin, Hans Willgerodt and Karl Hohmann, 187–92. Stuttgart: Fischer.

Röpke, Wilhelm. [1950] 1982b. 'Is the German Economic Policy the Right One'? In *Standard Texts on the Social Market Economy – Two Centuries of Discussion*, edited by Wolfgang Stützel, Christian Watrin, Hans Willgerodt and Karl Hohmann, 37–48. Stuttgart: Fischer.

Röpke, Wilhelm. 1987. *2 Essays by Wilhelm Röpke*. London: Lanham.

Röpke, Wilhelm. [1951] 1989. 'Interdependence of Domestic and International Economic Systems'. In *Germany's Social Market Economy*, edited by Alan Peacock and Hans Willgerodt, 68–81. London: Palgrave.

Röpke, Wilhelm. [1958] 1998. *A Human Economy*. Wilmington, DE: ISI Books.

Röpke, Wilhelm. [1962] 2000. *Europa in der Welt von heute*. Zürich: Schulthess.

Röpke, Wilhelm. [1944] 2002. *The Moral Foundation of Civil Society*. New Brunswick, NJ: Transaction Publishers.

Röpke, Wilhelm. [1942] 2009. *The Social Crisis of Our Time*. New Brunswick, NJ: Transaction Publishers.

Rossiter, Clinton L. 1948. *Constitutional Dictatorship. Crisis Government in the Modern Democracies*. Princeton, NJ: Princeton University Press.

Roth, Karl-Heinz. 2001. 'Klienten des Leviatans'. *1999: Zeitschrift für Sozialgeschichte des 20. und 21. Jahrhunderts* 16 (2): 13–41.

Rüstow, Alexander. 1942. 'General Sociological Causes of the Economic Disintegration and Possibilities of Reconstruction'. In Afterword to Wilhelm Röpke, *International Economic Disintegration*, 267–83. London: Hodge.

Rüstow, Alexander. 1953. 'Soziale Marktwirschaft als Gegenprogramm gegen Kommunismus und Bolschewismus'. In *Wirtschaft ohne Wunder*, edited by Albert Hunold, 97–127. Zürich: Rentsch.

Rüstow, Alexander. 1954. 'Vom Sinn der Wirtschaftsfreiheit'. *Blätter der Freiheit* 6 (6): 217–22.

Rüstow, Alexander. [1929] 1959. 'Diktatur innerhalb der Grenzen der Demokratie'. *Vierteljahreshefte für Zeitgeschichte* 7 (1): 87–111.

Rüstow, Alexander. [1932] 1963. 'Die staatspolitischen Vorraussetzungen des wirtschaftspolitischen Liberalismus'. In *Rede und Antwort*, 249–58. Ludwigsburg: Hoch.

Rüstow, Alexander. 1963. *Rede und Antwort*. Ludwigsburg: Hoch.

Rüstow, Alexander. 2005. *Freiheit und Herrschaft*. Münster. LIT Verlag.

Rüstow, Alexander. 2009. *Die Religion der Marktwirtschaft*. Berlin: LIT Verlag.

Ryner, Magnus. 2015. 'Europe's Ordoliberal Iron Cage: Critical Political Economy, the Euro Area Crisis and Its Management'. *Journal of European Public Policy* 22 (2): 275–94.

Scheuerman, William. 1996. 'Introduction'. In *The Rule of Law under Siege*, edited by William E. Scheuermann, 1–25. Berkley, CA: University of California Press.

Scheuerman, William. 1999. *Carl Schmitt. The End of Law*. Boulder CO: Rowman & Littlefield.

Scheuerman, William. 2016. 'Crises and Extralegality from Above and from Below'. In *Critical Theories of Crisis in Europe: From Weimar to the Euro*, edited by Poul FR. Kjaer and Niklas Olsen, 197–212. London: Rowman & Littlefield.

Schlesinger, Arthur. 1958. *The Age of Roosevelt*. Cambridge, MA: Riverside Press.

Schmidt, Alfred. [1962] 2014. *The Concept of Nature in Marx*. London: Verso.

Schmidt, Vivien. 2006. *Democracy in Europe*. Oxford: Oxford University Press.

Schmitt, Carl. 1934. *Über die drei Arten des rechtswissenschaftlichen Denkens*. Hamburg: Hanseatische Verlagsanstalt.

Schmitt, Carl. [1922] 1985. *Political Theology. Four Chapters on the Concept of Sovereignty*. Chicago, IL: Chicago University Press.

Schmitt, Carl. [1923] 1988a. *The Crisis of Parliamentary Democracy*. Cambridge, MA: MIT Press.

Schmitt, Carl. [1932] 1988b. *Legalität und Legitimität*. Berlin: Duncker & Humblot.

Schmitt, Carl. [1927] 1996a. *The Concept of the Political*. Chicago, Ill: University of Chicago Press.

Schmitt, Carl. [1931] 1996b. *Der Hüter der Verfassung*. Berlin: Duncker & Humblot.

Schmitt, Carl. [1932] 1998. 'Sound Economy – Strong State'. In Appendix to Renato Cristi, *Carl Schmitt and Authoritarian Liberalism*, 212–32. Cardiff: University of Wales Press.

Schmitt, Carl. [1928] 2008a. *Constitutional Theory*. Durham, NC: Duke University Press.

Schmitt, Carl. [1970] 2008b. *Political Theology II*. Cambridge: Polity Press.

Schmitt, Carl. [1921] 2013. *Dictatorship. From the Origin of the Modern Concept of Sovereignty to Proletarian Class Struggle*. Cambridge: Polity Press.

Schmitt, Carl. [1942] 2015. *Land and Sea*. New York: Telos.

Schmitt-Beck, Rüdiger. 2016. 'The "Alternative für Deutschland in the Electorate": Between Single-Issue and Right-Wing Populist Party'. *German Politics*, Onlinefirst. doi: 10.1080/09644008.2016.1184650.

Schumpeter, Joseph. 1950. *Capitalism, Socialism and Democracy*. London: Routledge.

Schwab, Georg. 1985. 'Introduction'. In Carl Schmitt, *Political Theology. Four Chapters on the Concept of Sovereignty*, xxxvii–lii. Chicago, IL: Chicago University Press.

Schwander, Hanna, and Philip Manow. 2016. 'Modernise *and* Die? German Social Democracy and the Electoral Consequence of Agenda 2010'. *Socio-Economic Review*, Onlinefirst. doi: 10.1093/ser/mww011.

Schwarz, Gerhard. 1992. 'Marktwirtschaftliche Reform und Demokratie – Eine Hassliebe'? *ORDO* 43: 65–90.

Sheppard, Eric, and Helga Leitner. 2010. 'Quo vadis neoliberalism'? *Geoforum* 41 (2): 185–94.

Siems, Mathias, and Gerhard Schnyder. 2014. 'Ordoliberal Lessons for Economic Stability: Different Kinds of Regulation, Not More Regulation'. *Governance* 27 (3): 377–96.

Sievert, Olaf. 1993. 'Geld, das man nicht selbst herstellen kann: Ein ordnungspolitisches Plädoyer für die Währungsunion'. In *Währungsunion oder Währungschaos?* edited by Peter Bofinger, Stefan Collignon and Ernst-Moritz Lipp, 13–24. Wiesbaden: Gabler.

Simons, Henry. 1948. *Economic Policy for a Free Society*. Chicago, IL: Chicago University Press.

Sinn, Hans-Werner. 2014. *The Euro Trap: On Bubbles, Budgets, and Beliefs*. Oxford: Oxford University Press.

Smith, Adam. [1776] 1976a. *The Wealth of Nations*. Oxford: Oxford University Press.

Smith, Adam. [1759] 1976b. *The Theory of Moral Sentiments*. Oxford: Oxford University Press.

Smith, Adam. [1763] 1978. *Lectures on Jurisprudence*. Oxford: Oxford University Press.

Soederberg, Susanne. 2014. *Debtfare States and the Poverty Industry: Money, Discipline and the Surplus Population*. London: Routledge.

Stiglitz, Joseph. 2016. *The Euro and Its Threat to the Future of Europe*. London: Allen Lane.

Stockhammer, Engelbert. 2016. 'Neoliberal Growth Models, Monetary Union and the Euro-Crisis. A Post-Keynesian Perspective'. *New Political Economy* 21 (4): 365–79.

Strange, Susan. 1998. *The Retreat of the State*. Manchester: Manchester University Press.

Strauss, Leo. [1932] 1996. 'Notes on Carl Schmitt'. In Appendix to Carl Schmitt, *The Concept of the Political*, 97–122. Chicago, IL: The University of Chicago Press.

Streek, Wolfgang. 2015. 'Heller, Schmitt and the Euro'. *European Law Journal* 21 (3): 361–70.

Streit, Manfred, and Michael Wohlgemuth. 2010. 'The Market Economy and the State: Hayekian and Ordoliberal Conceptions'. In *The Theory of Capitalism in the German Economic Traditions*, edited by Peter Koslowski, 224–69. Berlin: Springer.

Strong, Tracy. 1985. 'Foreword'. In Carl Schmitt, *Political Theology. Four Chapters on the Concept of Sovereignty*, vii–xxxii. Chicago, IL: University of Chicago Press.

The Economist, 2015. 'Germany and Economics: Of rules and order'. Accessed 8 March 2017. http://www.economist.com/news/europe/21650565-german-ordo liberalism-has-had-big-influence-policy-during-euro-crisis-rules-and-order

Tönnies, Ferdinand. [1887] 2001. *Community and Civil Society*, edited by Jose Harris. Cambridge: Cambridge University Press.

Tönnies, Sybille. 2009. 'Nachwort: Die liberale Kritik des Liberalismus'. In *Die Religion der Marktwirtschaft*, edited by Alexander Rüstow, 159–95. Berlin: LIT Verlag.

Tribe, Keith. 1995. *Strategies of Economic Order: German Economic Discourse, 1750–1950*. Cambridge: Cambridge University Press.

Tribe, Keith. 2009. 'The Political Economy of Modernity: Foucault's Collége de France Lectures of 1978 and 1979'. *Economy and Society* 38 (4): 679–98.

Tullock, Gordon. 1976. *The Vote Motive*. London: The Institute of Economic Affairs.

Tuori, Kaarlo. 2015. *European Constitutionalism*. Cambridge: Cambridge University Press.

Tuori, Kaarlo, and Klaus Tuori. 2014. *The Eurozone Crisis*. Cambridge: Cambridge University Press.

Vanberg, Viktor. 1988. ' "Ordnungstheorie" as Constitutional Economics. The German Conception of a 'Social Market Economy' '. *ORDO* 39: 17–31.

Vanberg, Viktor. 2001. *The Constitution of Markets*. London: Routledge.

Vanberg, Victor. 2002. *Rules and Choice in Economics: Essays in Constitutional Economics*. London: Routledge.

Vanberg, Viktor. 2011. 'The Freiburg School: Walter Eucken and Ordoliberalism'. *Freiburg Discussion Papers on Constitutional Economics*. Accessed 15 June 2016. http://www.eucken.de/fileadmin/bilder/Dokumente/Diskussionspapiere/04_11bw. pdf.

Vanberg, Victor. 2014. 'Ordnungspolitik. The Freiburg School and the Reason of Rules'. Freiburger Diskussionspapiere zur Ordnungsökonomie, 14/01. Accessed

25 November 2016. http://www.eucken.de/fileadmin/bilder/Dokumente/DP2014/ Diskussionspapier_1401. pdf.

Vanberg, Viktor. 2015. 'Ordoliberalism, Ordnungspolitik and the Reason of Rules'. *European Review of International Studies* 2 (3): 27–36.

van Gerven, Walter. 2003. 'European Political Integration, Comparative Law and Private Enforcement of Competition Law'. In *Spontaneous Order, Organization and the Law: Roads a European Civil Society*, edited by Tania Einhorn, 393–412. The Hague: Asser Press.

van Horn, Rob. 2011. 'Chicago's Shifting Position on Concentration of Business Power'. *Seattle University Law Review* 34 (4): 1527–44.

van Horn, Rob, and Phillip Mirowski. 2009. 'The Rise of the Chicago School of Economics and the Birth of Neoliberalism'. In *The Road from Mont Pélerin. The Making of the Neoliberal Thought Collective*, edited by Philip Mirowski and Dieter Plehwe, 139–78. Cambridge, MA: Harvard University Press.

Van Rompuy, Herman. 2012. 'Towards a Genuine Economic and Monetary Union'. Accessed 1 March 2016. www.consilium.europa.eu/uedocs/cms_Data/docs/press data/en/ec/134069.pdf.

Varoufakis, Yannis. 2013. 'From Contagion to Incoherence: Towards a Model of the Unfolding Eurozone Crisis'. *Contributions to Political Economy* 32 (1): 51–71.

Varoufakis, Yannis. 2016. *And the Weak Suffer What They Must?: Europe, Austerity and the Threat to Global Stability*. London: Bodley Head.

Voegelin, Eric. 1965. 'Die dritte Phase der Industriegesellschaft. Die Interdependenz als Wesensmoment der "Formierten Gesellschaft"'. *Gesellschaftspolitische Kommentare* 12: 123–28.

von Mises, Ludwig. 1947. *Planned Chaos*. Irvington-on-Hudson, NY: Foundation for Economic Education.

von Mises, Ludwig. [1927] 1985. *Liberalism in the Classical Tradition*. San Francisco: Cobden Press.

Wagenknecht, Sahra. 2011. *Freiheit statt Kapitalismus*. Frankfurt: Eichhorn.

Watrin, Christian. 2010. 'Alfred Müller-Armack – Economic Policy-Maker and Sociologist of Religion'. In *The Theory of Capitalism in the German Economic Tradition*, edited by Peter Koslowski, 192–220. Berlin: Springer.

Weber, Max. [1918] 1994a. 'Sozialismus'. In *Political Writings*, edited by Peter Lassman and Ronald Speirs, 272–303. Cambridge: Cambridge University Press.

Weber, Max. [1919] 1994b. 'The Profession and Vocation of Politics. In Max Weber, *Political Writings*, edited by Peter Lassman and Ronald Speirs, 309–369. Cambridge: Cambridge University Press.

Weber, Max. [1922] 2013. *Economy and Society*. Berkeley, CA: University of California Press.

White, Jonathan. 2015. 'Emergency Europe'. *Political Studies* 63 (2): 300–18.

White, Jonathan. 2017. 'Between Rules and Discretion: Thoughts on Ordoliberalism'. In *Ordoliberalism: An Irritating German Idea*, edited by Christian Jörges and Josef Hien. ARENA, Oslo: Centre for European Studies.

Wigger, Angela. 2008. *Competition for Competitiveness: The Politics of the Transformation of the EU Competition Regime*. PhD Thesis, The Free University of Amsterdam. Available at http://dare.ubvu.vu.nl/bitstream/handle/1871/15601/8237.pdf; jsessionid=655AB7B29 5D025EF4F2D7D7AF9C2319C?sequence=5.

Wilkinson, Michael. 2013. 'The Spectre of Authoritarian Liberalism: Reflections on the Constitutional Crisis of the European Union'. *German Law Journal* 14 (5): 527–60.

Wilkinson, Michael. 2014. 'Politicising Europe's Justice Deficit'. *LSE Law, Society and Economy Working Papers* 8/2014. London: LSE, Law Department.

Wilkinson, Michael. 2015. 'Authoritarian Liberalism in the European Constitutional Imagination'. *European Law Journal* 21 (3): 313–39.

Willgerodt, Hans. 1986. 'Der Neoliberalismus – Entstehung, Kampfbegriff und Meinungsstreit'. *ORDO* 57: 47–89.

Willgerodt, Hans, and Alan Peacock. 1989. 'German Liberalism and Economic Revival'. In *Germany's Social Market Economy*, edited by Alan Peacock and Hans Willgerodt, 1–14. London: Palgrave.

Williams, John, Karel Williams and Colin Haslam. 1992. 'Leap before You Look'. In *Towards a New Europe?: Structural Change in the European Economy*, edited by Ash Amin and Michael Dietrich, 212–33. Aldershot: Edward Elgar.

Wolf, Martin. 2001. 'The Need for a New Imperialism'. *Financial Times*, 10 October 2001.

Wörsdörfer, Manuel. 2012. 'Walter Eucken on Patent Laws: Are Patents Just Nonsense upon Stilts'? *Economic Thought* 1 (2): 36–54.

Young, Brigitte. 2014. 'German Ordoliberalism as Agenda Setter for the Euro Crisis: Myth Trumps Reality'. *Journal of Contemporary European Studies* 22 (3): 276–87.

Index